Media, Culture and Society in Putin's Russia

Studies in Central and Eastern Europe

Edited for the International Council for Central and East European Studies by Roger E. Kanet, University of Miami, USA

Titles in the Series include:

Thomas Bremer (*editor*)
RELIGION AND THE CONCEPTUAL BOUNDARY IN
CENTRAL AND EASTERN EUROPE
Encounters of Faiths

Joan DeBardeleben (*editor*)
THE BOUNDARIES OF EU ENLARGEMENT
Finding A Place for Neighbours

Graeme Gill (*editor*)
POLITICS IN THE RUSSIAN REGIONS

Stephen Hutchings (*editor*)
RUSSIA AND ITS OTHER(S) ON FILM
Screening Intercultural Dialogue

Roger E. Kanet (*editor*)
RUSSIA
Re-Emerging Great Power

Rebecca Kay (*editor*)
GENDER, EQUALITY AND DIFFERENCE DURING AND
AFTER STATE SOCIALISM

Stanislav J. Kirschbaum (*editor*)
CENTRAL EUROPEAN HISTORY AND THE EUROPEAN UNION
The Meaning of Europe

Katlijn Malfliet, Lien Verpoest and Evgeny Vinokurov (*editors*)
THE CIS, THE EU AND RUSSIA
Challenges of Integration

John Pickles (*editor*)
STATE AND SOCIETY IN POST-SOCIALIST ECONOMIES

Stephen Velychenko (*editor*)
UKRAINE, THE EU AND RUSSIA
History, Culture and International Relations

Stephen White (*editor*)
MEDIA, CULTURE AND SOCIETY IN PUTIN'S RUSSIA

Forthcoming titles include:

John Pickles (*editor*)
GLOBALIZATION AND REGIONALIZATION IN POST-SOCIALIST ECONOMIES
Common Economic Spaces of Europe

Stephen White (*editor*)
POLITICS AND THE RULING GROUP IN PUTIN'S RUSSIA

Studies in Central and Eastern Europe
Series Standing Order ISBN 0-230-51682-3 hardcover
(*outside North America only*)

You can receive future titles in this series as they are published by placing a standing order. Please contact your bookseller or, in case of difficulty, write to us at the address below with your name and address, the title of the series and the ISBN quoted above.

Customer Services Department, Macmillan Distribution Ltd, Houndmills, Basingstoke, Hampshire RG21 6XS, England

---

Media, Culture and Society in Putin's Russia

Edited by

Stephen White
Professor of International Politics
University of Glasgow, UK

First published 2008 by
PALGRAVE MACMILLAN
Houndmills, Basingstoke, Hampshire RG21 6XS and
175 Fifth Avenue, New York, N.Y. 10010
Companies and representatives throughout the world

PALGRAVE MACMILLAN is the global academic imprint of the Palgrave
Macmillan division of St. Martin's Press, LLC and of Palgrave Macmillan
Ltd. Macmillan® is a registered trademark in the United States,
United Kingdom and other countries. Palgrave is a registered
trademark in the European Union and other countries.

ISBN-13: 978–0–230–52485–9   hardback
ISBN-10: 0–230–52485–0   hardback

This book is printed on paper suitable for recycling and made from
fully managed and sustained forest sources. Logging, pulping and
manufacturing processes are expected to conform to the
environmental regulations of the country of origin.

A catalogue record for this book is available from the British Library.

A catalog record for this book is available from the Library of Congress.

10   9   8   7   6   5   4   3   2   1
17 16 15 14 13 12 11 10 09 08

Printed and bound in Great Britain by
CPI Antony Rowe, Chippenham and Eastbourne

Contents

List of Tables and Figure

Preface by the General Editor

When the International Council for Central and East European Studies (ICCEES) was founded at the first international and multidisciplinary conference of scholars working in this field, held in Banff, Alberta, Canada, on 4–7 September 1974, it was given the name International Committee for Soviet and East European Studies (ICSEES). Its major purpose was to provide for greater exchange between research centres and scholars around the world who were devoted to the study of the USSR and the communist states and societies of Eastern Europe. These developments were the main motivation for bringing together the very different national organizations in the field and for forming a permanent committee of their representatives, which would serve as an umbrella organization, as well as a promoter of closer co-operation. Four national scholarly associations launched ICSEES at the Banff conference: the American Association for the Advancement of Slavic Studies (AAASS), the National Association for Soviet and East European Studies in Great Britain (NASEES), the British Universities Association of Slavists (BUAS), and the Canadian Association of Slavists (CAS).

Over the past three decades six additional Congresses have been held: in Garmisch-Partenkirchen, Germany, 1980; Washington, USA, 1985; Harrogate, UK, 1990; Warsaw, Poland, 1995; Tampere, Finland, 2000; and Berlin, Germany, 2005. The next Congress is scheduled for 2010 in Stockholm, Sweden. The original four national associations that sponsored the first congress have been joined by an additional seventeen full and six associate member associations, with significantly more than a thousand scholars participating at each of the recent congresses.

It is now a little over three decades since scholars felt the need to coordinate the efforts in the 'free world' to describe and analyze the Communist political systems, their societies and economies, and East–West relations in particular. Halfway through this period, the Communist system collapsed, the region that was the object of study was reorganized, and many of the new states that emerged set out on a path of democratic development, economic growth, and, in many cases, inclusion in Western institutions. The process turned out to be complex, and there were setbacks. Yet, by 2004, the European Union as well as the North Atlantic Treaty Organization had welcomed those post-Communist states that had met all of the requirements for membership. Not all of the applicant states achieved this objective; but the process is ongoing. For this reason, perhaps even more than before, the region that encompassed the former Communist world demands study, explanation, and analysis, as both centripetal and centrifugal forces are at work in each state and across the region. We are most fortunate that the community of scholars addressing these issues now includes many astute analysts from the region itself.

ROGER E. KANET

Notes on the Contributors

Risto Alapuro is Professor of Sociology at the University of Helsinki, and currently Academy Professor at the Academy of Finland. His main publications in English include *State and Revolution in Finland* (1988) and *Beyond Post-Soviet Transition: Micro Perspectives on Challenge and Survival in Russia and Estonia*, edited with Ilkka Liikanen and Markku Lonkila (2004). His main research interests include social movements, social networks and the association at organization in a comparative perspective, and he currently directs a research project that examines associational activity in Russia, Estonia, Finland, and France.

Birgit Beumers is Reader in Russian at the University of Bristol. She completed her doctorate at St Antony's College, Oxford, and takes a special interest in contemporary Russian culture, especially cinema and theatre. Her publications include *Burnt by the Sun* (2000), *Nikita Mikhalkov: Between Nostalgia and Nationalism* (2005), *PopCulture: Russia!* (2005) and, as editor, *Russia on Reels: The Russian Idea in Post-Soviet Cinema* (1999) and *24 Frames: Russia and the Soviet Union* (2007). She is editor of the online journal *KinoKultura* and of the journal *Studies in Russian and Soviet Cinema*, published by Intellect. She is currently working on post-Soviet cinema and on the history of Russian animation.

Katja Koikkalainen is a doctoral student in the Department of Journalism and Mass Communication at the University of Tampere, and has also been working as a researcher at the Aleksanteri Institute of the University of Helsinki. Her research focuses on the Russian news media, especially business journalism; she also has working experience as a sub-editor on a Finnish business newspaper, and as a lecturer in journalism at the University of Tampere. She has published several articles on Russian business journalism, including 'The Local and the International in Russian Business Journalism: Structures and Practices', which was published by *Europe-Asia Studies* in 2007.

John M. Kramer is Distinguished Professor and Chair of the Department of Political Science, University of Mary Washington, Fredericksburg, Virginia. He received his BA in Political Science from La Salle University and his MA and Ph.D. degrees in International Relations and Russian Area Studies from the University of Virginia, where he was a Du Pont Fellow, a University Fellow, and a Woodrow Wilson Fellow. His publications include *The Energy Gap in Eastern Europe* (1990), as well as papers and articles in professional journals and symposia; much of his recent work has focused on drug abuse in post-communist polities, including published articles in *Problems of Post-Communism, Slavic Review* and the *Modern Encyclopedia of Russian and Soviet History.*

David Lane is Senior Research Associate in the Faculty of Social and Political Sciences, University of Cambridge, and was previously Professor of Sociology at the University of Birmingham. He is currently the recipient of a Leverhulme Trust research award on the relationship of class to transformation in Ukraine and Russia, and also holds a British Academy network award on elites and the European Union. His recent books include *Revolution in the Modern World* (editor, with John Foran and Andreja Zivkovic, and contributor, 2007), and as editor and contributor, *The Transformation of State Socialism: System Change, Capitalism or Something Else?* (2007).

Ilkka Liikanen is Director of the Karelian Institute at the University of Joensuu and head of the Finnish national 'Russia in Europe' postgraduate school. His research focuses on nationalism and political mobilization in Finland, postcommunist change in Russia and Estonia, and European integration, borders and cross-border cooperation. At the moment he heads the Finnish-Russian case study within the 'Eurodimensions' project, studying the external borders of the European Union. His publications include, as coeditor and coauthor, *Curtains of Iron and Gold. Reconstructing Borders and Scales of Interaction* (1999), *Education and Civic Culture in Post-Communist Countries* (2001), *Beyond Post-Soviet Transition. Micro Perspectives on Challenge and Survival in Russia and Estonia* (2003), and *Karelia – A Cross-Border Region? The EU and Cross-Border Region-building on the Finnish-Russian Border* (2007).

Marie-Hélène Mandrillon has been a member of the Centre for Russian, Caucasian and Central European Studies in Paris since 2000, where she has been leading a collaborative project devoted to the study of the environmental legacy of communism. As the first outcome of this project, she edited a special issue on 'L'Environnement à l'Est: le modèle européen à l'épreuve' for the *Revue d'Etudes Comparatives Est–Ouest* in 2005. Trained as a historian, she coedited together with Marc Ferro *L'État de toutes les Russies: Les Etats et les nations de l'ex-URSS* (1993) and *Russie: Peuples et civilizations* (2005). Her work currently focuses on the environmental history of the Soviet era.

Svetlana Pasti is a member of the Department of Journalism and Mass Communication at the University of Tampere. For two decades she worked as a journalist in the Russian media, and for the last decade she has been working as a researcher, lecturer and expert on academic and educational projects in Russia, Eastern and Central Europe. Her monograph *Rossiiskii zhurnalist v kontekste peremen: Media Sankt-Peterburga* (2004) examined the work attitudes and values of two generations of journalists of the late 1990s with the aim of describing their professional roles in society. Her new monograph on *The Changing Profession of a Journalist in Russia*, presented as a doctoral dissertation at the University of Tampere in 2007, examines the professionalization of Russian journalism in the light of its history and present circumstances.

Jukka Pietiläinen is currently a researcher at the Aleksanteri Institute at the University of Helsinki. His doctoral dissertation on 'The Regional Newspaper in Post-Soviet Russia' (2002) dealt with changes in media structure and journalistic conventions in contemporary Russia. His recent research has focused on the Russian media and journalism, on Russian society, and on foreign news and news flows in general.

Diana Schmidt-Pfister is a Research Fellow at the Institute for Intercultural and International Studies at the University of Bremen, Germany. Over the past decade she has focused on the development of Russian civil society with a particular focus on the attempt to introduce global environmental, human rights and good governance principles into the post-Soviet context, and on the transnational networking of Russian civil society actors through internet communication technologies and foreign financial assistance. Her monograph *Transnational Networks on the Ground* (2008) discusses the nature and implications of local civil society involvement in transnational anti-corruption campaigns in three Russian cities during the Putin era. Her current research interests include practical and methodological questions related to corruption and crime prevention at the international level as well as in postcommunist Eastern Europe.

Markus Soldner is currently completing a doctorate on 'The Russian Mass Media between the State and Big Business', and also works as a freelancer in the field of citizenship education. Until recently he was a research fellow at the Institute for Political Science, Dresden University of Technology, where together with Wolfgang Ismayr he coedited *Die politischen Systeme Osteuropas* and *Die politischen Systeme Westeuropas*. His main research interests include comparative politics, transformation in

Eastern Europe and the Former Soviet Union, German politics and theory of democracy. He has published a monograph on Russian policy towards Chechnya during the 1990s (*Russlands Čečnja-Politik seit 1993*, 1999) and has just completed a study of direct democracy in Germany, together with Kerstin Pohl. With Klemens Schrenk, he is currently coediting a volume on the comparative analysis of democratic government.

Introduction

Stephen White

One of the defining features of the Soviet system was its virtual elimination of a space for autonomous citizen activity. Everything, it used
to be said, was either banned or compulsory. There was a single ruling party, and it dominated the life of the society through its 'leading
role'. The party itself was dominated by its top leadership, and above all
by its General Secretary. Party rule was subject to no effective challenge,
either from the courts, or the trade unions, or the mass media. There was
a detailed censorship, whose existence was itself subject to censorship;
foreign radio broadcasts were jammed; movements across international
frontiers were strictly regulated. If there was a civil society in Brezhnev's
USSR, it was an official one: more than 98 per cent of the working population were enrolled in trade unions, for instance, but their leadership was
appointed by the party and their primary role was to mobilize support
for party policy in the workplace. Women were organized in the Soviet
Women's Committee on the same kind of basis; writers had the Writers'
Union; and so forth. All of these were 'transmission belts': the term was
used without any embarrassment to make clear that it was their responsibility to mobilize support for party policy rather than to articulate the
concerns of their members.

All of this had begun to change before the end of Soviet rule. The new
watchword, as Gorbachev explained in his *Perestroika* (1987), was that
'everything that isn't banned is legal'. The ruling party abandoned its
monopoly, indeed it soon ceased to be a party at all. Elections became
competitive, and elected deputies began to hold government ministers
to account. Public life was 'destatified', as ordinary citizens were allowed
and even encouraged to organize to advance their common concerns.
There were anti-government demonstrations, miners' strikes, and calls
for independence in the non-Russian republics. Most striking of all were

1

the developments that were taking place in the cultural world, where *glasnost'* allowed all kinds of 'forbidden themes' to be discussed once again. History was transformed, as the archives opened and the boundaries for discussion widened dramatically; literature was enriched by the publication or republication of work that had been banned in earlier years; the social sciences took advantage of new census data, new survey opportunities, and a greater willingness to rethink official orthodoxies and (in some cases) borrow conceptually from the West.

Putin's Russia, for many, was a regression in almost all of these respects. Public life was dominated once more by the Kremlin, operating as an all-powerful presidency rather than a Politburo but from the same buildings and using at least some of the same people. The parties that enjoyed the support of the Kremlin took firm control of elected institutions. The state was subordinated to an 'executive vertical'. State ownership and control began to extend in the media, particularly in national television. Businessmen who showed signs of political ambition found themselves in an increasingly difficult situation; in the worst case, as with Mikhail Khodorkovsky in 2005, they were sentenced to periods in prison. A number of the regime's most outspoken critics, notably Anna Politkovskaya in 2006, were assassinated. Bolstered by its oil revenues, the Kremlin became increasingly assertive in its relations with other countries, particularly in former Soviet republics. This, some suggested, was 'managed democracy', or (as some within the regime itself suggested) 'sovereign democracy', or perhaps (some Western scholars suggested) a form of authoritarianism – although it was one in which competitive elections continued to take place and some basic freedoms (such as freedom of conscience) were still respected.

This complex, hybrid but apparently stable and self-reproducing system provides the context for the chapters of this book, which stem from the Berlin Congress of the International Council for Central and East European Studies in 2005 but which have been entirely rewritten, updated and extended for this collection. They focus on three key inter-related themes. First of all, 'civil society': in quotes, because the applicability of the term in contemporary Russia is itself open to question, and in various locations: in Karelia, in the context of Western attempts to engage in 'democracy assistance', and in connection with the discourse that is used to address these concerns in Russia and Estonia. Secondly, the media: in printed as well as broadcast form, and looking at journalists themselves as well as the role of big business and the state, and the coverage of environmental issues. And thirdly, some wider issues of culture and society: whether contemporary Russia is 'capitalist' or, if it is, what that might mean; how government and society are responding to the challenges of drugs and HIV/AIDS; and how these and other changes have been reflected in the *blokbastery* of the Putin era.

Varied in theme and in conclusion, there are nonetheless some common elements that unite all these chapters and mark out new research frontiers in the study of transitional societies. One of these is the collaborative nature of such research: no longer Westerners pronouncing on a remote society from outside it, but Westerners and their Russian counterparts sharing the primary research, debating concepts, and writing up their results together. Another is the strong emphasis in these chapters on the collection of primary data, particularly of qualitative data drawn from interviews, focus groups and discourse. Perhaps still more important is the strongly comparative orientation of these chapters: sometimes across the Russian regions, but more often across East and West. It is 'not an accident' that northern Europe features frequently among the authors as well as the subject matter of the chapters of this book. The Scandinavian countries, the Baltic republics and the northern regions of Russia share much in common historically and geographically, but have experienced a variety of political regimes in a manner that makes them an ideal research laboratory. The appropriateness of a north European location for research on contemporary Russia was matched by the numbers of scholars from those locations that attended the Berlin Congress, and it will again be matched when the next world Congress convenes in Stockholm in 2010.

Finally, a note on technical matters. We have standardized on 'British' English, except for contributors based in the United States, but have balanced this by standardizing on the Library of Congress transliteration system (except when other forms have become established in English) and the 'Harvard' reference system. We hope these 'mid-Atlantic' conventions will make good sense in a volume that seeks to present the best of the work on its subject that is currently being conducted in North America as well as in Europe and further afield. A special word of thanks is due to Roger Kanet and Sarah Oates, for their thoughtful and constructive comments on an earlier version of the manuscript.

Part 1
Civil Society in Russia

1
Civil Society and the Reconstitution of Russian Political Space: the Case of the Republic of Karelia

Ilkka Liikanen

Ever since the early days of *perestroika* prophecies of the emergence of civil society in Russia have been a prime subject of the academic discussion on late and post-Soviet politics. At the same time, the end of Russian civil society and of Russian democratization have been predicted constantly since the collapse of the Soviet system. Questions of this kind have also inspired high-level political discussion, for instance in the European Parliament, and provoked open letters to world leaders by prominent politicians, scholars and ex-government officials.

Probably the most notable example is the open letter that leading American and European politicians and scholars drafted in September 2004 after the Beslan tragedy. The 'Open Letter to the Heads of State and Government of the European Union and NATO' was signed by scholars such as Timothy Garton Ash, André Glucksmann and Francis Fukuyama, as well as former heads of states such as Giuliano Amato, Carl Bildt, Vaclav Havel and Vytautas Landsbergis. The letter sharply condemned the 'weak policy of the West' in regard to Russia and claimed that ever since coming to office President Vladimir Putin had 'systematically undercut the freedom and independence of the press, destroyed the checks and balances in the Russian federal system, arbitrarily imprisoned both real and imagined political rivals, removed legitimate candidates from electoral ballots, harassed and arrested NGO leaders, and weakened Russia's political parties' (http://www.freedomhouse.org/uploads/press_release/pr_238.pdf).

The open letter evoked a response by prominent scholars and Russia specialists who urged a more balanced approach and summarized their message by stating: 'The unfortunate impression fostered by the wording

of the open letter is that Russians must choose between effective government and democratic values. Given this Hobson's choice, Russians will
of course prefer the former, particularly after the tragedy of Beslan. But,
as Mr Putin never tires of saying, this is a false choice. Russia simply has
no other option but to simultaneously strengthen both state and civic
institutions' (http://www.npetro.net/OpenLetter.html).

By stressing the need to simultaneously strengthen both state and
civic institutions, the response, evidently, touched the key issue in the
Western discussion of Russian civil society. From the outset, even the
academic discussion of Russian social and political transformation has
been characterized by a sharp juxtaposition of state and civil society and
a tendency to measure the development of civil society in terms of 'push-
ing back the state'. The merits of this type of civil society concept have
been the object of critical discussion since the rise of alternative civic
organizations in Eastern Europe in the 1980s, and for good reason still
are (Arato 1989; cf. Keane 1988; Schöpflin 2000, p. 36; Brubaker 2004,
pp. 132–46).

Though the argumentation of the response to the open letter is in this
respect in line with recent scholarly reasoning, in one sense it is remarkably reminiscent of the line of argument of the original letter. While
arguing for a more balanced approach to contradictory and multilay-
ered developments in Russia, the response, too, addresses the question
of democratization at an artificially uniform Russian national level – as
a question concerning a single integrated Russian political space.

Considering how intrinsically democratic structures and civic institutions are a phenomenon emerging from below, from local and regional-
level civic engagement, it is obviously rather problematic to interpret
their development simply in terms of national-level politics. In order to
achieve a more balanced picture of the prospects for Russian civil society
and, indeed, Russian democracy, it is clearly necessary to complement
the perspective of federal-level governmental politics with an approach
from below, addressing the relationship between civic and governmental institutions at the local and regional level. In terms of political space
Russia is not one but many. In order to understand what is happening
to the state and civil society as a whole, we maybe need to distance ourselves from the idea of a single Russian political space and look at the
process more from the perspective of regional and local actors. Perhaps
we should still be careful with conclusions regarding *Russian* civil society and *Russian* democracy (as a national-level phenomena) and instead
look at the constitution of the Russian political arena as an open process,
as something that is still in the process of formation.

This chapter approaches the question of Russian political space by a close study of local and regional voluntary associations in the Republic of Karelia during the late and post-Soviet period. The development of civil society is analysed in relation to the transformation of the field of political action and the reconstruction of federal and regional state structures. The formation of a new kind of political space is outlined on the basis of observations on the interconnection between civic action and changing modes of identification in statements and the everyday practices of clubs, societies and political groupings.

Analysing the development of Russian Karelia offers an alternative to Moscow-centred approaches that address questions of Russian democracy by focusing on the deeds of President Putin and his government, or on the real and imagined power struggles inside Kremlin. Even in regard to the forces of opposition and activities of non-governmental organizations, a look outside the capital can reveal more about Russian civil society than often-studied developments in the big metropolitan cities, which even in this respect differ fundamentally from the rest of the country.

Just as important, the Republic of Karelia does not represent a direct opposite to the federal centre. It is not a separate historical political community – neither in the sense of the Baltic ex-Soviet republics, which after the collapse of the Soviet Union were able to build on a tradition of independent political organization, nor in the sense of the more ethnically homogenous subjects of the Russian Federation that today seek to maintain or enlarge their autonomy. As one of the 21 republics, it enjoys somewhat greater powers than an ordinary region; but its population of just over 700,000 is the second-smallest of any of the republics or regions of the north-western federal district. It is overwhelmingly Russian (nearly 77 per cent, in the 2002 census), but with substantial minorities of Karelians, Belarusians, Ukrainians and Finns. Its wood and paper industries are particularly well-developed.

Civic organization and identity politics

In the Russian case, the relationship between the state and civil society is far from a simple dichotomy of two opposed blocs, and it is only through a complicated network of mediating structures that the level of local voluntary association encounters federal-level state politics. This makes it appropriate to address the question of Russian democracy starting from a regional perspective and considering the development of civil society in relation to local and regional power structures. It is first in this light that we can understand the role that President Putin's policies have played in the matter. Indeed, along with the sharp juxtaposition of state and civil society, the tendency to view civil society formation as something happening within a single integrated *Russian* national political space – controlled by President Putin – is probably the pattern that has most seriously distorted Western visions of democratization in Russia.

As is well known, the Putin administration has not only tightened the legislation concerning civic organizations but also ostentatiously encouraged the development of civil society by organizing large scale civic forums that have demonstrated the goodwill of the government towards voluntary associations.

> Currently, the already laborious and slow formation of civil society in Russia has slowed down. In separate sectors it has come to a halt or even gone backwards.... A system of so-called 'managed democracy' is developing in Russia instead of a democratic society predicated on civil institutions. Under this system, citizens are gradually restricted from decision-making processes which may have direct impacts on their interests, and society in general is deprived of the opportunity to control governmental activities. Consequently, a situation emerges in which governments do not serve the public interest and are not controlled by the public. On the contrary, the public becomes more and more subordinate to the government. (http://gadfly.igc.org/russia/forum.htm)

The response to Putin's initiatives has, however, not been exclusively positive. The above quote is from a statement that a group of Russian non-governmental organizations issued before the so-called Civic Forum held in Moscow in November 2001. This meeting of Russian civic organizations was initiated and chaired by Putin himself, and attracted considerable publicity in the media; it even brought questions of Russian civil society to the pages of Western newspapers. A similar thunderous discussion also followed the second civic forum that President Putin organized in the summer of 2006 (probably, largely in order to neutralize the heavy criticism that his new legislation on civic organizations had aroused).

Obviously, the tone of the statements of Russian civic organizations cannot be regarded as an example of a humble 'Eastern' flattering of the ruler and his government. In more than one sense, the basic line of argument is rather 'Western'. Indeed, it is reminiscent of and perhaps even reflects hegemonic modes of thought in Western public discussion and the scholarly literature. As in the open letter quoted above, the basic question is set along the lines of classical political liberalism: the citizen and the state are set against one another and the question is whether Russia is witnessing the emergence of modern civil society or the restoration of state-centred forms of social communication and political culture.

When scholars and commentators today analyse the 'end' or 'closing' of Russian civil society, the problems of the ambiguous Russian federal structure are seldom invoked. Increasing authoritarianism and restrictions on media freedom are in most cases analysed in terms of an unproblematic state/civil society division which bypasses the problems of regional power structures and the particular regional conditions in which civic organizations define their goals, friends and enemies (e.g. Lipman 2005). In regional-level identity politics, however, the federal government does not necessarily represent a bigger threat than the regional power structures. Hence, even Russian national rhetoric and identification should not be understood simply as tools for building a strong state from above. Indeed, the critical question is to what extent regional civic organization has been accompanied by the formation of new identities that frame policy issues in a new national frame and thus contribute to the creation of a national political space (Urban 1997, p. 26).

The obvious interconnection between civic action and the reconstitution of political space raises critical questions in regard to the study of Russian nationalism as well. Considered from the perspective of individual associations, it is quite impossible to distinguish between 'civic', non-governmental action and 'nationalistic' state-oriented forms of organization – which seems to be a leading tendency in the contemporary study of nationalism in Eastern Europe (see for instance Schöpflin 2000, pp. 4–6). At the level of statements and practices of individual associations, action cannot be separated from the definition of the field of action – and organization and identification are part of one and the same process.

This chapter summarizes the results of my earlier research on voluntary associations in Russian Karelia during the late and post-Soviet period. It then provides new information on civic organization in Karelia during the period of the Putin administration and analyses this information in relation to the federal reforms Putin has initiated. The main part of the study focuses on how local-level associations have defined their field of action, goals, enemies and allies. In the final section, this micro-level analysis of spatial identification is employed as a tool for examining the logic of Russian nation-building, reform of the federal structures and, ultimately, the formation of a nationally defined Russian political space.

Organization and identification during the late Soviet period

In the frame of Soviet Russia, Karelia formed an autonomous administrative entity from the beginning of the 1920s. In 1940, in connection to the so-called Winter War with Finland, it was even given the status of a Soviet republic. Still, even though Russian Karelia held this status till the end of the 1950s, during the entire Soviet period it never formed an ethnically defined political space where the titular nationality, the Karelians, would have formed the ruling majority. In the early phase during the 1920s, the Karelians still were the majority in regard to the Russian population, but at that time it was the Finnish Reds, who after the abortive revolution of 1918 fled to Soviet Russia, that formed the elite of Soviet Karelia. In the 1930s the special status of Finns was ruthlessly suppressed, Russian migrants and forced labour were brought into the area and after the war Russian became the dominant language of the republic. During the late Soviet period the share of the Karelian and Finnish population in official statistics was no more than 10 and 2 per cent of the total, respectively. The Karelians were rapidly being assimilated into the Russian-speaking majority, and in terms of social and cultural traditions the republic was more Soviet than anything else (Laine 2002). The new forms of civic organization that emerged with the politics of *perestroika* during the late Soviet period, however, opened a totally new horizon for cultural and political identification.

New local ties within the Soviet system, 1985–1986

In regard to social institutions, public life in the Karelian Autonomous Socialist Soviet Republic (as the republic had become in 1956) was completely channelled through official Soviet institutions when Mikhail Gorbachev came to power in 1985. We may of course surmise that below the official surface a 'second society' or perhaps even a hidden 'semi-public sphere' with its own norms and values existed (Voronkov 1996, pp. 146–9; Hankiss 1988). In the Finnish-language main newspaper that acted as an organ of the government, however, we find no trace of this. News items centred around the undertakings of the state and party administration and, at the grass-roots level, the activities of regional and local soviets and party units. Among reform-minded Communists there was, however, a discussion about how to bring the party closer to the everyday life of citizens. In the case of Karelia, it is evident that the first initiatives for establishing organizations formally independent of state and party structures came from within party circles. On the other hand, we have to be cautious about this conclusion as the very nature of the official newspaper material provides poor preconditions for evaluating the degree to which voluntary association was at the same time based on personal contacts and social networks typical of Soviet society (Ledeneva 1998; Lonkila 1999).

In 1984 there were only two clubs that could be perceived as even partly representing a new type of voluntary association. Both of these were athletics clubs, and as such not a very convincing indication of new civic activity. During the Soviet period sport clubs had been tightly bound to the system in the sense that they had their origins in other Soviet organizations such as workplaces, army units, schools or universities. In this sense, the two new clubs established in 1984 seem to represent a different idea. According to the information available they seem to function on a locally defined voluntary basis outside the Soviet structures, even if in both cases their opening ceremonies were attended by local party officials (*Neuvosto-Karjala* 20 January 1984).

In this sense, the voluntary organizations of the mid-1980s did not mark a mobilization from below. Even if there were some unprecedented features in the forms of organization, they were established very much in the old manner, from above, with the local party and Komsomol secretaries as the initiators. In this sense the breakthrough of voluntary associations was very much a 'revolution from above' – as was also the case even in Estonia (cf. Park 1995). The younger generation of party officials was either personally looking forward to a renewal of the structures of Soviet society or opportunistically calculating that this was what the new party leadership expected of them. In these conditions, it is quite clear that even the reformers did not aim directly at strengthening civic culture outside party control. The idea was still that the new societies and clubs would recognize the 'leading role' of the party.

Questions of nationality or ethnicity were not on the agenda at this stage but the new form of organization in itself advanced a kind of local identification and new localism by stressing local horizontal ties instead of vertical Soviet structures. The frame of action and the identification of the first voluntary associations were in this sense more local and pro-*perestroika* than Soviet. Local action was promoted, but at the same time the authorities wanted to limit the new forms of civic culture to the local level. Even so, this localism could be seen as an alternative to the ideals of the uniform Soviet patriotism of the Brezhnev period, which tended to bypass both ethnic and local identification as in the well-known song: 'My address is not a house or a street, my address is the Soviet Union'.

During the years 1985 and 1986 the number of associations mentioned in the newspaper *Neuvosto-Karjala* rose slowly (to 9 and 15 respectively). The degree to which they operated on a voluntary basis and outside official Soviet structures was still in many cases a complicated question. Eleven of the organizations were cultural clubs and societies established at the local Palace of Culture. Even if still under the control of the Soviet authorities, they can be seen as part of a gradually widening public space or at least a reflection of expectations that it was becoming possible to create new arenas for public discussion. Openly critical political statements were, however, not uttered out loud. The non-political nature of the phenomenon is clearly seen in the fact that the second largest group of associations was still sport clubs, which hardly represented societal renewal in any other sense than their mode of organization and perhaps an alternative local identification.

Still, a political element is evident in one sector of the new organizations, in the emerging temperance societies that arose after Gorbachev had started his first big political campaign – the war on alcohol. The sudden mobilization of new advocates of temperance was reminiscent of the old Soviet pattern of activating party cadres through campaigns from above. In connection with the change at the top of the party hierarchy, it might even be seen as proof of the opportunistic eagerness of the *apparatchiki* to demonstrate their loyalty to a new master. Considering the fight for hegemony inside the party, it is, however, more likely that the members of the temperance societies consisted primarily of younger generation officials and intellectuals who identified themselves with Gorbachev and the reform politics they expected him to initiate. If this, however, was the case, the political character of the phenomenon was more in the nature of 18th-century secret societies than modern voluntary organizations. Even in their most radical form, associational initiatives obviously came from above and the new forms of civic culture were supposed to be limited to the local level and within the boundaries of the Soviet system. In this respect the following years brought a dramatic change.

Sub-structures and counter-identities, 1987–1988

During 1987 *glasnost'* and *perestroika* attained hegemonic status as key concepts for reforming Soviet society. As catch-phrases in Mikhail Gorbachev's campaign to revitalize the stagnating society and economy, *glasnost'* and *perestroika* also served to rejuvenate human and national rights activity and to encourage the founding of civic organizations independent of official Soviet structures. This backing from above also had an effect in the Karelian Republic. Over the following years the number of associations mentioned in *Neuvosto-Karjala* rose to 25 and 26 respectively, which meant that the average doubled from the previous period. Half of the new bodies were still cultural organizations and discussion clubs, but they were now more orientated towards political issues and social problems. A second group was the youth associations which dissociated themselves from the Komsomol and the official ideals of Soviet culture. Some of the youth organizations represented a clear tendency to form their own sub- or even counter-culture, which was now reported openly in the press for the first time.

The intensification of the political climate can be seen in the fact that there were now clubs that openly declared politics as their main field of interest. This meant, however, still more space for opening up political discussion than for manifesting alternative political programmes. Typical examples of the period were the Political Film Club established in Petrozavodsk in April 1987 (the Filmmakers' Union had already taken the lead in the radicalization process by demanding a year earlier the release of previously banned films), the Friends of Political Literature Club (formed on 1 May 1987) or the Debating Club at the university that gathered regularly during the years 1987–1988 (*Neuvosto-Karjala* 26 April 1987, 6 May 1987, 22 May 1987 and 30 March 1988). Political topics were legitimized by citing Gorbachev's *perestroika* programme, and in this sense these organizations still represented more a political sub-culture than an oppositional counter-culture.

A change in this balance was, however, on its way especially on the level of youth culture, as can be seen in the activities of the Prospect Youth Club that was reported to operate as a 'combination of theatre, agitation brigade and discotheque'. The club organized performances handling social problems and injustices, alcoholism and other vices, shortcomings of the system and bureaucracy 'which disturbed our life and against which we all have to fight' (*Neuvosto-Karjala* 13 December 1987). In this sense, the club demonstrated a break with the official Komsomol tradition, but even more striking was its cultural break with formal Soviet culture. The group clearly aimed at establishing its own values, which deviated from Soviet norms, and in this sense it was balancing between a sub- and counter-cultural identity. References to Western youth culture and the open sexuality of its performances departed provocatively from the Soviet manner (Zdravomyslova 2001, pp. 151–67).

In 1988 political discussion clubs began to adopt a more critical role. The Debating Club of the University of Petrozavodsk added to its agenda questions like student self-government, renewal of higher education, democratization of Soviet society, and *perestroika* inside the Komsomol. Its declared aim was to launch a constructive debate to help its members participate in social life and in *perestroika* through concrete measures (*Neuvosto-Karjala* 30 March 1988).

During the period 1987–1988, new forms of counter-culture developed which deliberately set themselves outside Soviet society. Political discussion was intensified and new space for public discussion was created. Still, most of the open political discussion was incorporated inside the frame of the Soviet system and even its most radical forms sought legitimation by citing Gorbachev's *perestroika* programme. It was not until the end of this period that openly critical clubs and societies were formed which attacked the system and the party from the outside. In November and December 1988 *Neuvosto-Karjala* reported actions to form a Memorial Society in Petrozavodsk and at the university to commemorate and study Stalin's victims and crimes. Even earlier, three independent political clubs had been formed in Petrozavodsk and in Kostamuksa although they were not mentioned publicly in the press: the History and Literature Club and Socialist Pluralism in Petrozavodsk and Democratic Initiative in Kostamuksa (Tsygankov 1995). Similarly, the founding of the Popular Front of Karelia in November 1988 was initially greeted by silence in the press, but soon afterwards the new political front lines were brought into the open.

The years 1987 and 1988 witnessed a breakthrough of voluntary association outside the Soviet system. In terms of identification a clear dissociation from Soviet identity took place first in the form of subcultural youth clubs and later politically oriented counter-culture clubs. The frame of action was still primarily concerned with broadened autonomy within Soviet society at the local level, and it did not represent a direct challenge to power in a particular spatial frame. Towards the end of the period, however, part of the new organizations started to link their local activities to opposition forces in Moscow, Leningrad and the Baltic states seeking to change the whole Soviet system.

Politicization in the frame of the republic, 1989–1990

The intensifying struggle for hegemony at the top of the Communist Party and inside the Soviet system in general fuelled new kinds of regional level political mobilization in the union republics and autonomous areas during the last years of the 1980s. Despite the fact that the Karelian Autonomous Soviet Socialist Republic was mixed in its ethnic composition and weak in its economic and political status, even there an openly political challenge to the old power structures was manifested by emerging new social and political movements. During the years 1989–1990, the number of new associations mentioned in the Finnish press rose to 41 in 1989 and 47 in 1990. Alternative cultural associations, trade unions and ethnic organizations then became the most significant form of organization. More important than the forms of organization, however, was the open politicization of voluntary associations.

New independent labour unions and ethnic organizations first anchored their protest in basic social relations and everyday cultural traditions. The movement of the Ingrian Finns was organized in February 1989 and was the first to openly contest the myth of the unity of the Soviet people (*Neuvosto-Karjala* 22 February 1989, 21 June 1989; Klementjev 1996, pp. 142–5). By claiming recognition for the history and culture of the Ingrians it presented a symbolic challenge to the power-holders in the name of the people.

At the same time, the repertoire of collective action widened. Though small in number, environmental associations occupied a special place in the development of civic activity. The environmental movement was the first to make its demands in the form of collective mass protest. In December 1989, a demonstration was organized in the capital, Petrozavodsk, against plans to build a nuclear power station in the republic (*Neuvosto-Karjala* 13 December 1989; Liikanen 2001a). In 1990 new independent trade unions were established which soon broadened the repertoire of collective action to include strikes and new forms of social protest. In September 1990 the unions organized a protest meeting in the capital, which was the first to address open demands to the government (*Neuvosto-Karjala* 26 September 1990, 31 October 1990).

The most momentous expression of the politicization of voluntary organization was, however, the founding of the Popular Front of Karelia, which took place in November 1988. During the following years the Front was the first organization to publicly present rival economic and political reform programmes to those of the communist leadership of the republic. More importantly still, it was the first organization to strive openly for mass mobilization in support of its programmes.

As a political force, the Front won its greatest victories in the elections of 1989 to the USSR Congress of People's Deputies, when it successfully challenged and defeated the candidates of the party apparatus in the capital city of the republic, Petrozavodsk, and a few other *raions* (Tsygankov 1998, pp. 6–60). The Popular Front did not get much publicity in the press, but during the election campaign and again during the republican elections of 1990 it managed to function in the public sphere as an alternative to the official candidates. When the Soviet system collapsed, however, it was unable to institutionalize itself as a popular political movement. The Front split into rival parties and quarrelling national groupings. Neither the Front nor its successors was strong enough to destroy the old power structure. Individual members of the old elite remained in positions of power until the end of the 1990s (Tsygankov 1996, pp. 53–7).

In this sense it can be said that despite its name and aims, the Popular Front of Karelia did not represent a particularly successful popular movement; at first it was more a reflection of the 'rebellion of the intellectuals' (Liikanen 2001b; cf. Park 1995). It subsequently played an important role as the first organized political opposition recognized by public opinion, but this only occurred during a particular phase, in the quasi-parliamentarianism of the elections of 1989 and 1990. By challenging the hegemony of the Communist Party in the name of the people, the Front laid the foundation for a new political culture where the will of the people was in principle the final legitimation of power. In organizational terms, the Front, however, failed to establish itself as a new kind of political force which could have mobilized popular mass support and achieved a hegemonic position in the emerging Karelian political arena.

In Karelia, the Popular Front formed the first internal opposition to the Soviet system, and later it openly challenged the hegemony of the CPSU. The Front, however, achieved only limited success in its desire for mass organization. At its height it had about a thousand members (Tsygankov 1995, pp. 86–94). When compared to Estonia and the other Baltic countries, a simple explanation can be found in the fact that the Karelian Front did not have similar mobilization resources in terms of identity and culture. In Karelia the opposition had no access to similar cultural and organizational capital (memories of how to act collectively and voice things publicly), which the Estonian opposition had as a heritage from the period of independence (Ruutsoo 1996, pp. 101–8).

As in the case of Estonia, the group establishing the Front consisted predominantly of members of the intelligentsia, scholars, journalists, artists and actors. In this sense it was a product of the 'rebellion of the intelligentsia' as the Estonian scholar Andrus Park has described the first phase of political mobilization (Park 1995; Stranius 1996, pp. 150–5). In the case of Karelia the social base for mass mobilization was perhaps even narrower in the sense that the ruling elite did not fragment and ally itself with the mass organizations to the same degree as it did in Estonia and the other Baltic states. Although the Karelian leadership adhered to the reform politics of Moscow, it only did so reluctantly, and adopted a clearly negative attitude towards the political mass actions represented by the Popular Front.

More important, however, was the fact that the Front did not succeed in gathering together the opposition and uniting it into a single political project. Whereas in the Baltic states the Popular Fronts managed to gather under one umbrella the ethnic, environmental and trade union movements, in Karelia they went their separate ways, each broadening the public space and repertoire of collective action in its own way.

In the case of the Karelian Republic it is evident that Soviet power structures did not collapse because of a broad public mobilization and contentious collective action. Voluntary association and its politicization certainly broadened the sphere of public and political discussion and in the end were strong enough to challenge the powerholders in the quasi-democratic conditions of the late Soviet period. The principle of mass organization was adopted, but no successful mobilization followed. Populist anti-Soviet identification gained ground partly through such new ethnic organizations as Inkerin Liitto (the Ingrian Association) and Karjalan Rahvahan Liitto (the Karelian Union), but this could not generate a national political mobilization as in the Baltic republics. Even if the mobilization failed to establish and control an autonomous political space, a major change took place during this period. The frame of action shifted from the local level to that of the republic. The power hierarchy and the opposition confronted one another in the Karelian frame and the Karelian Soviet Republic even became the main frame of action for the organizations dominated by the Russian-speaking majority.

Challenge of the regions – and challenge in the regions, 1991

In its final phase the collapse of the Soviet system was greatly speeded by the challenge that the regions posed to the central authorities in Moscow. The opposition forming around the so-called Inter-Regional Group in the Supreme Soviet and around the heads of the Soviet Republics, most notably the President of the RSFSR, Boris Yeltsin, was in many cases supported by powerful regional level mobilization. Inside the regions, however, the nature and volume of this mobilization varied significantly. In the case of Karelia, the emergence of new voluntary associations during the late Soviet period culminated in the crucial year of 1991, but never achieved sufficient strength to shake the regional power structure. In 1991, the number of new associations rose to 64. Trade unions, ethnic organizations and readily established political party units were the most active forms of voluntary association. The Social Democrats and the Democratic Russia movement had already organized themselves the previous year and dominated the public scene, but none of the new party organizations was able to take the lead in uncertain political conditions. When the Soviet system collapsed in Moscow, in Petrozavodsk the old regime managed to maintain its position and the head of the government, Viktor Stepanov, remained in power until 1998.

In regard to the range of collective action, the introduction of new rival political parties was of course a momentous shift. During the first part of the year the Greens, for example, were reported to have organized party units in many of the major towns of the republic (*Neuvosto-Karjala* 2 April 1991). In the longer run, none of the new political parties managed to build stable organizational structures or inspire broader political mobilization. It is obvious that one reason for this development was the dual power situation in Moscow, the rivalry between reformers and old-guard Communists, which led to caution and inactivity in the periphery. In some sense, this uncertainty was felt even more deeply in the periphery than in the centre. For example, the speeches during the Red Army Day parade in Petrozavodsk in 1991 were filled with warnings to those who endangered the social order. Presented by unchallengeable armed power, they represented a very concrete threat to all who took part in opposition activities. Similarly, members of the opposition encountered pressure at their workplaces and if they were still party members, in their grass-roots party cells.

The ethnic movements avowed open alternative historical interpretations and cultural traditions which could have reinforced a popular mobilization. Because of immigration and assimilation, however, the ethnic signs and symbols could only reach a small minority. The Karelians and the Finns were in the best position to speak out in the name of the people, but compared to the Baltic states this was just a heroic episode in a lost battle. Among the Russians, the Memorial Society spread alternative images of history and there were even some attempts to organize support for Yeltsin during his struggle with the Russian parliament. These attempts, however, remained modest and were unable to win broader sympathy among the administrative elite or to create widely supported campaigns in the public sphere (*Neuvosto-Karjala* 6 June 1991, 11 July 1991).

The attitude of the elite and inactivity of the Russian-speaking majority of the population were exposed during the critical days of the attempted Moscow coup in August. The leadership of the republic remained silent, which could be taken as indirect support for the putsch. This later gave the Popular Front and the new party organizations, Democratic Russia, the Greens and Social Democrats, reason to demand the resignation of President Stepanov. In September 1991 a mass meeting was called in the main Kirov Square, but only a handful appeared. As a result, the organizers were unable to orchestrate even a symbolic overthrow of the old. The local newspaper reported: 'Unfortunately the majority of the quiet, peace-loving people stayed home. Because of the small number of demonstrators the resolution demanding the resignation of Stepanov could not be approved' (*Neuvosto-Karjala* 28 September 1991). As no 'taking of the Bastille' could be performed in the name of the people, the opposition forces themselves had to retreat.

The focus of public life in the republic started to move at this point from the political to the social sphere. Two weeks later the government and the labour unions concluded an agreement to guarantee the living standards and social welfare of the people (*Neuvosto-Karjala* 12 October 1991). After the unsuccessful attempt of the opposition to combine local activism with all-Soviet politics, the government and the interest groups found common ground in organizing things as best they could at the level of the republic itself. Strengthening the autonomy of this frame and withdrawing from ventures that could shake it became the main guideline for social organization. As for the peripheral Karelian Republic, it can be said that in the minds of the people the threatening dual power situation did not end in 1991, but ultimately only after the bombing of the White House in Moscow in 1993. Prior to that the people of the periphery chose to mind their own business and act at a republican level. Under the conditions of the economic crises of the following years the scope of voluntary action turned into strategies of everyday survival.

Civic organization and regional power in post-Soviet conditions

Reorganization of interest representation in a Karelian frame, 1992–1994

After a continuous increase in the number of new voluntary associations throughout the Gorbachev period, the dissolution of the Soviet Union led to a sharp fall in civic activity. In 1992 the number of new associations was barely half the level of the previous year. In 1993 it again reached the 1991 level and exceeded it slightly in 1994. The collapse in 1992 concerned almost every type of organization. Political parties still formed the biggest group, but the number of party groupings mentioned was only half that of the previous year. Paradoxically, the hegemonic upswing of the opposition forces was undermined by the collapse of communist rule. The new political parties lost the enemy that had given them their ideological credibility as forces of renewal. They were now drawn into the unromantic administration of the most unfavourable social and economic problems and caught up in party struggles that could hardly appeal to the public after the great drama of the previous years. Political life became a constant fragmentation and reconstitution of party alliances, which can be seen as an indication that the real power centres were elsewhere (*Karjalan Sanomat* 17 July 1993, 27 November 1993, 4 December 1993).

After the dissolution of the Communist Party of the Soviet Union, attempts at a communist revival were soon being made, but at least initially, without much success. After an unsuccessful communist demonstration in March 1992 the Finnish-language newspaper (which had by then changed its name from *Soviet Karelia* to *Karelian News*) declared in its headline: 'No return to the past' (*Karjalan Sanomat* 17 March 1992). During the next two years the Communists were, however, able to build the only functioning party network in the republic, and the First of May and October Revolution festivities again became the most popular ideological public manifestations in the republican capital (*Karjalan Sanomat* 7 November 1992, 30 March 1993, 25 September 1993, 9 November 1993, 5 May 1994, 10 November 1994).

The leadership of the republic, however, remained very much in the same hands as before. In the public discussion the labour unions and the ethnic organizations could largely set the agenda. Demonstrations, strikes and cultural manifestations were organized. The significance of such movements was, however, no longer a function of their ability to seize the public space, but was dependent more on negotiations with the government than demonstrations against it. In the new situation both the trade unions and the mainstream ethnic organizations joined with the Stepanov government to promote their own interests. At the end of 1992 the president of the republic and the leadership of the central trade union celebrated the anniversary of the October revolution side by side (*Karjalan Sanomat* 7 November 1992). After the elections of 1994 the trade union chairperson, Valentina Pivnenko, was nominated to head the representative chamber of the republic. In a way, she personified the new line of combining co-operation with the republican administration and sharp criticism of the Yeltsin government and Moscow businessmen (*Karjalan Sanomat* 5 May 1994, 9 June 1994).

During this period the Ingrian and Karelian ethnic mobilization was confronted by a Russian counter-organization, and the radical claims of the Karjalan Liike evoked aggressive reactions in the Russian-language press (*Karjalan Sanomat* 21 August 1993). The government, however, chose to work in co-operation with the representatives of ethnic groupings that symbolized the distinctiveness of the republic. In July 1993 the Ingrians were officially rehabilitated (*Karjalan Sanomat* 6 July 1993), and at the end of the year Viktor Stepanov was nominated as one of the candidates of the ethnic organizations in the Russian Federation Duma elections; the Karelian radical Anatolii Grigor'ev became his leading spokesman (*Karjalan Sanomat* 21 October 1993).

During the period 1992–1994, the Republic of Karelia served as an arena for negotiation over the scant resources at hand. It provided a frame for promoting the economic, social and cultural demands of different interest groups. At the same time, the Stepanov government managed to bind its old rivals to its side in the fight to defend the autonomy and the resource base of the republic in relation to Moscow. For all the actors, governmental and non-governmental alike, the Karelian Republic clearly formed the frame of action which they wanted to use in defending their interests against outside interference.

Organizing everyday life from below, 1995–1997

Starting in 1995 the number of associations active in the Karelian Republic doubled in comparison with the average for the previous period. New forms of organization emerged and an extensive diversification of civic culture took place. Smaller interest groups started organizing as self-help associations and pressure groups. Local trade unions were activated, women's, youth and various social organizations started to resolve everyday problems at the grass-roots level. The need to create a relationship between local organizations representing particular interests and administrative institutions came to the fore and resulted in a constant request for 'roundtable negotiations'. To some degree, this system probably reflected idealized attempts to restore the harmony between administration and civic culture that the Soviet system was said to represent. In practice, this obviously concealed contradictory tendencies similar to those of the Soviet era: government seeking to control the voluntary sector and civic organizations wanting to obtain resources and support from the administration.

On the whole, however, the characteristic feature of this period was not centralization but diversification in the field of civic action. There were new organizations established that did not focus on interests or politics and the reorganization of the relationship between government and the citizen. There were dozens of new cultural, ethnic and religious organizations that served the everyday needs of their members without the conscious desire to participate in the identity-political struggle for power and hegemony (the Club of Local History Lovers, Friends of Norway and others). As in the first phase of voluntary association in Western Europe, civic culture still served the needs of citizens to make social distinctions. Several associations promoting the status or professional prestige of their members emerged in the mid-1990s in Petrozavodsk (such as the Lions, Elite Women, Business Women, Lawyers' Union, and the Architects' Guild). In the social sphere charitable and self-help organizations were established (the Society of Big Families, the Invalids' Sporting Club). The clearest examples of this new emphasis on everyday problems and particular interests were of course found among hobby and leisure societies (such as the Kennel Club, Cat Lovers, the Fitness Club, the Dance Club and others).

Some of these associations were supported by Finnish organizations, EU programmes or other forms of Western aid. This presumably created organizational structures that would not have otherwise emerged, but as a whole the Finnish influence in Karelian public life started to wane when people with Finnish or Ingrian family backgrounds were allowed to move to Finland. At the same time the Karelian power bloc based on cooperation between the government and the trade unions was cracking under the pressure of the economic crises, which led to strikes and demonstrations (*Karjalan Sanomat* 6 November 1996, 18 December 1996). The trade unions sought a new ideological direction by participating in the foundation of the Karelian branch of the Patriotic Union of the Russian People (*Karjalan Sanomat* 15 January 1997, 22 January 1997). At the same time, the ethnic organizations that had given the bloc credibility in terms of identity politics started to distance themselves from the politics of the government (*Karjalan Sanomat* 1 January 1997).

In most cases the identification of the new voluntary associations was apolitical, but in more and more cases it reflected an all-Russian civic culture, and central organizations and ideologies that had their origin in a nationwide Russian frame. For example, new women's and party organizations were streamlined according to the models that existed at the federal level. As to political discussion, the frame of action was still predominantly the Karelian Republic, though in some cases the new organizations clearly reflected politics in the context of the Russian Federation. In particular, the war in Chechnya led to mobilization and demonstrations both in support and against the war effort. The local organization of Soldiers' Mothers was formed in late 1994 and a group petitioning against the war managed to collect nearly 25,000 names in 1996 (*Karjalan Sanomat* 20 November 1994, 1 June 1996). In the end, however, it seems that these activities were overshadowed by patriotic demonstrations signalling the rise of Russian nationalism. A report on the Victory Day parade in 1996 stated: 'It seemed that there were even more people than in the obligatory parades of the Soviet period' (*Karjalan Sanomat* 29 May 1996).

Civil society and the redefinition of Russian federal relations

Re-politicization and stabilization beyond the regional frame, 1998

Towards the end of the 1990s organizational activity in the Karelian Republic seemed to stabilize at a level roughly double that of the first half of the decade. During the period from 1998 to 2001 the number of voluntary associations mentioned annually in *Karjalan Sanomat* varied between 117 and 157 and reached a new peak at the beginning of the new millennium in the year 2000. The period was characterized first by a new politicization and shift within the regional power structures followed by gradual stabilization beyond the regional frame.

In 1998 the economic crises deepened as salaries and pensions went unpaid, and the trade unions and social charitable organizations played an important role in the field of civic organization. Ethnic and cultural organizations lost much of their previous visibility in public life and the forms of organization were further diversified with all kinds of new organizations being established in the fields of leisure and everyday life. The most notable feature of the year was, however, the emergence of a broad range of new political organizations and movements during the election year of 1998.

The deepening of the economic crisis led to angry demonstrations among teachers, doctors and other employees in the public sector. These actions were mostly organized on a local basis by groups blocking roads and streets, declaring hunger strikes or even threatening to prevent the elections from being held (*Karjalan Sanomat* 12 February 1997, 8 March 1997, 20 December 1997, 24 December 1997, 21 January 1998, 11 March 1998, 1 August 1998). The central trade union had previously entered into an agreement with the government and supported the Stepanov administration in the elections. In 1997 intensifying local demonstrations gradually forced the central trade union to act, and eventually it left the coalition (*Karjalan Sanomat* 26 February 1997, 1 March 1997, 5 March 1997, 29 March 1997, 25 February 1998). During the presidential elections that followed the central trade union was first reported to be supporting Stepanov as part of the Patriotic Front of the Russian People coalition (*Karjalan Sanomat* 21 January 1998), but later, during the campaign, the union changed its course and declared that it was neutral and supported none of the candidates, which in practice meant distancing itself from the Stepanov bloc (*Karjalan Sanomat* 14 February 1998).

During the late 1980s, ethnic movements had played a crucial symbolic role by signalling the popular nature of the protest against Soviet rule. Later, they provided an important identity-political credibility to the new power structure organized in the frame of the Karelian Republic. After the mid-1990s the organizations of the titular people, the Karelians, as well as those of the Finns and the Ingrians, started losing their status. In 1997, the Karelian Congress announced that Karelian organizations were being discriminated against when governmental bodies were appointed (*Karjalan Sanomat* 26 March 1997). At the same time, Ingrian organizations and the entire Finnish-language culture suffered badly from an increasing migration to Finland. The 7th Annual Congress of the Ingrian League reportedly was 'reminiscent of a gathering of pensioners' (*Karjalan Sanomat* 26 February 1997). The withering of ethnic radicalism was symbolized by the fact that its best-known representative, Anatolii Grigor'ev, acted at the same time as the head of the Karelian Congress and co-ordinator of the local party unit of Our Home is Russia (*Karjalan Sanomat* 21 March 1998).

Ethnic organizations had previously allied themselves with the government but after the mid-1990s this alliance started to show signs of friction. The expectations of protecting Finnish culture and revitalizing the Karelian language and culture were thwarted and many of the Fenno-Ugric organizations declared their support for rival candidates to Stepanov, who – though a Russian speaker – was by origin an ethnic Karelian (*Karjalan Sanomat* 21 August 1998).

Throughout most of the 1990s, Russian nationalist voices had remained in the background in Karelian politics. Most notably, they were represented by small extremist groups like the paramilitary 'Russian National Unity' and the liberal democrats who successfully organized local party units in the Karelian countryside during the election campaign of 1998 (*Karjalan Sanomat* 26 April 1997, 4 February 1998). To some degree, nationalist slogans had been employed by the Patriotic Front of the People coalition, which had earlier linked the trade unions and the local Communists in an electoral bloc supporting Stepanov. The 1998 election campaign did not bring a great change in the use of nationalist sentiments but in practice the frame in which politics was conducted was clearly changing from the Karelian Republic to an all-Russian frame. The political parties as well as civic organizations turned their attention more to a Russian perspective and planned their activities as part of the Russian field of action. In this sense the relationship between civic culture and nationality shifted in a new direction. The fall of Stepanov can be seen as both a symptom and a result of this tendency. In the new millennium, civic culture and politics in the Karelian Republic started to be increasingly reorganized in relation to the burgeoning civic culture of the Russian Federation.

The language question and the status of the republic, 1999–2001

In succeeding years, the ethnic organizations of Karelians and Finns came to dominate much of the Finnish-language public scene in the Karelian Republic. This was, however, not a sign of their increasing authority but, on the contrary, of a defensive action to restore the crumbling basis of an ethnic-based organization and of their political rhetoric.

At the end of 1999 the Ingrian League celebrated its 10th anniversary. The League had been one of the pioneers of the emergence of new social and ethnic movements during the years of *perestroika*. Lately, it had, however, been hit hard by the so-called return migration to Finland, which led to a situation where a major part of the Ingrian population in Karelia had moved to Finland, among them many of the most educated and language-skilled actors in Karelian public life. In an interview given in connection to the anniversary, the chairman of the League, Juho Mullonen, stated: 'During the last years migration to Finland has greatly weakened our intellectual resources, but we are still alive and we will go on with our activities' (*Karjalan Sanomat* 15 December 1999).

Similarly, the Union of the Karelians was very visible in the public discussion but this happened mostly in connection with the conflict over the official languages of the republic, where the status of the titular people of the republic was in the end further weakened. During the post-Soviet years Karelian organizations had at least occupied a symbolically important role in the power structures of the republic. In conditions of deepening assimilation, the Union had managed to build its organization and promote the status of Karelian language and culture. In the spring of 2000 the Union was proud to announce that it had held its meeting for the first time in the Karelian language – but at the same time it had to report that there were not too many people present (*Karjalan Sanomat* 22 March 2000). The following year enthusiasm for the Karelian language suffered a further blow as Russian was made the only official language of the republic. The summer meeting of the Karelians was held in a gloomy atmosphere, and discussions were again held mainly in

Russian – as interpretation was not available (*Karjalan Sanomat* 27 June 2001).

The language question had become topical at the end of the previous year when the House of Representatives rejected a government proposal not to give Karelian the status of second official language of the republic. When plans to make Russian the only official language became public, Karelian organizations protested stridently and all the Fenno-Ugric ethnic organizations joined in a common appeal to the head of the government (*Karjalan Sanomat* 23 September 2000, 4 November 2000, 23 December 2000, 14 March 2001).

Paradoxically, the ethnic organizations found more support from the old power bloc built around President Stepanov in the early post-Soviet years than among the elected representatives who gained more power after the fall of Stepanov in 1998. The ethnic organizations then tried to primarily appeal to members of the government who were interested in safeguarding the status of the republic against federal reforms planned in Moscow. In a round table discussion on the language question Aleksandr Lukin formulated this point: 'Russia is moving towards a unitary state, on the principle: we do not need many regional subjects, it is easier to rule if the country is uniform. On these grounds Karelia can be incorporated into the Murmansk or Vologda region. For this reason, to deny the special national status is pure political ignorance.' According to Lukin the question was: 'Do we, indeed, want to say no to the Karelian Republic?' (*Karjalan Sanomat* 21 February 2001).

The following year brought more defeats along the same lines. In the autumn of 2001, the national organizations first protested against the closing down of the Ministry of Nationality Affairs by President Putin (*Karjalan Sanomat* 27 October 2001). At the end of the year, an initiative to allocate specific seats to minority groupings was defeated in the Karelian parliament, which led the Karelian Congress to declare that the very existence of the republic was in danger (*Karjalan Sanomat* 19 December 2001). Developments culminated in parliament's symbolic decision that in future the official version of the national anthem of Karelia would only be in Russian (*Karjalan Sanomat* 15 December 2001).

Among minority groupings all this raised questions about the intentions of the federal government and of President Putin in particular. Zinaida Strogalstsikova of the Vepsian Cultural Society stated in the heat of the language debate: 'The position of the aboriginal peoples in Russia has worsened. The new age of "controlled democracy" has led to the alienation of small peoples from power and to the closing down of the state committee of the Northern areas' (*Karjalan Sanomat* 28 April 2001).

The ethnic organizations seemed to find some support at the highest levels of the Karelian government after the language decision when the head of the republic, Sergei Katanandov, proposed that a council of the indigenous population should be included in the administrative structures (*Karjalan Sanomat* 2 June 2001). In August 2001 this presidential council was formed from representatives of the ethnic organizations, but its status and authority remained unclear (*Karjalan Sanomat* 18 August 2001).

In a way the founding of the council can even be seen as a continuation of the tendency of binding voluntary organizations to the administration, a tendency that had been typical of the whole post-Soviet period. In 1999 a plan was announced to incorporate civic organizations into the town administration of Petrozavodsk (*Karjalan Sanomat* 15 September 1999), and in the autumn of 2001 a civic forum 'State, Civic Organizations and their Opportunities for Co-operation' was held in Petrozavodsk under the guidance of President Katanandov (*Karjalan Sanomat* 24 October 2001). As the forum was taking place just prior to – and most likely as part of the preparations for – President Putin's grand civic forum in Moscow, it can also be taken as a new sign of the shift in political framing from the republican to the federal level.

New winds in the relations between civic organizations and state institutions also started to blow in the field of cultural organizations. The old Soviet Union of Karelian Writers lost its official status and gained two rival organizations to work at its side. Symptomatically, the old union managed to keep most Karelian and Finnish writers who were oriented to the frame of the Karelian Republic in its ranks while the new organizations seemed to attract Russian writers interested in the status of writers at the level of the Russian Federation (*Karjalan Sanomat* 6 November 1999, 31 January 2001, 29 December 2001).

Even if the ethnic and cultural organizations engaged in the language strife achieved a strong position on the Finnish-language public scene, this did not automatically mean that they would dominate the field of civic action. During the years following the 1998 economic crisis, labour unions formed a third form of organization that was most often mentioned in the press. In comparison with the late and post-Soviet periods, information on labour union activities in *Karjalan Sanomat* was exceptionally voluminous between 1999 and 2001, and it reached its all-time peak in 2000. At the same time, it should be remembered that even during this period most voluntary associations were not involved in social or political skirmishes but operated at the level of people's everyday concerns and hobbies. In this sense basic structures of civil society were evolving without making the headlines.

The tendency to link regional and federal-level activities in a new manner was clearest in politics. In spring 2000, the Karelian branch of Putin's new Unity party was founded and the news reported that it was expanding rapidly (*Karjalan Sanomat* 11 March 2000). Other new coalitions followed, and the Forces of the Right founded their Karelian branch in the summer of 2000 (*Karjalan Sanomat* 1 July 2000). The federation-wide political arena was also employed by the opposition, such as when four Karelian 'pacifist organizations' issued a declaration against the war in the Caucasus in late 1999 (*Karjalan Sanomat* 22 December 1999). This federation-wide organizing, however, concerned not only Moscow-based politicians and political parties, but paradoxically even ethnic organizations, as is indicated by the acceptance of the Organization of Vepsian Youth as a full member of the nation-wide Youth Conference of Aboriginal Peoples (*Karjalan Sanomat* 4 August 1999).

Going beyond a Karelian frame did not stop at the Russian federal level but was also manifested in the form of new international links. Many types of voluntary organizations engaged in everyday co-operation with Finnish or Western sister-organizations like the Youth Organization of the Karelian Red Cross (*Karjalan Sanomat* 25 September 1999). New friendship societies were founded, and in 2001 it was announced in Petrozavodsk that there were active friendship organizations with ten countries (*Karjalan Sanomat* 4 April 2001). This internationalization also concerned ethnic organizations, as evidenced by the joint meeting of Ingrian organizations of Finland, Sweden, Estonia, Karelian Republic and St Petersburg in the spring of 2001 (*Karjalan Sanomat* 30 May 2001).

Colonizing the regional political platform – or opening up a national political arena? 2002–2005

After 2002, references to voluntary associations in the Finnish-language public discussion in the Karelian Republic fell to a level approximately one-third below those of previous years. Ethnic and cultural societies still dominated the field but towards end of the period 2002–2005 ethnic associations were losing their position as the most discussed form of organization, and cultural bodies, musical and sport clubs as well as all kinds of associations connected to everyday life and hobbies became more important.

Can this be read as a sign of the weakening of civil society and the loss of its political significance? An answer to the first question during this period can no longer be given based on the basis of newspaper information. The number of associations mentioned in the press at this point is nothing more than a weak indicator of what is happening in the society as a whole. Associations had become part of everyday life and their founding in some neighbourhood was no longer news that interested the republic-level media. We know from published data that during 2002–2003 there were about 2000 associations officially registered in the Karelian Republic, and according to estimates there was an equal number of unregistered organizations. Civic action of this kind did not concern the republic as a whole, however, and 75 per cent of the new organizations operated in the capital, Petrozavodsk (*Karjalan Sanomat* 21 January 2004).

Being eased out of public discussion can of course be seen as a sign of weakening political influence. The ethnic organizations of Finns and Karelians were still in the centre of public discussion over the official languages of the republic, but they were losing their battle and in the end also losing their previously strong mandate to speak in the name of the titular people of the republic. On the other hand, voluntary associations were at the same time becoming an elementary part of the rhetoric of the Putin regime both in Karelia and in the federation as a whole. The eagerness of the ruling elite to define, control and co-ordinate the role of voluntary associations seems to hint that fears and expectations concerning the political potential of civic organizations had not disappeared.

In 2002 and 2003, the hectic discussion over the official languages ensured that ethnic organizations had a more visible position in the Finnish-language press than any other form of civic organization. Even though the goal of making Karelian the second official language alongside Russian was not achieved, the battle itself did have at least a temporary mobilizing effect, and the organization of the Karelians, Karjalan Rahvahan Liitto, was reported to have revived its activities (*Karjalan Sanomat* 5 March 2003), although heavy losses again led to infighting and inactivity. There were differing opinions on which of the Karelian dialects should be made the basis of the literary language, and whether the vocabulary should be modernized on the basis of Finnish or Russian in order to preserve its authenticity. The leader of the radical Karjalan Kongressi, Anatolii Grigor'ev, wrote that the only way was to adopt the missing modern terms and concepts from Finnish. He noted that the Karelians had no time to waste: 'If the small group of linguists just continue their futile dispute over the Karelian language, the language will die. No laws can help this' (*Karjalan Sanomat* 29 October 2003). In the end a new association emerged with the opposite aim of reviving the 'original' Karelian literary language that had been composed after the liquidation of the Finnish Reds in 1937 and then forgotten for decades (*Karjalan Sanomat* 27 July 2005).

In the midst of the quarrels over the proper form of Karelian literary language the ethno-sociologist Yevgenii Klement'ev published studies that revealed the depth of the assimilation of the Karelian population and directed the discussion away from the status of the language to practical questions of teaching Karelian and Finnish in the schools (*Karjalan Sanomat* 14 August 2002, 28 December 2002). During 2004 and 2005, the language question was no longer the object of hectic public debate between representatives of civic organizations but became more a matter of negotiation between such organizations and the government. The council of representatives of the Finns, Karelians and Vepsians that worked under the chairmanship of President Katanandov was closely involved in the preparation of legislation over state subsidies to the Karelian, Vepsian and Finnish languages (*Karjalan Sanomat* 16 January 2002, 18 February 2004, 8 June 2005). This brought positive results in terms of language teaching in schools but at the same time reinforced the tendency to incorporate civic organizations into administrative structures in a manner that was typical of the Soviet period.

The inclusive strategy of the Katanandov government was also evident in other fields of social and political life. In terms of party politics, the most notable example was the merging of the rival party branches of Unity and Fatherland. The new umbrella organization, Reconciliation of Karelia, was supposed to prevent disintegration and instability. Katanandov declared his aim to be the building of a modern civil society which would be achieved through reconciliation and compromise between the different population groups (*Karjalan Sanomat* 23 January 2002).

The tendency to organize broader umbrella organizations working in close contact with the authorities concerned – for instance – women's and religious organizations (*Karjalan Sanomat* 15 September 2004, 4 February 2004). Under Katanandov's leadership a council of religious organizations was formed, which followed the model of the council of ethnic organizations (*Karjalan Sanomat* 12 May 2004). Towards the end of the period religious organizations, especially the Orthodox Church, achieved an increasingly prominent position in public life and in the politics of the government (*Karjalan Sanomat* 4 February 2004, 18 February 2004, 21 April 2004).

The comprehensive reconciliation between civic organizations and administrative structures, however, was not frictionless. The labour unions were able to organize large demonstrations against the government when they felt the social welfare of their members had been prejudiced (*Karjalan Sanomat* 19 October 2002, 27 October 2004). In early 2005 there was a serious attempt to politicize the protest movement when the Communists and the Yabloko Party organized a joint demonstration against cuts in welfare benefits. A notable feature of the protest action was its direct link to federal politics. Grigorii Yavlinsky, the Yabloko leader, appeared as the main speaker at the demonstration and the main demand of the demonstrators was no less than the resignation of the federal government (*Karjalan Sanomat* 9 February 2005).

The demonstration signalled a new dimension of social and political life that had been maturing in the republic since the late 1990s: a turn towards the Russian federal political arena. In approaching the new millennium, even the ethnic and national movements that were trying to protect the autonomy of the Karelian Republic and its ethnic bases began to act and make demands at the federal level. Paradoxically, the radical Karjalan Kongressi was the first to shift its field of action from the Karelian frame to the federal by starting to make claims and demands on the federal government (*Karjalan Sanomat* 19 January 2002). By 2005 Anatolii Grigor'ev had appealed to President Putin no less than five times to improve the status of small ethnic communities. It is notable that at this point in his framing of the political field, enemies and allies had shifted completely to the federal level when he declared: 'The nationality policy of the government is threatening to bring disharmony between peoples and shake the foundations of statehood. Russia has to be multinational and multilingual; it has to have many faces. Only in this way can it preserve its unity' (*Karjalan Sanomat* 26 January 2005).

Karelian civic organizations, in fact, were adopting the rhetoric of the federal government. The role of civic and ethnic organizations was acknowledged and even praised, but only when co-ordinated with the politics of the government itself and as part of building national unity and social and political uniformity. This tendency was evident, for instance, in the foundation of a council of civic organizations that was to work under the chairman of the Karelian legislative assembly (*Karjalan Sanomat* 21 January 2004). The message that this policy had the backing of the highest level of federal government was made clear when foreign minister Sergei Lavrov visited the republic in early 2005. Lavrov emphasized the role of voluntary associations in cross-border co-operation and in social and political life as a whole. He stated that while Russia had not advanced far in developing civil society, positive changes were under way, and added that 'In the near future a Public Chamber [would] be formed to unite all the country's non-governmental organizations and coordinate their activities' (*Karjalan Sanomat* 26 January 2005). This close interest of the federal authorities in the activities of voluntary associations leaves open critical

questions about their objectives: is the real intention of the administration to promote the development of civil society or to control it?
Similarly it can be asked in relation to the development of civil society in
Karelia whether we are witnessing the colonization of the regional political platform – or the opening up of a new kind of national political arena.

Conclusions

During the late Soviet period voluntary association and identity politics developed an antagonistic relationship with the Soviet state and
Soviet identity. In Karelia, civic culture matured from a locally defined
sub-culture to an open counter-culture and finally to a direct political
challenge to Soviet rule and the ideology with which it was associated.
As in the larger union republics the challenge in the name of the people
was first channelled through ethnic organizations seeking to strengthen
the autonomy of the republic in regard to the central state. After the
collapse of the Soviet Union the identification expressed by voluntary
associations followed the new framing of their field of action, which
in most cases was the Karelian Republic. Relations with politics on the
federal level were initially cautious, and up to the mid-1990s collective
action was still conceptualized mainly in a regional Karelian frame, but
gradually issues of the national political agenda became more and more
important. Since 1998, when the regime of the old Soviet-time president
Stepanov fell, the field of action of voluntary associations has been more
and more defined in a federal or Russian national frame.

In regard to present-day Russian political culture, three themes concerning identity politics among voluntary associations in Russian Karelia
seem to offer new elements to recent scholarly and political discussion.
Firstly, it seems that the strengthening of federal structures initiated by
President Putin does not necessarily represent simply nation-building
from above, but is linked to a profound redefinition of political space and
the sphere of action even at the level of civil society. Secondly, identifying with regional political structures typical of the 1990s was obviously
not just a result of ethnic mobilization but rather an adaptation to a
frame through which very limited resources could best be negotiated
and battled over. Thirdly, it is possible that the ongoing change of political frame towards the federal level does not necessarily signal a mere
shift in the balance of power between civil society and the state – from
the regions to the centre. It can be perceived even from below in terms
of the formation of new alliances and hegemonic blocs operating within
a federal frame.

It is perhaps too early to speak of the reconstitution of Russian political space, but if the case of Karelian voluntary associations indicates a more general tendency in the Russian regions, steps in that direction seem evident. It seems that politics and civic culture in Russia are no longer simply shifting on a centre-periphery axis but turning more towards an arena of multiple actors where cross- and multi-regional alliances are possible. At the moment, it remains far from obvious what the long-term consequences of this development may be for the democratization of Russian political culture. Still, it seems clear that in the future the development of regional level civic culture will play a key role in the reconstitution of Russian political space.

References

Newspapers

Karjalan Sanomat 1992–2005
Neuvosto-Karjala 1984–1991

Books and articles

Alapuro, R. 1993. 'Civic Society in Russia?' in J. Iivonen (ed.), *The Future of the Nation State in Europe*, Aldershot: Edward Elgar, pp. 194–218.

Arato, A. 1989. 'Civil Society, History and Socialism: Reply to John Keane.' *Praxis International* 9: 141–4.

Brubaker, R. 2004. *Ethnicity without Groups*. Cambridge: Harvard University Press.

Fish, M. S. 1994. *Democracy from Scratch. Opposition and Regime in the New Russian Revolution*. Princeton: Princeton University Press.

Hankiss, E. 1988. 'The Second Society.' *Social Research* 55: 13–42.

Keane, J. (ed.) 1988. *Civil Society and the State*. London: Verso.

Klementyev, Y. 1996. 'Formation of a Civil Society and National Movement in the Republic of Karelia,' in K. Heikkinen and E. Zdravomyslova (eds), *Civil Society in the European North. Concept and Context*, Centre for Independent Social Research, St Petersburg, pp. 142–5.

Laine, A. 2002. 'Rise and Fall of Soviet Karelia', in A. Laine and M. Ylikangas (eds), *Rise and Fall of Soviet Karelia*. Helsinki: Kikimora Publications, pp. 7–24.

Ledeneva, A. 1998. *Russia's Economy of Favours: Blat, Networking and Informal Exchange*. Cambridge: Cambridge University Press.

Liikanen, I. 2001a. 'Environmental Campaigns and Political Mobilisation in the Northwestern Border Areas of the Former Soviet Union,' in P. Ganster (ed.), *Cooperation, Environment and Sustainability in Border Regions*, San Diego: San Diego State University Press, pp. 275–86.

Liikanen, I. 2001b. 'Educational and Political Capital and the Breakthrough of Voluntary Association in Russian Karelia,' in S. Webber and I. Liikanen (eds), *Education and Civic Culture in Post-Communist Countries*, Basingstoke: Palgrave, pp. 28–41.

Lipman, M. 2005. How Russia is Not Ukraine: The Closing of Russian Civil Society. *Carnegie Endowment for International Peace, Policy Outlook,* January 2005. http://www.carnegieendowment.org/files/PO8lipmanfinal.pdf

Lonkila, M. 1999. *Social Networks in Post-Soviet Russia. Continuity and Change in the Everyday Life of St Petersburg Teachers.* Helsinki: Kikimora Publishers.

Luukkanen, A. 2001. *Hajoaako Venäjä? Venäjän valtiollisuuden kehitys vuosina 1862–2000.* Helsinki: Edita.

McDaniel, T. 1996. *The Agony of the Russian Idea.* Princeton: Princeton University Press.

Park, A. 1995. 'Turning-points of post-communist transition: Lessons from the case of Estonia,' *Proceedings of the Estonian Academy of Sciences* 44, pp. 323–32.

Patomäki, H. and Pursiainen, C. 1998. *Against the State, With(in) the State, or a Transnational Creation: Russian Civil Society in the Making?* UPI working papers 4. Helsinki: The Finnish Institute of International Affairs.

Petro, N. N. 1995. *The Rebirth of Russian Democracy. An Interpretation of Political Culture.* Cambridge, MA: Harvard University Press.

Putnam, R. D. 1993. *Making Democracy Work.* Princeton: Princeton University Press.

Ruutsoo, R. 1996. 'Formation of Civil Society Types and Organisational Capital of the Baltic Nations in the Framework of the Russian Empire,' in K. Heikkinen and E. Zdravomyslova (eds), *Civil Society in the European North. Concept and Context,* St Petersburg: Centre for Independent Social Research. pp. 101–8.

Ruutsoo, R. 2002. *Civil Society and Nation Building in Estonia and the Baltic States. Acta Universitatis Lapponiensis 49.* Rovaniemi: Lapin yliopisto.

Sakwa, R. 1996. *Russian Politics and Society.* London: Routledge.

Schöpflin, G. 2000. *Nations, Identity, Power.* London: Hurst & Co.

Stranius, P. 1996. 'The Role and Drama of the Russian Intelligentsia,' in K. Heikkinen and E. Zdravomyslova (eds), *Civil Society in the European North. Concept and Context,* St Petersburg: Centre for Independent Social Research. pp. 150–5.

Tsygankov, A. 1991. *K grazhdanskomu obshchestvu.* Petrozavodsk: Kareliya.

Tsygankov, A. 1995. 'Nuutuneen riemun aika,' *Carelia* 4, pp. 86–94.

Tsygankov, A. 1998. *Prishestvie izbiratelya. Iz istorii vybornykh kampanii v Karelii 1989–1996.* Petrozavodsk: Kareliya.

Urban, M. with V. Igrunov and S. Mitrokhin 1997. *The Rebirth of Politics in Russia.* Cambridge: Cambridge University Press.

Voronkov, V. 1996. 'Dissidenttien rooli kansalaisyhteiskunnan muotoutumisessa,' in I. Liikanen and P. Stranius (eds), *Matkalla kansalaisyhteiskuntaan. Liikettä ja liikkeitä Luoteis-Venäjällä. Karjalan tutkimuslaitoksen julkaisuja 115,* Joensuu: Joensuun yliopisto, pp. 143–50.

White, A. 1999. *Democratisation in Russia under Gorbachev 1985–91.* London: Macmillan Press.

Zdravomyslova, E. 1996. 'Kansalaisyhteiskuntakeskustelu Venäjällä,' in I. Liikanen and P. Stranius (eds), *Matkalla kansalaisyhteiskuntaan. Liikettä ja liikkeitä Luoteis-Venäjällä. Karjalan tutkimuslaitoksen julkaisuja 115.* Joensuu: Joensuun yliopisto, pp. 17–26.

Zdravomyslova, E. 2001. 'Hypocritical Sexuality of the Late Soviet Period,' in S. Webber and I. Liikanen (eds), *Education and Civic Culture in Post-Communist Countries.* Basingstoke: Palgrave, pp. 151–67.

2
What Kind of Civil Society in Russia?*

Diana Schmidt-Pfister

Throughout the 1990s, new possibilities of participation have triggered the emergence and development of a civil society or third sector in post-Soviet Russia. At the turn of the millennium, assessments were made not only as this marked the end of the first decade of development, but also the onset of a new era of government with Vladimir Putin assuming the presidency in 2000. By then, many scholars responded with rather optimistic prospects to the frequently asked question whether Russia would be 'on its way towards civil society' (see for instance the contributions in Gorzka and Schulze 2000; Schrader et al. 2000; vanden Heuvel 2000). Yet some remained more cautious regarding this new political era, envisaging that all the crucial societal achievements of the last few years might be put to test (Schulze 2000, p. 151). Recently, increasing international awareness of Russia's deviance from the path of democratization and the government's imposition of restrictive regulations on civil society have spurred renewed attention to the issue. Current assessments are overly pessimistic, while recent attempts at drawing a balance have been confusing at best. Many have argued that Russian civil society remains weak, internally fragmented, underdeveloped,

---

* This chapter builds on a paper presented at the VII ICCEES World Congress in Berlin, Germany, 25–30 July 2005 (see *How to Explain Russia's Post-Soviet Political and Economic System?* Bremen: Forschungsstelle Osteuropa, Working Paper No. 69, September 2005, pp. 23–45). For insightful comments on earlier versions I am grateful to Dmitry Vorobyev, Valerie Bunce, Agnes Gilka-Bötzow, Masha Lipman, and Guido Müntel. The first drafts would not have been written without the hospitality of the Centre of Independent Social Research, St Petersburg, and the Centre of Independent Social Research and Education, Irkutsk. The financial contributions of Queen's University Belfast and of BASEES through grants for field research in Russia are gratefully acknowledged.

co-opted, repressed, or even non-existent. Other accounts have taken the rather different view that civil society does exist in Russia, and is building on longstanding traditions. Others have emphasized novel incentives and forms of mobilization. Consensus has emerged, at least, that it is problematic to compare Russian civil society with Western standards.[1]

It is by now impossible to remove the term 'civil society' from both the bulk of Western political science literature and the terminology of international governance. It has become one of the main points on the agendas of most international organizations. Moreover, the state of civil society in contemporary Russia is of central concern to American and European actors who have provided considerable democracy assistance to post-Soviet Russia, including targeted civil society development programmes and the involvement of NGOs as mediators or implementers of issue-related programmes. In this context, the issue has grown increasingly relevant to both political practice and scholarly study over the last decade or so. Still, it has remained difficult to introduce the term into Russian scholarly debates and official discourses in a meaningful way. At the sight of a puzzling range of diverse arguments, we must realize that our understanding of Russian civil society is still partial.

Is the ambivalent picture found in the scholarly literature and expert assessments a problem of lacking empirical evidence? Or, to the contrary, is it a problem of applying concepts, rhetoric and expectations that have been heavily influenced by Western thought to the Russian realities of civil society formation? Or is it a problem of the lack of communication between Western and Russian researchers and experts? Certainly, these three problems are intertwined. The ongoing processes of civil society development (and repression) in contemporary Russia are insufficiently analysed in the academic literature; and assessments often generalize on the basis of very specific empirical data (certain points in time and space of post-Soviet Russia). Most analyses start from conventional assumptions that are in the minds of Western scholars and donors, in order to arrive at *ex post* insights that these are difficult to apply in this case. On the other hand, Western concepts are often not taken up by Russian scholars, on the *a priori* premise that they would not be applicable anyway. As a result, many authors on both sides come to conclude that there is not much to discuss about 'civil society' in Russia. Unfortunately, these tendencies have hampered constructive discourse between Western and Russian experts on the multitude of meanings attached to the concept of civil society according to different research traditions, changing experiences of non-/democratic governance in Russia as well as connotations with the different terms used in different languages.

What kind of civil society does Russia have? This chapter will not offer a straightforward answer. Rather, it seeks to provide a broader overview of relevant approaches and findings by revisiting recent scholarly contributions of both Western and Russian origin and against the background of empirical developments. While in fact adding even more question marks to the debate, this is still done with a view to furthering our understanding of where we find ourselves, empirically as well as analytically. This effort to identify and systematize recent controversial trends and concepts will also assist in demarcating areas of disagreement, common interest and potential future collaboration. The purpose of the chapter is thus not to revisit longstanding fundamental debates in the various literatures around civil society as such or its role in transformation/democratization processes or globalizing politics.[2] Nor does it summarize the comprehensive debates on civil society formation in Russia during the *perestroika* or even Soviet periods.[3] Rather, it seeks to systematize a variety of seemingly different stories on the particularities of civil society in present-day Russia. It thus localizes existing boundaries between conceptual approaches, Western and Russian views, and scholars' and practitioners' discourses, and underlines the benefit of stepping beyond such confines.

The chapter starts with a brief outline of the current empirical puzzle concerning civil society development in Russia. It then proceeds to a systematic review of Western and Russian publications on these and related developments by categorizing them into four main blocs: (i) civil society within a context of transformation, (ii) as presenting a 'third sector', (iii) as being part of transnational civil society, and (iv) as comprising uncivil elements. The literature discussions draw on empirical insights gained from the author's own interviews and fieldwork.[4] Finally, on the basis of these insights into trends in research and practice, potential cross-fertilizations between communities of Western and Russian researchers as well as scholars and practitioners are suggested.

Excursus: what's the problem with civil society in Russia?

Empirically, recent developments in Russia have been puzzling to analysts no less than to practitioners involved in civil society formation. Efforts of declared civil society building have been undertaken in Russia by international together with domestic partners since the late 1980s.[5] This emphasis of Western donors on fostering the growth of Russian civil society or involving NGOs in democratization programmes has been reflected in increasing numbers of Moscow-based foreign field offices,

Internet portals, handbooks of various kinds, regular newsletters and reports. In the domestic context, civic activity has flourished during the 1990s. When President Putin assumed office and claimed civil society formation to be among his reform priorities this raised mixed feelings. Obvious governmental efforts to constitute a formal framework for civic activity started with the Civic Forum in 2001,[6] have proceeded with the establishment of a 'Council for the Support of the Development of Civil Society Institutions and Human Rights' in November 2004,[7] and the creation of a Public Chamber (*Obshchestvennaia Palata*)[8] in 2005 as 'an additional opportunity for the development of civil society in the country'.[9] In an effort to mobilize public participation and opinion, the Kremlin has also supported the growth of a civic youth movement, *Nashi*, founded in April 2005.[10] Western donors and Russian activists became very concerned when a new law on civic organizations was enacted in 2006 that will control the foreign financing of Russian civic action.[11] Foreign foundations who have not withdrawn earlier, disillusioned at the sight of meagre results, failed strategies or wasted budgets, are now finally tempted to leave.[12] In any case, while cutting their budgets, donors are currently reconsidering their strategies and revising their civil society assistance programmes for Russia.

While the above-mentioned key measures have attracted the attention and concerns of Western observers, continuous and more subtle developments into the direction of recentralizing state–civil society relations have remained out of sight. Yet a more procedural and contextualized view would help not to misinterpret these actions as sudden assaults by the Kremlin. The Russian government has, for example, already a fairly long time openly scrutinized civic organizations for their reliance on funding from influential foreign foundations or dubious interest groups.[13] At the same time, proposals to increase governmental support have remained limited to groups close to the Kremlin. Alternative domestic support from Russian business corporations used to be minor, given the fact that companies that are officially obliged to finance social and infrastructural projects in their regions have little incentive to provide further resources to voluntary civic projects. Financial support from oligarchic or corporate sources has further been discouraged with the trial of Yukos founder Mikhail Khodorkovsky (in 2003), whose foundation, *Otkrytaia Rossiia* (Open Russia), was eventually incapacitated in 2006, removing essential financial resources from ongoing and future civic initiatives.[14]

In sum, criticisms regarding a troublesome situation of Russia's civil society persist from various directions, in view of strategic governmental top-down civil society building, legalized state control on civil society financing, of additional barriers to association and free reporting, but also given persisting interpersonal relations or cleavages among activists and a lack of popular trust or participation. At the same time, some recent evidence indicates that civic initiatives are not completely curtailed or missing. Some activities have perhaps grown even more determined, especially those concerning proximate societal issues, and some recent occurrences would come close to the beginnings of 'real bottom-up' civil society formation as foreign donors would have wished to see ten years ago. For example, there has been increasing activism in form of street protests and mass mobilization, mainly in response to reforms affecting pensioners and students in early 2005.[15] Regional/local level activities have been intensifying, such as locally initiated referenda[16] or more systematic collaboration through regular roundtables of smaller local activist communities.[17] Besides formal organizations, most of which are led by experienced and internationally well connected experts, there is also a very young activism emerging with a generation whose initial life planning has been dominated by the *perestroika* period and who are working in many places without formal structures or offices but with considerable social and political commitment. Other dynamics of horizontal and vertical organization seem to arise from more strategic voluntary initiatives, such as efforts by representatives of grass-roots environmental associations to establish a political party as a 'political wing to the green movement'.[18]

Given these and other events or trends, it can hardly be said that Russian civil society remains weak or totally absent. Nor does it continue to exist along enduring traditions. Rather, recent empirical evidence indicates the emergence of new strategies, reflection and adaptation on part of all parties involved and in reaction to each others' changing courses. As various empirical trends seem to follow contradictory logics, it is interesting to ask how civil society in this context is studied and conceptualized by scholars and analysts.

Western vs. Russian perspectives?

Western researchers who tend to look for forms of civil society on the grounds of their preset hypotheses have difficulties finding them in contemporary Russia – and thus tend to criticize Russian civil society for its weakness, fragmentation, or even its non-existence. When Russian researchers undertake efforts to apply Western hypotheses on civil society to empirical phenomena in their country, they find that most of them are of little help in explaining Russian realities. Responses on this research front thus come in the form of either stretching the (Western) concept or insisting on specifically Russian hypotheses. Moreover, the discrepancy between expectations and observations is quite well reflected in political practice. A key incident in this respect was perhaps the first meeting of the *Petersburger Dialog*[19] in 2001, where German participants posed the irritated question why representatives of the actual Russian civil society were excluded from the gathering. The response that 'there is no civil society in Russia'[20] did not provide a satisfying answer. Yet it was also much disliked by Russian activists as well as the Kremlin, with the former arguing that civil society had long traditions in Russia, whereas the latter proclaimed to promptly install civil society in view of its absence (cf. Wehner 2002).

The bulk of Western literature on civil society in general is enormous. Accordingly, research on civil society in Russia has been primarily guided by these debates, which are based on longstanding concepts as well as more recent approaches in the light of post-communist democratization and globalizing governance. Four main conceptual clusters can be distinguished in the Western literature, which have primarily guided scholarly efforts to assess the development of Russian civil society: (i) civil society in the context of post-communist transformation, (ii) civil society as a third sector supplementing the state and the market sectors, (iii) transnationalizing civil society, and (iv) deviant forms of uncivil society. The following sections review the latest contributions along these four (overlapping) clusters. This reassessment does not aim at testing theoretical hypotheses or concepts. Rather, it systematically discusses a wider range of recent conceptual contributions in this field while taking into account recent empirical evidence and integrating Western and Russian literatures.

Civil society and transformation

In the Western academic literature, civil society formation in Russia is generally seen within the context of post-Soviet transformation. This was for a long time based on presuming a transition towards democratic consolidation.[21] From a Western normative perspective and on the basis of democratic theory, the development of an active civil society is regarded as an essential cornerstone to back-up this democratization process. Russia, in contrast to other CEE countries, is commonly categorized as a case where no democratic traditions prior to communist rule could be recovered and where 'civil society had to be rebuilt from scratch' (McFaul 2001, p. 320). Yet meanwhile scholars are referring to the importance of three peculiar legacies while trying to explain the seemingly persisting weakness of Russia's civil society: (a) the Soviet experience, (b) the failed democratization under President Yeltsin, or (c) the authoritarian governance climate under President Putin.

The communist legacy, in particular Russian citizens' tendency to mistrust and avoid any public organizations, is mainly emphasized by historical and cultural approaches to explain the distinctive weakness of civil society (e.g. Howard 2003). From a more structural cultural perspective, also its notorious resistance to *network building* is criticized. In critical response to the predominantly Western view that there would be no civic traditions in the sense of voluntarily organized non-state activity, some Western and Russian experts have emphasized that Russia's present civil society would be rooted in previous traditions of self-organizing community networks and regime-critical citizens initiatives (see e.g. Beichelt & Kraatz 2000; Evans 2006a; Fein 2002; Skalaban 2004). Others argue that the general assumption of Russian citizens being apathetic and apolitical may lead scholars 'to overlook the *civic organizing* that is occurring' (Sundstrom and Henry 2006, p. 307, emphasis added). Some authors describe how within confined spaces patterns of collective problem solving may emerge, which are based on the persisting primacy of social connections in the daily lives of ordinary people (e.g. Caldwell 2004; Shomina et al. 2002). Yet even among Russian experts, the argument persists that the weakness of Russian civil society may be explained by its fragmentation and atomization, as it would exist only in 'small islands' or 'single dots' rather than network configurations.[22]

The failed democratization throughout the 1990s provides the basis for other systemic explanations of Russia's weak civil society. In this light, the population's experience with a chaotic democratization may have caused a rejection of democratic ideas, including the idea of civil society. Moreover, perceiving the period of democratization and pluralization as an episode of crisis, chaos, and privations, citizens would be inclined to support the idea of a strong and effective state. What people wanted and needed, was a 'good government', not necessarily a democratic one (e.g. Levada 2000; Tschepurenko 2001). In retrospect, the short peak during the late 1980s and early 1990s and subsequent decline in overt political activity by civic groups is also interpreted as part of general anti-communist mobilization and a tendency to disassociate from the Soviet past at that time (McFaul 2001, p. 320).

The legacy of the Putin era has most recently entered scholarly debates with acknowledgement of an authoritarian trend, which may serve to explain the weakness of civil society initiatives as a consequence of systematic repression. Both systemic and systematic obstacles to civil society formation are thus considered in recent assessments, making arguments more complex. In addition to persisting structural or institutional impediments to the development of civil society, a change in the government's direct approach towards civil society brings new restrictive policies, institutions, and laws. The repressive or co-opting tendencies that scholars only started to identify a few years ago (e.g. McFaul and Treyger 2004, p. 159 et seq.) are now commonly acknowledged. Yet thorough insights and conceptual elaboration of the precise processes of weakening Russian civil society during the Putin era are still missing.

Overall, the transformation perspective has paid much *impact*-oriented attention to what civil society may accomplish as a central pillar of a democratizing society, based on concepts of representation, participation, and deliberation. The successes and failures of Russian civil society development have been assessed according to these envisioned results. Accordingly, over the last years, authors and observers have become increasingly concerned about their findings that civic groups have played a much smaller role than expected in the reorganization and reformation of state policy and politics. However, few contributions have actually analysed the problems during the early stages of *civil society development* within this context of a comprehensive transformation process affecting all spheres of politics, economy, and society. While it has been overemphasized that civil society would positively influence the process of transition towards democracy, the reciprocal effects of the ongoing transformation on civil society formation have rarely been addressed. Only now, have some scholars come to propose that weak institutionalization of civil society, rather than weak impact, would require more research attention since empirical insights 'provide us with a more complicated depiction of Russian civil society' (Sundstrom and Henry 2006, p. 305). These scholars argue that continuing patterns inherited from Soviet times include not only citizens' general reluctance to participate in civic associations, but also a dominant role of the state as well as a need of civic groups to communicate with this state via connections with key individuals.

More comparable in-depth studies on difficulties of civic groups and foundations within the current operational context would be desirable. In single cases, analysts have documented how newly established organizations, regardless of their enthusiasm and former experience within a variety of cultural contexts, tended to be caught up in the process of transformation rather than leading this process in Russia. An amalgam of innovative and traditional styles of interaction, communication, and alliance building among individuals and groups have caused problems and setbacks. Kaufman (2003), for example, describes such complex challenges in the case of the Soros Foundation's efforts to set up office in Moscow in an ambition to finance civil society building and to serve as a 'pioneering vanguard of a new economic culture' (ibid., p. 226) – based on the idea of a market-oriented open sector generating profit for the benefit of charitable programmes.[23] Also striking difficulties of journalists, activists and researchers to provide information on politically sensitive issues, including human rights, corruption, environmental or military affairs, have been addressed.[24] Current patterns of horizontal and vertical network building or spontaneous mass mobilization at local or regional levels, while obviously difficult to fit into a conventional (Western) 'civil society' concept, might still be addressed from more socio-cultural or procedural social capital or social movements perspectives.

Among Russian scholars, a significant decrease in using the concept of 'civil society' in the wake of ongoing transformation is noticeable. A peak of Russian publications on the issue was reached during the 1990s, the time when the number of NGOs in Russia rapidly increased. That this process was significantly initiated by Western civil society building efforts is not a secret. Correspondingly, the Russian-language scholarly literature of that time consists for a substantial part of translated leading Western classics and contemporary monographs in the field. Otherwise, it comprises a variety of voices from different Russian communities of academics and activists who sought to contribute their knowledge about and opinions on the Western ideas, Russian experience or future possibilities. The decade of the 1990s may hence be referred to as the time of most intense discussion on this issue, including efforts to link conventional concepts to developments in the post-Soviet context. Russian publications appeared in newly emerging social and political sciences journals[25] and in form of monographs. Some seminal reviews have assessed these Russian debates on civil society during the 1990s (e.g. Belokurova 2001; Dorosheva 2002; see also Temkina 1997). These scholars have also traced changes in dominant interpretations of civil society with reference to the changes in the Russian context. Belokurova (2001) finds that studies based on a 'political culture' approach have tended to be more pessimistic about Russian civil society development, while approaches with a focus on economic problems or state–society relations and social movements were more optimistic. As for the late 1990s, Khlopin (2002) also points to a presence of polarized opinions as well as to the rather abstract character of the discussion, supported by not more than fragmented interests and empirical evidence. At present, and contradicting the thesis that civil society ceased to exist in Russia, the interest in the concept seems to be reviving among Russian analysts (e.g. Carnegie Moscow Center 2005a; Carnegie Moscow Center 2005b).[26]

Civil society as 'third sector'?

Civil society is often understood as a 'third sector', operating independently of, but also mediating between, the two other societal sectors – the state and the market. Such a third sector would be composed of institutions which have a formal structure and independent administration, pay taxes and employ significant parts of the population, yet with a non-profit orientation. Regarding Russia, the debate around three-sectoral relations, however, has been dominated by a focus on *state–civil society relations*, while a separate research focus lies on *state–business relations*, in particular big businesses. A perspective on the remaining nexus of such a tripartite constellation is largely missing: *business–civil society relations*.

With a predominant focus on *the third sector vis-à-vis the state* this debate centres on concepts of independence and power balancing. Mainly from a Western perspective and closely connected to the debate on civil society and transformation, Russian civil society was hoped to play an oppositional and influential role. Given the changing state–civil society relations in the Putin era, such a vantage point may now serve to confirm a weakening of Russian civil society under the strengthening state. Yet, as mentioned, there is a research deficit on the relations of Russian civic groups with their currently authoritarian state. It seems that earlier conceptualizations of state–civil society relations within a context of authoritarian rule are more appropriate than the democratization literature. This would demand a shift in focus from concepts of independence and influence more towards the locus of civil society as acting both outside and inside the state while the latter dominates the political and public sphere. Examples like the Civil Forum, the Public Chamber, or state-supported movements illustrate tendencies similar to those documented in Latin American studies, where the central administration constitutes a force that 'destroys self-organized and autonomously defined political spaces and substitutes for them a state-controlled public arena *in which* any discussion of issues must be made in codes and terms established by the rulers' (O'Donnell and Schmitter 1986, p. 48, emphasis added). Furthermore, Soviet studies generated valuable insights on civil society and individual activists acting *from within* the Soviet state (e.g. Lewin 1991), which still have some relevance to the current situation in

Russia. Yet short-sighted analogies should be prevented when comparing the Soviet and the present regime in this regard, not least because the intermediate *perestroika* period must not be neglected (Evans 2006b). Recent studies that provide insight into general governance patterns and restructurings within the state during the Putin era[27] are therefore important sources to draw on. Still, given changing views among Russian activists, more in-depth empirical research on actors' perspectives is needed. For example, some activists were initially optimistic about the course initiated under Putin and on this ground also envisioned the newly created frame of the Civic Forum as a potential solution to the problem of a (self-imposed) separation of civil society from the state.[28]

Moreover, the argument could be resumed that '[a]uthoritarian rulers tend to interpret the ensuing lack of perceivable opposition as evidence of "social peace" among previously conflicting classes and of "tacit consensus" for their policies' (O'Donnell and Schmitter 1986, p. 48). This is in turn closely related to another perspective, which is based on democratic theory and also seems to be supported by current empirical evidence: In response to growing Western criticism towards the increasingly authoritarian governance style, President Putin repeatedly claims that he is seeking a more balanced system of government. He is grounding his argument more on the chaotic democratization experience throughout the 1990s, underlining the trends of changing power relations and implied dangers of increasing influence of economic clans in Russia's regions. While his position is thus diverging from democratic visions based on pluralism, elections, decentralized governance and a liberal market system, it perfectly goes in line with democratic visions that see a balance of forces between competing groups, rather than a high level of economic development, as a crucial precondition, and monopolization of governance a key danger for modern democracies (e.g. Whistler 1993, p. 19). It also draws on hypotheses on the potentially negative influence of civil society on democratization (e.g. Schmitter 1997, pp. 247–8), as will be discussed in more detail in the next section.

Relations between the business sector and civil society remain neglected in the literature on Russian civil society. Conventional Western perspectives tend to conceptualize the third sector as separate from a second sector that comprises corporations and business associations. More recently, as the concept of corporate social responsibility (CSR) is entering civil society debates, more attention is paid to the business sector in this field as well.[29]

However, in a Western context, this concept emerged primarily from transnational companies' reaction to pressure from consumer movements. This is of less relevance to the Russian case, where the 'common' history of the governmental, business and civil society sectors is different in many respects. Importantly, Russia is one of the countries where efforts of building civil society were (and remain) not devoid of combining market-oriented and charitable ideas, as it has been exemplified by the Soros Foundation (cf. Kaufman 2003) or Charities Aid Foundation (cf. Hinterhuber and Rindt 2004). Some authors include businesses in their concept of civil society (e.g. Pleines 2005; Rutland 2006). Yet it should be noted that such an inclusive approach might not reflect the inter-relations between the two sectors. For example, in the course of ongoing transformation of the business and civic sectors, having emerged separately, actors from both spheres find each other on a common problematic playground where they discover common interests vis-à-vis the state, such as the removal of administrative barriers, the media landscape, independent expertise, regulations concerning workers/employees, and regular inspections. This applies primarily to small and medium enterprises (SMEs). However, research on the Russian business sector is heavily focused on big corporations, including multinational companies, and largely neglects the role of SMEs. Big industrial businesses remain a main opponent of one of the most important parts of the Russian third sector – the environmental movement. At the same time, newly emerging partnerships between activists and businesses are challenging traditional understandings of civil society, which prefer to exclude industrial and trade organizations and other actors guided by private interests. Respective developments are thus only hesitantly included into the debate.

Essentially, a conception of society as composed of three sectors seems more appropriate if perspectives on the mutual interrelations between all three sectors are developed. Looking at recent governance reforms in Russia, it becomes evident that all three spheres are much more intertwined than acknowledged in the literature. Given the dominant role of the state in leading comprehensive reforms and the simultaneous entanglement of the political and economic as well as political and civic spheres, it is rather surprising that there is little inquiry about intersectoral relations in Russia.[30] For example, in contrast to the concept of state-capture, as predominant in the Western literature, Russian analysts not only speak of business-capture, but also of NGO-capture. New questions have further arisen with regard to philanthropy supported by Russian foundations as additional mediators within state–business–civil society relations (see Hinterhuber and Rindt 2004). Finally, a view on civil society as a third sector within a domestic sphere of governance that excludes *international* influences on these domestic inter-relations seems too short-sighted in an era of globalizing governance and transnational networking. Yet, unfortunately, research looking at domestic civil society–state relations has largely ignored donor–recipient relations, and vice versa, so that the more complex interrelations between all these entities have remained unaddressed.

Transnationalizing civil society

A third possible way of analysing civil society considers the increasing integration of local/domestic groups into transnational movements and networks. This discourse is rather young and further characterized by a heavy focus on NGOs as the main representatives of civil society.[31] Central to these approaches is the conceptualization of NGOs as carriers of ideas across cultural boundaries for the benefit of transferring international norms into domestic contexts. This includes a normative bias against civil society actors as 'good', and pro-democratic norm-promoting and inherently oppositional forces[32] and against the accused state and state decision-makers as 'bad', norm-deviant but also 'passive and reactive' targets.[33] This also applies to another body of literature, which brings together transnational networking and civil society development within countries undergoing transformations: studies on democratization assistance. Regarding Russia, in addition to the role of ideas and norms (e.g. Schmidt and Bondarenko 2005; Sundstrom 2005), this debate puts much emphasis on the aspect of foreign funding in relation to domestic civil society development (e.g. Carothers 1999; Henderson 2003; Mendelson and Glenn 2002). Furthermore, although rather marginal, some contributions have examined the limited fulfilment of Western expectations that the introduction of modern technological infrastructure, internet communication in particular, would be automatically beneficial to transnational networking and the diffusion of democratic ideas and practices via Russian activists (Lenhard 2003; Schmidt 2006a).

Research on transnational influences on Russian civil society is mainly of Western provenance and increasingly very critical. 'Managing civil society' (Crotty 2003) is not any longer an issue related solely to state–civil society relations. Some analysts point to dysfunctions arising from transnational aid and networking grounded on foreign funding. One of the main arguments is that the support from donors and transnationally active organizations, since it has largely been the only available source for funding, has significantly shaped the topical agendas and organizational capacities of domestic NGOs. As a result, '[t]he version of civil society that has been brought into being by western design – the third sector – is far from what Russian activists desired and what donor agencies promised' (Hemment 2004). Some argue that the financial ties between foreign donors and Russian NGOs may entail unintended consequences that disturb desired mechanisms of persuasion and pressure. Suggesting that Russian NGOs have become involved in rather asymmetrical or hegemonic relations, Henderson sees a mirroring of unintended consequences of foreign aid in these relations, which she terms 'supply-driven civic development', 'principled clientelism', and 'guardian civil societies' (Henderson 2003, pp. 155–66).

It is important to note that financial assistance to Russia involves civic groups in two ways: by directly supporting civil society development and by channelling aid for issue-related programmes through NGOs. This distinction should be kept in mind when assessing the successes and failures of Russian civil society and/or of foreign donors. With a view to environmental activism, for example, Powell (2002, p. 141) concludes that, if assistance to domestic environmental groups 'is understood to compromise two separate but related goals – the development of post-communist third-sector groups and the progressive resolution of environmental issues – it is manifestly clear that greater progress has been achieved on the first front than on the second'. Apart from that, foreign sponsored projects are often criticized for lacking connection to local needs and realities. Behavioural impacts within local movements have thus frequently been attested in a negative sense: 'Despite its claims to allow a grassroots to flourish, the third sector is a professionalized realm of NGOs, inaccessible to most local groups and compromised by its links to a neoliberal vision of development' (Hemment 2004; see also Crotty 2003; Henry 2002).

Besides misdirection and a lack of contextualization of foreign assistance, local circumstances are also seen as conditioning (passive) project design, for example when local NGO workers adopt foreign ideas and say precisely what foreign donors want to hear out of fear of losing their job or income (Powell 2002, p. 142). These positions need to be somewhat mitigated. First, there is also recent evidence that local groups and individuals actively question the procedures and issue preferences of their Western donors, even if only discussing among themselves related problems and more sensible approaches according to local expertise, experience and circumstances.[34] Certainly, local expertise tends to be better acknowledged by Western agencies when not based on direct grantee–donor relations. Yet to what extent critique on the part of Russian activists reaches into grant making structures and grant programmes remains to be explored. Second, different funding strategies have been pursued by US or European (EU) donors, with the former paying more attention to the professionalization of the NGO sector itself, to grant making and philanthropy and a normative standpoint that seeks to foster civil society control over state power. EU assistance, in contrast, is more concerned with interaction with (and professionalization of) regional/local authorities, fostering input from recipients, civic education, and expert exchange from normatively understanding civil society as complementary to the state (Belokurova 2005; Freise 2005; Wedel 1998).

Further, scholarly approaches towards norms, based on transnational advocacy and the social movements literature, prove relevant in the current Russian context. For example, taking mechanisms of issue framing and normative contexts of activists into account, Sundstrom (2005, p. 422) suggests that failure of foreign assistance might not only be due to political barriers. Rather, foreign assistance may lead to successful mobilization if it is used to promote a universal norm, but may not do so if promoting non-universal norms that originate in the specific context of the foreign donors. Comparing the soldiers' rights movement and the women's movement in Russia, Sundstrom finds that civic initiatives that face more hostile political structures may even experience greater public support and progress in changing state conduct than those which face more open political structures. But depending on what kind of norms they support, activities may also face resistance within society itself. Central to this approach is also the concept of trust, more precisely the problem of distrust, in connection with foreign assistance. Western-funded local tend to be suspicious of (local and federal) authorities, businesses as well as the population, all the more if they pursue specific goals that are alien to Russian society. Besides being less successful (Sundstrom 2005, p. 423), they are thus easily blamed for inefficiency and mismanagement, considered as money-laundering devices, dubious enterprises seeking to evade taxes, elite-driven clubs, or alien institutions trying to impose foreign norms while abandoning traditional approaches and values (Henderson 2003; Powell 2002). Russian experts argue that distrust directed towards reliance on foreign funding is essentially reinforced by a lack of information about third sector organizations and foundations.[35] Still, existing myths that NGO are corrupt, money laundering, tax avoiding, profit making devices are only rarely discussed by Russian analysts (Dorosheva 2002, pp. 20–5). Respective scrutinizing remarks made by the government on NGO funding, even while becoming manifest in new legislation, have received critical response through discussions among Russian activists and in some newspapers rather than entering scholarly debates.

Some of these arguments are not entirely new. Earlier studies on transnational activism have pointed to the challenges of far-flung networking, including aspects of location, access to resources, ambiguity and opportunism (e.g. Keck and Sikkink 1998). From a Russian perspective, the interrelations between transnationalization and compromising the independence of Russian civil society organizations had even been problematized earlier. For example, in the midst of initially emerging assistance structures, Yanitsky (1994; 1998) criticized the Westernization of the Russian environmental movement as a turn from self-replication of resources towards receiving financial assistance from the West.[36] Although he understands this strategy as a 'logic of self-protection', he critically points to the multiple risks involved. Summarizing his main points, many parallels with today's Western critics become obvious. Due to overwhelming effort directed at the exploration and allocation of financial resources and technical support, he sees the social behaviour, mentality and politics of the ecological movement changing with trends towards (a) more organizational and communication services, and less mass protest campaigns and public discussions, (b) increasing corporatist and vertical structures with a growing bureaucratic elite, and decreasing ability to promptly react to new problems, (c) strengthening of the reformist and service character of single movement units that seek to deliver 'constructive' projects, therewith also growing atomization, isolation and disunity, (d) commercialization and monopolization of organizations that are bigger and closer to the financial sources, thus enjoying better chances of receiving further grants, their reputation, and bureaucratization.

Yanitsky also contends that the fundamental idea of free association and civic initiatives is inapplicable in this context. If environmental organizations are created for the purpose of receiving grants, activists would be turned into common employees within a 'normal service hierarchy', which replaces the idealistically emphasized links of friendship and like-mindedness. Moreover, leading organizations would be transformed into 'finance pumps', in order to channel in resources from the West. In accordance with the Western critique described above, he also points to the danger that agendas are increasingly defined by Western donors, 'replacing the objective interests of the citizens by subjective interests of the resource allocators' (Yanitsky 1994, p. 17), and that organizations are increasingly enhancing contacts with familiar Western organizations while decreasingly initiating mass campaigns with domestic fellow-organizations (Yanitsky 1998, p. 29). Yet, in contrast to the more recent Western normative arguments that such organizations may be criticized as co-opted by foreign agitation and unsuited to Russian conditions, Yanitsky (1994, p. 17) envisages the possible result that organizations concentrate even more on local problems, while 'thinking globally' would become an unaffordable luxury. He argues that projects focusing on the ideology and strategy of the green movement would never be financed. Regarding the relation to the state, besides opting for either protest or cooperation, he suggests a third way for Russian organizations: distancing themselves from the state and searching for their own experts and professionals. Meanwhile, as the problem of over-dependence on foreign grants is commonly acknowledged, the 'logic of self-protection' is perhaps more prevailing than ever. However, it also becomes clear that a third way as envisaged by Yanitsky is difficult to accomplish as it is vital for Russian organizations to maintain links with both Western partners and domestic/local authorities.

Despite the largely critical stance of this field of literature, it remains to be noted that some authors also underline 'unexpected signifying possibilities' (Hemment 2004) of civic engagement fostered by a third sector introduced by Western efforts at the local level, as indicated by the many social services undertaken by local groups that would otherwise not have been possible. Numerous small organizations have emerged, which are concerned with social and health services, education, culture and religion. Caldwell's (2004) research on soup kitchens run by an international food aid community and the Christian Church of Moscow, for example, describes sites of social stability and refuge, where provision of social support in various forms outweighs the importance of material resources. While such projects may be disconnected from the domestic political sphere and restricted to a confined local terrain, many rely on important international links. Some neighbourhood-based urban movements, in turn, may not rely on transnational networks but nevertheless provide links between social and legal spheres.[37] Others are not solely supported by Western donors but receive part of their funding from local sources. But also local support through Russian businesses has in some cases been induced through Western concepts such as CSR or community foundations.[38] In any case, the operational context constituted by the particular location of Russian organizations needs to be accounted for. Therefore, a focus on the transnational embeddedness of Russian civil society should be combined with a conceptual distinction between *domestic* and *local* levels. This would prevent from overgeneralizing conclusions about 'the Russian case', as many assistance programmes and network initiatives that involve Russian organizations are targeted at a particular city or region and are implemented at local rather than federal level. Analyses of international–domestic–local interrelations are important steps to rethinking the ways in which relationships between social and economic practices, as well as legal and political aspects, may be theorized. Such research may further supplement contributions on the continuing weakness of Russian civil society or mitigate statements which morally devalue civic groups as scapegoats operating in the grey areas between state, market and international donor community.

Uncivil society?

Another more recent field of study has emerged around the conception of *uncivil society* as a problematic type of or sub-sector within civil society. This may include groups with other than pro-Western, liberal democratic agendas or contentious social movements that are challenging conventional (Western) normative assumptions on civil society in general and within post-communist countries in particular (Kopecký 2003). From a Western perspective, assumptions about the character of civil society in general were largely coloured by optimism, presuming virtues such as fairness, pluralism, tolerance, voluntarism, independence and an interest in public affairs with an orientation towards communicative action. On these normative and moral grounds, civil society appears problematic or malfunctioning to analysts if it is not *per se* progressive, and if it breeds power monopolies or inequalities, or internal democratic deficits. The concept of uncivil society has become increasingly relevant in the Russian case.

Not a few analysts have turned to lamenting the undemocratic nature of civil society in Russia (Sundstrom and Henry 2006, p. 305). According to Umland (2002), for example, the 'civic public' or 'civic community' in Russia is not only developing slowly. In addition, the diversification of this sector during the *perestroika* period entails the emergence of groups, movements and trends that are 'unsupportive or explicitly critical of liberal democracy'. While he refers to right-wing ultra-nationalist and fundamentalist extremism, others point to an emergence of Islamism following the dissolution of the USSR. In this context, radical groups are considered as uncivil because they benefit from complicated economic circumstances, corruption and repression in order to lobby their own causes (Warkotsch 2004). Furthermore, a significant increase in illegal trafficking in Russia is attributed to 'uncivil' groups and networks operating outside the state and business spheres.

Criminal groups may fall into this ambiguous category of collective action in a common interest yet in anti-liberal and anti-democratic ways. Some authors explicitly exclude these from their definition of (Russian) civil society, underlining the for-profit nature of criminal organizations and the fact that they place themselves beyond the reach of the law (Howard 2003, p. 41; Sundstrom and Henry 2006). Others understand them as an ' "uncivil" part of' this civil society, arguing that they may even operate within the law and pointing more towards the network structure and transnational dimensions (Shelley 2001, p. 248; 2006). Most authors agree on the fact that criminal groups affect civil society development, be it by co-opting and threatening civic groups and journalists or by providing security and funding to fulfil basic needs in society (Shelley 2006), in any case thus 'changing the playing field for NGOs' (Sundstrom and Henry 2006) and impeding channels of healthy contact between civil society and the state (Shelley 2001). Conceptually, this debate further complicates arguments about the identity and functions of civic groups. Nevertheless, it should be noted that the mere *existence* of criminal groups may not simply be interpreted as serious impediment to civic action, since their activities also provoke new forms of counter-engagement (albeit often encouraged by Western or transnational initiatives), as illustrated by increased action against illegal trafficking in Russia.

Another trend is seen in 'creating uncivil society' on the grounds of a security-oriented debate in connection with the global antiterrorism agenda. Governments may use arguments of fighting against crime and terrorism to destroy their political opposition, gain control over or foster suspicion of civic groups within their countries. In Russia, also anti-corruption and anti-crime agendas, taken up by President Putin since 2000, have become a powerful tool in the hands of the leadership and have been turned selectively against unhelpful officials or political opponents (e.g. Krastev 2004; Savintseva and Stykow 2005, p. 200). The context of intensified debate on new terrorist threats and the colour revolutions has provided further fertile ground for the Russian government to identify civic organizations as undermining national security or stability.

Moreover, some phenomena which would generally count as part of the civic or public sphere in Western democracies fall into a conceptual twilight zone thanks to the particular characteristics attributed to them in the Russian case. Russian media, for example, have become perceived as untrustworthy state-owned or co-opted and scandal-ridden private outlets (cf. Oates and White 2003). A similar verdict would apply to business actors, insofar as these are to be included into the civil society concept. The Russian business sector, with its features of political entrepreneurship and informal or corrupt relations, is predestined to be categorized as uncivil. Moreover, even pro-Western activist groups may be considered as uncivil in some form, based on the argument that they have become increasingly uninterested in and disconnected from both state and population, while pursuing private interests or narrow agendas of their foreign donors (see also above).

Yet another peculiarity of the Russian civic sphere is the persisting importance of various forms of informal inter-personal networks. The most prominent example is *blat*, a social practice that includes Soviet-time traditions of protectionism, the using of profitable connections, or illegal dealings. Some scholars consider this kind of social interaction as a form of 'street level corruption' (Miller et al. 1997) or 'grassroots corruption' (INDEM 1998) and others as an informal exchange of favours that essentially opens access to scarce goods under conditions of economic shortages (e.g. Ledeneva 1998). In this vein, yet on a more theoretical basis, Kharkhordin (2000, p. 2) understands friendship networks in contemporary Russia as a 'complicated set of transformed elements of Soviet society and new social ties', which may present most fundamental means of social welfare, withstanding the temptations of jointly pursuing wealth and power on the one hand, or, in case of strong links to governmental and business spheres, may be regarded as 'clan politics' on the other. He argues that the 1990s legacy of a *weak state* has brought into existence a plethora of entities that use violent non-civil methods to ensure the more or less smooth functioning of businesses. Yet as even militant relations are penetrated by friendship ties, '[t]he central problem of contemporary Russian civil society thus may consist of making relations of uncivil violence conform to the principles of friendly networks' (Kharkhordin 2000, p. 3). With a view to the Russian context, the fundamental question persists whether the well-documented distrust of Russian citizens towards democratic institutions and continuing reliance on informal networks are necessarily an obstacle to the creation of civil society. Sundstrom and Henry (2006, p. 309) rightly argue that the informal relations and networks in Russia deserve study in their own right. It should be added that such study needs to be linked to an analysis of how civil transactions accommodate the interplay between new realities and enduring features.

Separate, contradictory, or combinable views?

The four categories identified and discussed above do not present a chronological sequence of distinct phases of Russian civil society development. Certainly, the presentation of these categories does follow successive changes in the scholarly discourse, which in turn have tried to keep up with empirical developments. Thus, the 1980s/90s literature has mainly focused on transformation and third sector emergence within Russia, the late 1990s contributions have included transnational influences, and recent works are accommodating a concept of uncivil society, but also of authoritarian operational conditions. Yet these various ways of understanding different aspects of civil society development are not either–or options. Not only are their different perspectives interrelated and overlapping in many respects, all four categories represent ongoing research programmes, which have remained relevant to assessing Russian civil society in the Putin era and will certainly continue to do so in future analyses. Civic groups will continue to develop survival strategies within a context of ongoing transformation, the third-sector perspective will remain relevant with increasing business–civil society collaborations, and the significance of transnational as well as undemocratic features within this sphere should hardly be reversible.

Empirically, it becomes obvious that contemporary Russian civil society is neither a vanishing nor traditional phenomenon, but rather in a process of evolving through a complex set of adaptive and original processes. However, the questions remain open to what degree Russian activist groups are establishing new ways of citizen participation and service provision, along which strategies and in which areas foreign aid is effective, and in which ways activities of the state and business sectors impact on civic initiatives as well as on Western assistance. Conceptually, there is an obvious need to reconsider mismatches between such empirical trends in the Russian case and conventional Western approaches. How to accomplish this task still remains an open question for the scholarly community.

> *Concept stretching, combined with the rapid pace of change in Russia, may have discouraged serious efforts at assessing precisely how far Russia had actually gone toward realizing a genuine civil society.* (Fish 1996, p. 53; original emphasis)

Fish's argument was made with regard to the first efforts of studying civil society in post-Soviet Russia. In particular, Fish (ibid., p. 52) had criticized that the foundation of much of this research, Sovietology, did not take enough account of longstanding civil society debates. However, this chapter has shown that the analysis of Russian civil society touches upon a variety of aspects in addition to the original (Western) civil society debates and Sovietological area studies. It is therefore argued here that combined efforts of various academic disciplines are required and that much potential to learn remains for both Western and Russian approaches. Russian scholars acknowledge that domestic politics and regional policy studies, for example, have not yet developed to a stage at which respective tasks may be dealt with (Mikhaleva and Ryzhenkov 2001b, p. 7). Yet also scholars in the Western political, social and regional sciences are only starting to scrutinize their longstanding assumptions with a view to the puzzles of civil society formation found in the Russian case. Moreover, civil society studies, having evolved into a virtually global discipline by now, are further changing in the context of empirical developments in international and regional contexts.[39]

While trying to assess the complex puzzle of contemporary civil society in Russia, an imbalance of dominating Western perspectives has remained to date. There are numerous examples where Russian authors are engaging in familiarizing themselves with Western propositions. But too often such efforts are devoid of debating the actual applicability of given concepts to the rapidly changing Russian context, in a sense of critically studying Western models. It is thus often more a process of familiarization which 'also implies a shallow knowledge of Russian realities by the Russians themselves and a lack of efforts on their part to go beyond fitting these realities into what is often a straightjacket of alien theoretical concepts' (Bogaturov, in Tsygankov and Tsygankov 2005, p. 24). Similarly, regarding the current Russian scholarship in its position to dominating Western approaches in IR studies, Tsygankov and Tsygankov (2005) identify pluralization, Westernization and isolationalism as key trends. They argue that isolationalism, meaning a rejection of concepts established in the West and a refusal to learn from each other, may lead to 'stiffening creative indigenous thought' (ibid., p. 25) at the cost of acquiring profound knowledge about Russian realities. Westernization, in turn, would mean 'delaying or subverting indigenous impulses of epistemological development' (ibid., p. 23). Both trends can be traced also in the Russian civil society literature.[40] Conversely, Russian research is often not accounted for in Western debates. This has a range of rather pragmatic reasons, as Russian contributions are more difficult to explore or unavailable via Western formal distributive markets or over the internet, being for substantial parts constituted by grey literature, *samizdat* booklets, conference proceedings, or publications in domestically circulated Russian journals. In addition, many experts on both sides remain separated from each other simply through language barriers.

Yet reconsidering this whole milieu of civil society studies with a critical view on given concepts and Russian developments does not have to be an impossible or unpleasant undertaking. For instance, the fact that Western sponsors are heavily influencing the civil society sphere, both in practice and academic discourse, must not necessarily entail its Westernization. Increasing presence of Western experts and researchers in Russia and international mobility of Russian researchers and activists does enhance dialogue through a new feature: an increasing number of coauthored or coedited Western–Russian contributions.[41] Such collaborative publications contribute to better identifying commonalities and differences across cultural boundaries. Machura, Donskow and Litinova (2003), for example, examine the recent development of 'legal culture' from a sociology of law perspective with a view to the social institution of lay judges, who act as links between society and the judiciary. By exploring these aspects in detail, they refrain from resting on historical explanations for Russia's notorious divergence from international norms and narrow views on mediation through NGOs. The wider debate on international influences on Russia's domestic development has also triggered more detailed research into civic action within the domestic context as well as interrelations across international–local dimensions.

Furthermore, there are numerous publications that have resulted from research projects conducted by Russian practitioners and experts with grants from foreign foundations. Some provide empirical data in the sense of action research, which is linking research and action within the civic sphere in an effort to create mutually supporting effects. Apart from, yet often inspired by, conventional theoretical reasoning, such texts may address questions of what civil society/NGOs/third sector means in the context of Russian realities (e.g. Dorosheva 2002; Dzhibladze and Ermichine 2002). Others issue practical guides on aspects of NGO management in the given legal context (Tereshchenko 2003) or large-scale surveys on the situation of NGO-governmental cooperation (Forum Donorov 2005; Sevortyan and Barchukova 2002). Many of these works thus support a transfer of knowledge between civic and academic communities or are of practical interest to government officials, civic associations, the business communities, journalists, lawyers, or international agencies. Unfortunately, many practitioners issue handbooks which are addressed to and remain within their professional or personal circle. Moreover, Russian civil society tends to provide little original and in-depth information about itself to the wider public. There are only few examples of insider accounts on the actual work of Russian organizations, which provide detailed insights by documenting examples, experiences and how these may trigger the development of new strategies (e.g. Deutsches Institut für Menschenrechte 2003). In general,

NGO surveys mainly have the character of large-n catalogues, while in-depth studies are often limited to presenting single-case projects or organizations. Comparative qualitative studies are largely missing.

Recent action research differs from earlier insider accounts, mostly American–Russian initiatives, which were primarily guided by the hopeful spirit of the late 1990s and a Western perspective on democratic consolidation. These optimistically took for granted civil society's abilities and prospects to ensure social, religious and political justice through an effective engagement with the Russian state, the role of mass education and the free press in inculcating new civic values.[42] By focusing on courageous insider experiences, one of the main ambitions of 1990s contributions was to go beyond existing problems and instead portray the human dimensions of civil society building efforts by underlining the energy, commitment, courage and intellect of individuals within a democratizing Russian society (e.g. vanden Heuvel 2000). However idealistic, these earlier contributions deserve a positive evaluation as they brought together authors from various backgrounds, including Western and Russian academics, civil society activists and entrepreneurs.

Recent coauthored works are important steps to moving beyond a separation between hollow conceptual debates and descriptive accounts. They also assist in reassessing normative biases. However, some crucial deficits are still remaining. First, in order to gain better insight into the country-specific contextual conditions for civic work, underlying socio-economic dimensions need to be better integrated. Second, the rapidly changing characteristics of administrative and market environments remain neglected issues in the literature on Russian civil society. In these respects, systematic inter-regional comparative studies are still underrepresented.[43] Third, if the normative values and moral qualities of Russian organizations are to be reassessed, closer attention needs to be paid to the self-presentation as well as behind-the-scenes activities of these organizations. A question hardly addressed is which objectives, morals, and meaning these (mostly local) organizations want to carry. Moreover, questioning the legitimacy of civic organizations, which claim to pursue goals that are in the public interest, would also necessitate research on organized civic action in combination with the general public interest. Finally, in-depth empirical analysis on the complex interplay between emerging and persisting formal regulatory norms as well as informal rules is scarce. Providing a deeper understanding of the realities of civic interaction and civic culture, such studies could enrich ongoing abstract conceptual discussions and offer the potential to engage Russian and Western students of civil society in a more constructive dialogue. In any case, given the complex and often contradictory connections between changes in civil society formation, political transformation, economic development and international influences in contemporary Russia, assessments of civil society require more complex multi-dimensional research than commonly acknowledged. To this end, the various frameworks reviewed in this paper need to be regarded as complementary perspectives rather than separate schools of thought.

The recapitulative discussion presented here does not claim to be exhaustive. Many more Russian and Western scholarly contributions are available but could not be dealt with in the limited scope of this chapter. Moreover, there are other conceptual or empirical issues which could not be explored but which would certainly be relevant when seeking to specify the possibilities of analysing civil society in Russia. Such endeavour also needs to be supplemented by comparatively exploring approaches towards civil society in Russia and in other post-Soviet contexts. This chapter has at least disclosed different conceptual trends that have emerged with regard to recent developments in the Russian case. This is but one step towards more effective cross-fertilization across discursive and cultural boundaries within the debates on civil society in Russia (and beyond), namely between different conceptual approaches, between Western and Russian perspectives, and between scholarly and practitioners' views.

Notes

1. A note on terminology: Civil society is understood here as the sphere of collective action between the state and the market (i.e. being non-governmental and non-commercial) and outside private households. In addition, the terms civic groups and activists are used in this chapter to subsume the more or less loose organizational units operating within this sphere. The narrower term non-governmental organizations (NGOs) is used only when referring to precisely this form of organization or to the works of other authors or bodies of literature that explicitly use term NGO. When strictly translating from Russian language texts, NKO (*nekommercheskaia organizatsiia*, non-commercial organization) or NPO (*nepravitel'stvennaia organizatsiia*, non-governmental organization) would be more correct. To simplify matters, only the more common English-language term NGO is used here. On the various organization types that may officially register as 'bodies of public independent activity' in Russia (e.g. associations, non-commercial organizations, non-commercial partnerships, foundations, movements, establishments), see Shvedov (2005) and Skalaban (2004).

2. In these respects, excellent reflections on the origins, usage and various meanings of the concept have been contributed by Alexander (1998), Hyden et al. (2004, chapter 3) and Keane (1988; 1998).

3. Although the Western literature on civil society development in Russia during the 1990s is vast, summarizing reviews are rare (possible starting points include Brown 2001; McFaul and Treyger 2004). For good reviews of the civil society debate in Russian social/political sciences during the 1990s, see Belokurova (2001), Mikhaleva and Ryzhenkov (2001a), Khlopin (2002) and Pro et Contra (1997).

4. More than 140 interviews have been conducted by the author with representatives of local civic groups, business associations, individual journalists, activists and experts as well as representatives of Western donor organizations or network partners in Moscow, St Petersburg, Irkutsk, Berlin and Brussels between 2001 and 2006. The author has also participated in round tables, conferences and semi-closed meetings of representatives of Russian civic groups, local authorities and/or Western partners.

5. To mention just a few: Since 1988, the Open Society Institute (OSI) of George Soros sponsored the salary of Russian scientists, artists and writers as well as Internet facilities in universities, textbooks and independent media. Since 1991, the EU has provided technical and financial assistance under the Tacis, EIDHR, ECHO, Tempus and IBPP programmes. Since 1992, USAID has operated democratization programmes in partnership with NGOs. Since 1993, the Charities Aid Foundation (CAF) has supported civil society development through grants, training and consulting, etc.

6. The Civic Forum (*Grazhdanskii Forum*) held on 21–22 November 2001 in the Kremlin was an unprecedented official gathering of Russian civic groups, government and the President. International observers tended to criticize the Civil Forum as a mere PR actually signalling governmental control, (e.g. Fein 2002; Meier 2003), whereas Russian civic groups have initially also been hopeful, seeing it as potentially helpful for bridging the immense gap between authorities and civic groups and paving a way towards better dialogue (author's interviews St Petersburg, 2003), (Dorosheva 2003).

7. This Council was established in November 2004 in order to replace the former Commission on Human Rights.

8. The creation of a Public Chamber was approved by the Duma in May 2005; the Federal Law on the Chamber took effect on 1 July 2005. The partly appointed, partly selected representatives of this formal civic organ can issue recommendations to the government. For critical evaluations, see Evans (2006a, p. 151) and Fein (2006).

9. Duma Speaker Boris Gryzlov, Moscow, 16.05.2005 (RFE/RL, 17.05.2005).

10. Although the Kremlin has denied any direct links to the pro-governmental Nashi movement, capacity-enhancing support became obvious in several recent actions (see the organization's own site: www.nashi.su).

11. See Schmidt (2006b) for more detail on the so-called 'NGO law', which has actually been part of a broader legal reform package that was approved as 'Federal Law No. 18-FZ of 10 January 2006 on introducing amendments to certain legislative acts of the Russian Federation', came into effect in April 2006, and will be implemented through additional decrees.

12. As the most prominent example, the Soros Foundation closed down its offices in Russia in 2003, after having sought to assist Russia in the transition from a closed to an open society through OSI (Open Society Institute) over a period of 15 years. It also became an issue that foundations might withdraw without appropriate exit strategies and leave both grantees and initiated efforts to their fates. While this has not entered scholarly debates, see Kortunov (2004) on the Russian point of view (Kortunov is now president of the newly established New Eurasia Foundation) and Soros (2004) on an exited donor's point of view.

13. President Putin, Foreign Minister Lavrov, and FSB spokespersons had repeatedly publicly criticized NGOs of pursuing the interests of foreign donors. In addition, more directly, the presence of the British Council in Russia was questioned with reference to their financial records in 2004, the difficulties surrounding the Moscow office of the Soros Foundation in 2002 implied the charge that it represented 'US interests,' and German political foundations were accused of supporting dubious institutions in Russia as early as 2001.

14. *Otkrytaia Rossiia* was audited several times by tax officials (in November 2003, April 2004, February 2005) and its offices searched by the Prosecutor General's Office (in October 2005); authorities have also probed NGOs that had received funding from the foundation. Eventually the foundation's bank accounts were frozen by a Moscow district court on 17 March 2006. By the time of writing, it remained unclear whether it had ceased or continued to work, having announced an appeal with Russia's Constitutional Court and if necessary the ECHR. Its website (www.openrussia.info) was closed on 10/07/2006.

15. As these occurred in the context of the Rose Revolution in Georgia and Orange Revolution in Ukraine, the Russian protests raised concerns among some and hopes among others that there would be another revolutionary wave in the post-Soviet space (e.g. Borisov 2005).

16. For an exemplary analysis on regional environmental referenda, see Vorobyev (2005a).

17. Author's participation in some foreign funded as well as relatively recent unsponsored meetings in St Petersburg and Moscow, 2003–2006.

18. Aleksei Yablokov (RFE/RL, Moscow, 6 June 2005). Efforts to establish the *Union of Greens* party started in June 2005, in prospect of running in the local/regional elections in December 2005 and Federal elections in 2007, see Vorobyev (2005b).

19. *Petersburger Dialog*: Bilateral partnership between Germany and Russia, initiated by and organized under the auspices of chancellor Schröder and president Putin. It aims at enhancing relations between *civil societies and governments* of both countries and transferring German civil society formation experiences to Russia.

20. Gleb Pavlovsky, counsellor of the presidential administration (quoted in Meier 2003, p. 19).

21. On earlier critiques of the unidirectional concept of *transition,* in contrast to the more open-ended and comprehensive concept of *transformation,* see Dawisha and Parrot (1997), also Carothers (2002).

22. Author's interviews, Russian researchers and activists, St Petersburg and Moscow, 2004–2006.

23. Unfortunately, Kaufman's account only refers to a period between the late 1980s and mid-1990s.
24. At least, some of the more prominent cases where information provision has been turned into allegations of espionage have been examined in more detail, see for example Pas'ko (2005) on Sutjagin, Siegert (2002) on Pas'ko, Martirossian (2004) on Zhirov.
25. E.g. Pro et Contra (1997); various core aspects related to the civil society debate have also appeared in the journals *Sotsiologicheskie issledovaniia, Politicheskie issledovaniia* and *Neprikosnovennyi Zapas*.
26. Also author's interviews, Russian researchers and practitioners, Moscow/ St Petersburg, 2005.
27. In particular: Evans (2006b); Fish (2005); Kryshtanskovskaya and White (2005); Reddaway and Orttung (2004; 2005); Petrov (2005); Sakwa (2004); White et al. (2005).
28. Hopeful views were expressed by most interviewees in 2003/2004 (researchers and activists, Moscow/St Petersburg).
29. E.g. among the first analyses on the role of business in social investment and societal development in Russia: Litovchenko (2004) and Deuber (2006).
30. This analytical deficit has recently also been criticized by Petrov (2005).
31. The recent literature on transnational networks contains prominent concepts such as the 'boomerang effect' (Keck and Sikkink 1998) or the 'spiral model' of network socialization (Risse et al. 1999), which focus on the strategic involvement of international actors by domestic NGOs in cases where states violate internationally accepted norms while blocking communication with civil society domestically.
32. According to Risse and Sikkink (1999) '[g]overnments want to remain in power, while domestic NGOs seek the most effective means to rally opposition'. NGOs are seen as actors 'who want to tell the truth' (Risse 2000, p. 203).
33. On the bias against states in the spiral model proposed by Risse et al. (1999), see also Checkel (1999, p. 5); Hawkins (1999).
34. Author's research on USAID-supported anti-corruption coalition in Irkutsk, 2005.
35. The most comprehensive survey on the image of non-governmental organizations undertaken by the Russian Donors' Forum (Forum Donorov 2005) shows that not only trust but also awareness of civic groups and donor organizations is low among Russian citizens.
36. Yanitsky extensively studied the Russian environmental movement during the *perestroika* time. The following paragraph builds on Yanitsky (1994, p. 17; 1998, pp. 28–9).
37. E.g. see Shomina (2002) on housing and property rights initiatives in Moscow.
38. The concept of CSR, suggesting commercial corporations to behave in socially responsible ways, includes donations to civic initiatives (cf. Deuber 2006). Community foundations, a concept promoted by the Charities Aid Foundation (CAF) are acting as mediators in order to redirect assets from local budgets, private donors or companies towards community projects implemented by civic groups (author's interview with CAF Russia, Moscow, 2005; see also Hinterhuber and Rindt 2004).
39. In addition, see an earlier debate on the controversial pros and cons of area studies vs. comparative research on transformation processes in

post-communist countries: Schmitter and Karl (1994), Bunce (1995b), Karl and Schmitter (1995), Bunce (1995a).

40. The trends in IR and civil society studies may not be directly compared as the former presents an established academic discipline and the latter a more practice-oriented field of study. Nevertheless, there are obvious and important parallels with a view to introducing the very core concepts into the Russian scholarly contexts.

41. Also some Western academic journals are publishing more Russian authors, and some Russian journals have featured articles of Western authors.

42. See also Marsh and Gvosdev (2002) on the role of the Orthodox Church as 'a principal unifier of civil society'.

43. A good deal of research has been undertaken in various regions and a number of researchers have elaborated on specific local units of civic activism. E.g. some contributions in the volume on Russian civil society compiled by Evans et al. (2006) creditably move beyond Moscow by studying civic action in various cities: women's organizations in Ivanovo and Cheboksary (Sperling 2006), environmentalists in Vladimir and Vladivostok (Henry 2006), organizations for disabled children in Saratov and Samara (Thomson 2006), civil society in the small towns of Achit, Bednodemianovsk, and Zubtsov (White 2006). However, these chapters stand detached from each other without any systematic comparison. As a rare exception, a more systematic cross-regional study of NGO activities in seven cities has been presented more recently by Sundstrom (2006).

References

Alexander, J. C. 1998. 'Introduction. Civil Society I, II, III: Constructing an Empirical Concept from Normative Controversies and Historical Transformations', in J. C. Alexander (ed.), *Real Civil Societies. Dilemmas of Institutionalization*, London/ Thousand Oaks: Sage: 1–19.

Beichelt, T. and S. Kraatz. 2000. 'Zivilgesellschaft und Systemwechsel in Rußland', in W. Merkel (ed.), *Systemwechsel 5. Zivilgesellschaft und Transformation*, Opladen: Leske + Budrich: 115–43.

Belokurova, E. B. 2001. 'Kontseptsiia grazhdanskogo obshchestva v rossiiskom prochtenii: obzor publikatsii poslednykh let', in G. M. Mikhaleva and S. I. Ryzhenkov (eds), *Grazhdan'e i vlast': problemy i podkhody*, St Peterburg: Letnii sad: 28–47.

—— 2005. *NGOs Role in the Policy-Making in the Russian NW Regions*, presentation at ICCEES Congress, Berlin, 25–30 July 2005.

Borisov, S. 2005. 'Russia: Gray Suits 1, Chintz 0', *Transitions Online* (14 February 2005), www.tol.cz.

Brown, A. 2001. 'Evaluating Russia's Democratization', in A. Brown (ed.), *Contemporary Russian Politics*, Oxford: Oxford University Press: 546–68.

Bunce, V. 1995a. 'Paper Curtains and Paper Tigers', *Slavic Review* 54 (4): 979–87.

—— 1995b. 'Should Transitologists Be Grounded?' *Slavic Review* 54 (1): 111–27.

Caldwell, M. L. 2004. *Not by Bread Alone. Social Support in the New Russia*, Berkeley: University of California Press.

Carnegie Moscow Center (ed.) 2005a. *Grazhdanskoe obshchestvo i politicheskie protsessy v regionakh*, Working Papers No. 3, 2005, Moscow.
—— (ed.) 2005b. *Grazhdanskoe obshchestvo: ekonomicheskie i politicheskie podkhody*, Working Papers No. 2, 2005, Moscow.
Carothers, T. 1999. *Aiding Democracy Abroad. The Learning Curve*, Washington, DC: Carnegie Endowment for International Peace.
—— 2002. 'The End of the Transition Paradigm', *Journal of Democracy* 13 (1): 5–21.
Checkel, J. T. 1999. *Why Comply? Constructivism, Social Norms and the Study of International Institutions*: ARENA Working Papers 99/24.
Crotty, J. 2003. 'Managing civil society: democratisation and the environmental movement in a Russian region', *Communist and Post-Communist Studies* 36 (4): 489–508.
Dawisha, K. and B. Parrot (eds) 1997. *Politics, Power and the Struggle for Democracy in South-East Europe*, Cambridge: Cambridge University Press.
Deuber, G. 2006. *Corporate Social Responsibility (CSR) und postsozialistische Transformation*, Diskussionspapiere an der Universität Bayreuth (Heft 11).
Deutsches Institut für Menschenrechte 2003. *Russland auf dem Weg zum Rechtsstaat? Antworten aus der Zivilgesellschaft*, Berlin (Published in Russian and German).
Dorosheva, N. and M. 2002. *Vse, chto vy khoteli znat' o nekommercheskom sektore, no boialis' sprosit'. Posobie dlia zhurnalistov*, Moscow: CAF.
—— (ed.) 2003. *Grazhdanskii forum. God spustia*, Moscow: Charities Aid Foundation (CAF).
Dzhibladze, Y. and K. Ermichine (eds), 2002. *Grazdanskoe obshchestvo: vzgliad iznutri*, Moscow: Tsentr razvitiia demokratii i prav cheloveka.
Evans, A. B. 2006a. 'Civil Society in the Soviet Union?' *Russian Civil Society: A Critical Assessment*, Armonk NY: M. E. Sharpe: 28–54.
—— 2006b. 'Vladimir Putin's Design for Civil Society', *Russian Civil Society: A Critical Assessment*, Armonk NY: M. E. Sharpe: 147–58.
Evans, A. B., et al. (eds), 2006. *Russian Civil Society: A Critical Assessment*, Armonk NY: M. E. Sharpe.
Fein, E. 2002. 'Zivilgesellschaftlicher Paradigmenwechsel oder PR-Aktion? Zum ersten allrussischen "Bürgerforum" im Kreml', *Osteuropa-Spezial* 52 (April): 19–40.
—— 2006. 'Potjomkinsches Parlament und Papiertiger. Die russische Gesellschaftskammer', *Russlandanalysen* (87): 2–4.
Fish, M. S. 1996. *Democracy from Scratch: Opposition and Regime in the New Russian Revolution*, Princeton NJ: Princeton University Press.
Fish, S. 2005. *Democracy Derailed in Russia. The Failure of Open Politics*, Cambridge and New York: Cambridge University Press.
Forum Donorov 2005. *Donorskie i nekommercheskie organizatsii: chto my o nikh znaem. Obzor materialov issledovanii*, Moscow: Forum Donorov.
Freise, M. 2005. 'Demokratie-Bildung. Die Förderung der Zivilgesellschaft in Ostmitteleuropa', *Osteuropa* 55 (8): 83–93.
Gorzka, G. and P. W. Schulze (eds) 2000. *Russlands Weg in die Zivilgesellschaft*, Bremen: Edition Temmen.
Hawkins, D. 1999. 'Transnational Activists as Motors for Change (Book Review)', *International Studies Review* 1 (Spring): 121–2.

Hemment, J. 2004. 'The riddle of the third sector: Civil society, international aid, and NGOs in Russia', *Anthropological Quarterly* 77 (2): 215–41.

Henderson, S. L. 2003. *Building Democracy in Contemporary Russia. Western Support for Grassroots Organisations*, Ithaca and London: Cornell University Press.

Henry, L. 2002. 'Two paths to a greener future: environmentalism and civil society development in Russia', *Demokratizatsiya* 10 (2): 184–206.

—— 2006. 'Russian Environmentalists and Civil Society', in Alfred B. Evans, L. A. Henry and L. M. Sundstrom (eds), *Russian Civil Society: A Critical Assessment*: Armonk NY: M. E. Sharpe: 211–28.

Hinterhuber, E. and S. Rindt 2004. *Bürgerstiftungen in Russland: Philanthropie zwischen Tradition und Neubeginn (Community Foundations in Russia: Philanthropy between Tradition and Rebirth)*, Arbeitshefte des Maecenata Instituts für Philanhtropie und Zivilgesellschaft Nr. 14, Berlin: Maecenata Verlag.

Howard, M. M. 2003. *The Weakness of Civil Society in Post-Communist Europe*, Cambridge: Cambridge University Press.

Hyden, G., et al. (eds) 2004. *Making Sense of Governance: Empirical Evidence from Sixteen Developing Countries*, Boulder, CO: Lynne Rienner.

INDEM 1998. *Rossiia i korruptsiia: kto kogo*, Moscow: Informatika dlia Demokratii (Fond INDEM).

Karl, T. L. and P. C. Schmitter 1995. 'From an Iron Curtain to a Paper Curtain: Grounding Transitologists or Students of Postcommunism?' *Slavic Review* 54 (4): 965–78.

Kaufman, M. T. 2003. 'Russia', in M. T. Kaufman (ed.), *Soros. The Life and Times of a Messianic Billionaire*, New York: Vintage Books: 222–34.

Keane, J. (ed.) 1988. *Civil Society and the State*, London: Verso.

—— 1998. *Civil Society: Old Images, New Visions*, Cambridge: Cambridge University Press.

Keck, M. E. and K. Sikkink 1998. *Activists Beyond Borders. Advocacy Networks in International Politics*, Ithaca and London: Cornell University Press.

Kharkhordin, O. 2000. *The Importance of the Politics of Friendship in Contemporary Russia*, PONARS Policy Memo 149, European University at St Petersburg.

Khlopin, A. 2002. 'Grazhdanskoe obshchestvo v Rossii: ideologiia, utopiia, real'nost' ', *Pro et Contra* 7 (1): 120–44.

Kopecký, P. 2003. 'Civil society, uncivil society and contentious politics in post-communist Europe', in P. Kopecký and C. Mudde (eds), *Uncivil Society? Contentious politics in post-communist Europe*, London and New York: Routledge: 1–18.

Kortunov, A. 2004. 'Twelve Commandments for Exiting Foundations', *Trust for Civil Society in Central & Eastern Europe* (Article No. 142, July).

Krastev, I. 2004. *Shifting Obsessions. Three Essays on the Politics of Anticorruption*, Budapest and New York: CEU Press.

Kryshtanskovskaya, Ol'ga and S. White 2005. 'Inside the Putin Court: A Research Note', *Europe–Asia Studies* 67 (7): 1065–1075.

Ledeneva, A. V. 1998. *Russia's Economy of Favours. Blat, Networking and Informal Exchange*, Cambridge: Cambridge University Press.

Lenhard, M. 2003. 'Netzwerkerinnen in Russland. Die digitale Vernetzung der Frauenbewegung', in M. Schetsche and K. Lehmann (eds), *Netzwerker-Perpektiven. Bausteine für eine Soziologie des Internet*, Regensburg: S. Roderer: 109–27.

Levada, Y. 2000. 'Homo Sovieticus Ten Years On', in E. Skidelsky and Y. Senokosov (eds) *Russia on Russia: The Fate of Homo Sovieticus*, Moscow: Moscow School of Political Studies, Centre for Post-Collectivist Studies: 13–28.

Lewin, M. 1991. *The Gorbachev Phenomenon. A Historical Interpretation*, Expanded edition, Berkeley and Los Angeles: University of California Press.

Litovchenko, S. (ed.), 2004. *Report on Social Investments in Russia. Role of Business in Social Development*, Moscow: Russian Managers Association.

Machura, S., et al. 2003. *Ehrenamtliche Richter in Südrussland. Eine empirische Untersuchung zu Fairness und Legitimität*, Münster: LIT.

Marsh, C. and N. K. Gvosdev (eds), 2002. *Civil Society and the Search for Justice in Russia*, Lanham MD: Lexington Books.

Martirossian, J. 2004. 'Russia and Her Ghosts of the Past', in R. A. Johnson (ed.), *The Struggle Against Corruption: A Comparative Study*, New York: Palgrave Macmillan: 81–108.

McFaul, M. 2001. *Russia's Unfinished Revolution. Political Change from Gorbachev to Putin*, Ithaca and London: Cornell University Press.

McFaul, M. and E. Treyger 2004. 'Civil Society', in M. McFaul, N. Petrov and A. Ryabov (eds), *Between Dictatorship and Democracy. Russian Post-Communist Political Reform*, Washington DC: Carnegie Endowment for International Peace: 135–173.

Meier, C. 2003. *Deutsch-Russische Beziehungen auf dem Prüfstand. Der Petersburger Dialog 2001–2003*, SWP-Studie S 10, März 2003, Berlin: Stiftung Wissenschaft und Politik / Deutsches Institut fur Internationale Politik und Sicherheit.

Mendelson, S. E. and J. K. Glenn (eds), 2002. *The Power and Limits of NGOs. A Critical Look at Building Democracy in Eastern Europe and Eurasia*, New York and Chichester, West Sussex: Columbia University Press.

Mikhaleva, G. M. and S. I. Ryzhenkov (eds), 2001a. *Grazhdan'e i vlast': problemy i podkhody*, St Petersburg: Letnii sad.

—— 2001b. 'Predislovie', in G. M. Mikhaleva and S. I. Ryzhenkov (eds), *Grazhdan'e i vlast': problemy i podkhody*, St Petersburg: Letnii sad: 6–10.

Miller, W. L., et al. 1997. 'How Citizens Cope with Postcommunist Officials: Evidence from Focus Group Discussions in Ukraine and the Czech Republic', *Political Studies* 45 (3): 597–625.

O'Donnell, G. and P. C. Schmitter 1986. *Transitions from Authoritarian Rule: Tentative Conclusions about Uncertain Transitions*, Baltimore MD: Johns Hopkins UP.

Oates, S. and S. White 2003. 'Politics and the media in postcommunist Russia', *Politics* 23 (1): 31–7.

Pas'ko, G. 2005. 'Der Spion, der keiner war. Der Fall Sutjagin ist nicht beendet', *Osteuropa* 55 (1): 91–102.

'Petrov', N. 2005. 'Model' "Gosudarstvo – biznes – grazhdanskoe obshchestvo" ne rabotaet tam, gde biznes i gosudarstvo – odno tseloe', in Carnegie Moscow Center (ed.), *Grazhdanskoe obshchestvo: ekonomicheskii i politicheskii podkhody, Working Papers No. 2, 2005*, Moscow: 18–21.

Pleines, H. 2005. 'The Political Role of Civil Society Organisations in Central and Eastern Europe', in H. Pleines (ed.), *Participation of Civil Society in New Modes of Governance. The Case of the New EU Member States. Part 1: The State of Civil Society*, Vol. Arbeitspapiere und Materialien No. 67 – May 2005, Bremen: Forschungsstelle Osteuropa: 30–9.

Powell, L. 2002. 'Western and Russian Environmental NGOs: A Greener Russia?' in S. E. Mendelson and J. K. Glenn (eds), *The Power and Limits of NGOs. A Critical Look at Building Democracy in Eastern Europe and Eurasia*, New York and Chichester, West Sussex: Columbia University Press: 126–51.

Pro et Contra 1997. *Grazhdanskoe obshchestvo*, Issue 2/4, Moskva: Moskovskii Tsentr Karnegi.

Reddaway, P. and R. W. Orttung (eds) 2004. *The Dynamics of Russian Politics. Putin's Reform of Federal-Regional Relations, Volume I*, Lanham MD: Rowman and Littlefield.

—— (eds) 2005. *The Dynamics of Russian Politics. Putin's Reform of Federal–Regional Relations, Volume II*, Lanham MD: Rowman and Littlefield.

Risse, T. 2000. 'The Power of Norms versus the Norms of Power: Transnational Civil Society and Human Rights', in A. M. Florini (ed.), *The Third Force. The Rise of Transnational Civil Society*, Washington DC: Carnegie Endowment for International Peace: 177–209.

Risse, T., et al. (eds) 1999. *The Power of Human Rights. International Norms and Domestic Change*, Cambridge: Cambridge University Press.

Risse, T. and K. Sikkink 1999. 'The socialization of international human rights norms into domestic practices: introduction', in T. Risse, S. C. Ropp and K. Sikkink (eds) *The Power of Human Rights. International Norms and Domestic Change*, Cambridge: Cambridge University Press: 1–38.

Rutland, P. 2006. 'Business and Civil Society in Russia', in A. B. Evans, L. A. Henry and L. M. Sundstrom (eds) *Russian Civil Society: A Critical Assessment*, Armonk NY: M. E. Sharpe: 73–94.

Sakwa, R. 2004. *Putin: Russia's Choice*, London and New York: Routledge.

Savintseva, M. and P. Stykow 2005. 'Country Report. Russia', in TI (ed.), *Global Corruption Report 2005*, London/Ann Arbor MI: Pluto Press, Transparency International: 199–202.

Schmidt, D. 2006a. 'Hard to Connect: Trans-national Networks, Non-Governmental Organisations and the Internet in Russia', in S. Oates, D. Owen and R. Gibson (eds), *The Internet and Politics. Citizens, voters and activists*, London and New York: Routledge: 163–82.

—— 2006b. 'Russia's NGO Legislation: New (and Old) Developments', *Russian Analytical Digest* (3): 2–6, http://www.res.ethz.ch/analysis/rad/documents/Russian_Analytical_Digest_3_2006.pdf.

Schmidt, D. and S. Bondarenko 2005. 'Good governance and anti-corruption mobilisation: do Russian NGOs have any say?' in I. I. Demirag (ed.), *Corporate Social Responsibility, Accountability and Governance. Global Perspectives*, Sheffield: Greenleaf Publishing: 291–311.

Schmitter, P. and T. L. Karl 1994. 'The Conceptual Travels of Transitologists and Consolidologists: How Far to the East Should They attempt to Go?' *Slavic Review* 53 (1): 173–85.

Schmitter, P. C. 1997. 'Civil Society in East and West', in L. Diamond, M. F. Plattner, Y. -h. Chu and H. m. Tien (eds), *Consolidating the Third Wave Democracies. Themes and Perspectives*, Baltimore MD: Johns Hopkins University Press: 239–62.

Schrader, H., et al. (eds), 2000. *Russland auf dem Weg zur Zivilgesellschaft? Studien zur gesellschaftlichen Selbstorganisation in St Petersburg*, Münster: LIT.

Schulze, P. W. 2000. 'Krise und Delegitimation der Macht in Russland', in G. Gorzka and P. W. Schulze (eds), *Russlands Weg in die Zivilgesellschaft*, Bremen: Edition Temmen: 143–68.

Sevortyan, A. and N. Barchukova 2002. *The Nonprofit Sector and Government in the Russian Regions: Patterns and Prospects for Collaboration. Regional Survey Report (in Russian and English)*, Moscow: Charities Aid Foundation (CAF).

Shelley, L. 2001. 'Crime and Corruption', in S. White, A. Pravda and Z. Gitelman (eds), *Developments in Russian Politics 5*, Basingstoke: Palgrave: 239–53.

—— 2006. 'Organized Crime Groups: Uncivil Society', in A. B. Evans, L. A. Henry and L. M. Sundstrom (eds), *Russian Civil Society: A Critical Assessment*, Armonk NY: M. E. Sharpe.

Shomina, Y., et al. 2002. 'Local activism and the prospects for civil society in Moscow', *Eurasian Geography and Economics* 43 (3): 244–70.

Shvedov, G. 2005. 'Grazhdanskoe obshchestvo v Rossii. Zametki praktika', in Carnegie Moscow Center (ed.), *Grazhdanskoe obshchestvo: ekonomicheskie i politicheskie podkhody, Working Papers No. 2, 2005*, Moskva: 22–5.

Siegert, J. 2002. 'Ökoheld oder Vaterlandsverräter? Der Fall Pas'ko – Ein Lehrstück über Rußlands defekten Rechtsstaat', *Osteuropa-Spezial* 52 (April): 41–54.

Skalaban, I. A. 2004. *Stanovlenie i razvitie nekommercheskikh organisatsii v Rossii. Khrestomatiia*, Novosibirsk: Novosibirskii Gosudarstvennyi Tekhnicheskii Universitet.

Soros, G. 2004. 'Putin's Heavy Hand Could Halt Russia's Rise. Choking Society', *International Herald Tribune*, (June 16).

Sperling, V. 2006. 'Women's Organizations: Institutionalized Interest Groups or Vulnerable Dissidents?' *Russian Civil Society: A Critical Assessment*, Armonk NY: M. E. Sharpe: 161–77.

Sundstrom, L. M. 2005. 'Foreign Assistance, International Norms, and NGO Development: Lessons from the Russian Campaign', *International Organization* 59 (Spring): 419–49.

—— 2006. *Funding Civil Society. Foreign Assistance and NGO Development in Russia*, Stanford CA: Stanford University Press.

Sundstrom, L. M. and L. A. Henry 2006. 'Russian Civil Society: Tensions and Trajectories', in J. Alfred, B. Evans, L. A. Henry and L. M. Sundstrom (eds), *Russian Civil Society: A Critical Assessment*, Armonk NY: M. E. Sharpe: 305–22.

Temkina, A. 1997. *Russia in Transition: The Case of New Collective Actors and New Collective Actions*: Kikimora Publications, Aleksanteri Institute.

Tereshchenko, I. I. 2003. *Pravovoe aspekty sozdania nekommercheskich organisatsii*, Moscow: Charities Aid Foundation.

Thomson, K. 2006. 'Disability Organizations in the Regions', in Alfred B. Evans, L. A. Henry and L. M. Sundstrom (eds), *Russian Civil Society: A Critical Assessment*, Armonk NY: M. E. Sharpe: 229–45.

Tschepurenko, A. 2001. 'Die Akzeptanz von Demokratie und Marktwirtschaft in der russischen Gesellschaft', in H. -H. Höhmann and H. -H. Schröder (eds), *Russland unter neuer Führung. Politik, Wirtschaft und Gesellschaft am Beginn des 21. Jahrhunderts*: Bundeszentrale für Politische Bildung: 201–15.

Tsygankov, A. P. and P. A. Tsygankov 2005. 'New directions in Russian international studies: pluralization, Westernization, and isolationalism', in

A. P. Tsygankov and P. A. Tsygankov (eds), *New Directions in Russian International Studies*, Stuttgart: ibidem: 13–36.

Umland, A. 2002. 'Toward an uncivil society? Contextualizing the decline of post-Soviet Russian parties of the extreme right wing', *Demokratizatsiya* 10(3): 362–91.

vanden Heuvel, W. (ed.), 2000. *Future of Freedom in Russia*, West Conshohocken: Templeton Foundation Press.

Vorobyev, D. 2005a. 'Ekologicheskie referendumy v Rossii', *Otechestvennye zapiski* (6): 179–91.

—— 2005b. *Strengthening Green Ideology in Russia under the Pressure of Globalisation and Authoritarianism*, Paper presented at the 3rd ECPR Conference, Budapest, 8–10 September 2005. Section 19/7. Environmental Politics: Globalisation, European Integration and Green Party Politics.

Warkotsch, A. 2004. 'Zentralasiens Regime und der Islam', *Osteuropa* 54 (11): 3–15.

Wedel, J. R. 1998. *Collision and Collusion. The Strange Case of Western Aid to Eastern Europe 1989–1998*, New York: St. Martin's Press.

Wehner, M. 2002. 'Oppositionelle müssen draußen bleiben. Rußlands Delegation beim Petersburger Dialog', *Frankfurter Allgemeine Zeitung*, 10 April: 5.

Whistler, D. E. 1993. 'The mainstream democratic vision', in G. D. Wekkin (ed.), *Building Democracy on One-Party Systems*, Westport CT: Praeger.

White, A. 2006. 'Is Civil Society Stronger in Small Towns?' in A. B. Evans, L. A. Henry and L. M. Sundstrom (eds), *Russian Civil Society: A Critical Assessment*, Armonk NY: M. E. Sharpe: 284–304.

White, S., Z. Gitelman and R. Sakwa (eds), 2005. *Developments in Russian Politics 6*, Basingstoke: Palgrave Macmillan.

Yanitsky, O. N. 1994. 'Ekologicheskaia politika: rol' dvizhenii i grazhdanskikh initiativ', *Sotsiologicheskie issledovaniia* 10: 10–20.

—— 1998. 'Ekologicheskoe dvizhenie v "perekhodnom" obshchestve: problemy teorii', *Sotsiologicheskie issledovaniia* 10: 22–33.

3
Russian and Estonian Civil Society Discourses Compared

Risto Alapuro

The concept of civil society is open to diverse interpretations, which undoubtedly explains much of its popularity since the 1980s.[1] It has appeared in such contexts as the criticism levelled against dictatorships in Latin America, the neoliberal critique of the welfare state, the antineoliberal critique of globalization, the communitarian critique of individualized modern societies, and the opposition to the Soviet-type system and the construction of democracies in Eastern and East-Central Europe. In addition to its importance in the contemporary social scientific repertoire, it has a rich history in a variety of different traditions (Keane (ed.) 1988 and Cohen and Arato 1992 are only two examples from the enormous literature on the subject).

Yet, seen from the perspective of the *history of concepts* (what in German is called *Begriffsgeschichte*) the ambiguity of the concept – its nature as a 'conceptual chameleon' (Kocka 2000, p. 21) – is not a problem but an object of study in its own right whose goal is to ascertain what the concept of civil society means in different countries and cultures, and in different languages. As Jürgen Kocka (2004, p. 65) and Michel Offerlé (2003, pp. 5–6) have pointed out, it is true not only that the concept has had a successful career in many languages, but also that the meanings of the terms denoting what is called 'civil society' in English are not identical in other languages. Thus the Russian term *grazhdanskoe obshchestvo* and the Estonian term *kodanikuühiskond* are not identical concepts.

My hypothesis is that a comparative study of the concept of civil society in different languages can provide new insights into the political cultures of the respective countries. As Mikko Lagerspetz has remarked, 'a study of how the concept [of civil society] is interpreted in a society can tell us more about its ... political culture than does a study of its formal political institutions' (2001, p. 11; see also Kocka 2000, pp. 26–9). In this comparison of the use of the concept in Russia and Estonia, and in Russian- and Estonian-language discourses, I will concentrate primarily on a sample of the scholarly utilization of the term, in order not to be immersed in the abundance of the material and to maintain comparability.[2]

The concept of civil society is expressive of political culture on account of its close relationship to the conceptions of the state, society, democracy, the public sphere, and most concretely, voluntary associations. This richness is common to its usage in different cultural contexts – whatever varieties the notion may otherwise display. Because the concept lies at the heart of fundamental issues in democratic politics, it can express, explicitly and implicitly, basic assumptions in the political culture, understood as the 'sociology of ordinary citizenship', which includes notably the ways people frame political questions, get angry, and act together (Cefaï 2001, pp. 97, 99).

Even though the focus is on the concept, the following remarks will also shed light on its proponents – the scholars – and their position in Russia and Estonia: the role of intellectuals will be discussed briefly from the perspective of the discourses in the two countries.

The 'purposive adoption' of a concept

The common context for the use of the notion of civil society in Russia and Estonia was opposition to the Soviet system and the construction of democracy after the disintegration of the USSR. This context provides the central starting point for the following comparison. In both countries the issue of the *adoption* of a culturally specific concept presents itself in an acute form. Civil society is an inherently Western idea, a 'product of the West' (Kocka 2004, p. 76), and in both countries it was introduced in reference to Western models. In the West the ideas of civil society and liberal democracy as a whole largely developed as unintended outcomes of the efforts of statemakers (Tilly 1975, p. 633). That is, the practices and conceptualizations of civil society evolved over centuries without taking the form of a preconceived project to be carried out. In present-day Russia and Estonia, in contrast, precisely the adoption of this idea, both in discourse and in practice, is at issue. The two countries have, in their own ways, embarked on Westernization, including the establishment of democratic and capitalist systems based on an ideal-typical Western model, of which civil society is an integral component (Howard 2003, pp. 49, 50). Therefore, views about civil society are expressive not only of the problems of democratization in general, including participatory democracy, but also of special problems attending a large-scale sociopolitical transformation. For this reason the analytic and the normative aspects, both of which are necessarily present in the civil society debate, may appear with different emphases and in different ways in the Russian and Estonian scholarly discussions on the one hand, and in established Western discussions on the other.

In reflecting on the use of the concept, it is helpful to link the issue to the constraints under which the institutions of civil society have been introduced or reintroduced in Russia and Estonia, or to what Claus Offe (1995, p. 117) has called the 'purposive adoption' of institutions. Whereas in several Western contexts voluntary associations and other institutions of civil society constitute an element in an established system of interlinked elements – the public sphere, articulation of interests and so forth – in postsocialist societies they had to be created or revived more or less at the same time as the actors in state institutions and in civil society were being defined or redefined and their mutual relations regulated: both the rules of the game and the players who play the game had to be defined simultaneously. For many people it was – or is – not only difficult to see who or which organizations were representing their interests, but simply what their interests were in the first place. Mikko Lagerspetz, Erle Rikmann and Rein Ruutsoo (2002, p. 85) capture an essential aspect of this problem when they remark that '[f]rom the point of view of democratic participation, the task of the Estonian (and more generally, Central and Eastern European) civil society is not to influence the existing channels of participation from "the outside", but *to create such channels in the first place*'. Moreover, the purposive adoption of an institution like a voluntary association may spoil the desired effect, because the process of designing and implementation of new institutions necessarily takes place in the shadow of the institutional patterns that are to be replaced – and these patterns are not easy to eradicate even if they can be shown to be grossly deficient in some instrumental respects (Offe 1995, pp. 117, 122). A formal set of rules and procedures may well be adopted, but not the shared meanings, values, and moral underpinnings that make people comply with those rules.

This problem is relevant here in two ways. First, a parallel exists between institutional adoption and the adoption of the concept of civil society in the sense that the latter process is also necessarily modified by the structures of the receiving culture. The adoption of the Western concept has taken place in a struggle against pre-existing Soviet conceptualizations, both in Russia and in Estonia, but at the same time it has implied a stance vis-à-vis other, possibly more entrenched domestic traditions of political thought. Second, the character of the institutional adoption itself – that is, the establishment of the actors of civil society and the rules of their game – directly affects reflections on the concept of civil society as well as where the proponents of these reflections, the scholars-intellectuals, locate themselves in relation to the new arrangements.

Russian civil society discourse

The Russian term *grazhdanskoe obshchestvo* goes back to the late eighteenth and early nineteenth century (Volkov 1997, pp. 82–3). It had a place in the Hegelian, Marxist and other philosophical literature in the nineteenth and the twentieth century (Gavra and Gomosova 2000, p. 32), but it never became important in empirical use before the challenge to the Soviet system gained momentum in the 1980s. At that time, the term was embraced by the rhetoric of the new mass action, along with other new or newly important terms referring to democracy, such as 'citizens' movements' (*grazhdanskie dvizheniia*), 'citizen initiatives' (*grazhdanskie initsiativy*), and the 'constitutional state' (*pravovoe gosudarstvo*). Almost simultaneously *grazhdanskoe obshchestvo* found its way into the scholarly vocabulary as well.

Rather than emerging as a concept at the end of the 1980s and the beginning of the 1990s, the term was a slogan conveying the idea that civil society was the prerequisite for the new or future democratic order. In most analyses applying the notion, the Soviet Union or Russia was viewed as another country that would follow the Western path more or less, and the term became a catchword to describe the conditions that were required to further *perestroika* and subsequently, democracy in the Western sense. Even the CPSU adopted it in 1990, declaring as its objective the formation of a 'civil society, in which people do not exist for the state but the state for people'. Usually the term conveyed similar aspects of economy and society as in the West. 'Proprietary rights . . . provide the basis for civil society'; the emergence of civil society presupposes 'the self-organization of the population in terms of dwelling areas, reconciliation of different group interests, . . . the creation of self-administrative councils and committees [and] of consumer cooperatives' (*potrebitel'skie obshchestva*); the consolidation of the 'democratic structure of civil society' requires, among other things, the 'development and expansion of socially significant middle classes' and 'social institutions guaranteeing the citizens' rights and freedoms'; and so on.[3] The juncture at the turn of the 1990s was seen as bringing Russia into the Western mainstream, with a 'normal society', 'normal historical process', or 'normal market democracy', and with the dominance of 'universal human values'.

This use of the term 'civil society' was thus an important conceptual tool in the dissociation from the Soviet system, a terminological resource needed for the conceptualization of the democratic development and its obstacles (Diligensky 1997, pp. 7, 12). Gradually it became the 'conceptual code of the epoch' (Golenkova 1999, p. 4).

However, with the decline of popular movements in the early 1990s, activists and scholars alike painfully realized that the creation of civil society was a more complicated and laborious task than had seemed in the days of *perestroika*. The disappointment led a number of scholars to reflect on and to analyse the concept in relation to Russia, especially the obstacles to its realization (Belokurova 2001, p. 41). Today it is a well established term in the Russian social science vocabulary.

In her informative overview of the Russian social scientists' 'reading' of the concept of civil society Elena Belokurova (2001) distinguishes between two mainstream Western traditions, called the 'L-tradition' and the 'M-tradition'. According to Oleg Kharkhordin (1997, p. 38), from whom Belokurova draws the distinction, the former tradition, 'going back to John Locke, ... considers civil society as an ethical community that lives under natural law prior and outside politics', and the latter tradition, 'named after Charles Montesquieu, ... presents civil society as a multitude of citizens' autonomous associations that are intermediaries between the individual and the state and, if needed, defend the freedom of the individual against the usurpation by the state'.

This distinction appears explicitly (Kharkhordin 1997; Gavra and Gomosova 2000, pp. 34–5; Belokurova 2001; Petrov 2005, p. 6; Belokurova and Iargomskaia 2005, p. 23) or implicitly (e.g. Golenkova 1999, p. 5; Vitalii Grigoriev's overview (2000, pp. 89–91); *Politicheskaia sotsiologiia* 2001, pp. 227–8) in a number of Russian reflections and studies. It seems to capture a division that exists in the Russian discussion in a more pronounced way than in the Western one.[4] The distinction implies that there are two types of 'purposive adoption' of a concept and points to a major dimension in the Russian scholarly debate on civil society in general. Schematically, on the one hand, civil society is presented as civilized and morally worthy, and on the other hand as a sustained organized capacity to lay claims to the state. Noteworthy is that the former, morally charged perspective is 'quite popular' (Belokurova and Iargomskaia 2005, p. 23) among Russian specialists. Its popularity seems reminiscent of the distinction between the 'uncivilized' Soviet system and 'normal society' that was current during *perestroika*.

Among those who represent the former view (the 'L-tradition') it is common to see the prospects of civil society in Russia in a more negative light than among those stressing people's self-organization. The former attribute the poor prospects to the absence of the middle class and to the ethnic heterogeneity of the population, factors that block the growth of a civic and egalitarian culture. More pessimistic still among these scholars are those who lament the nature of the political culture, the paternalist consciousness of the people, and the centuries-long cleavage between society and the state authorities (Belokurova 2001, pp. 36–40; Grigoriev 2000, p. 87). The problematic character of Russia's political culture allegedly manifests itself in a mentality that thwarts the activity necessary for the emergence of civil society. 'The historically formed ideotype of the Russian personality (*russkaia lichnost'*)' involves an aspiration to egalitarianism and the absence of the ethics of success, weak capacity to take responsibility for one's own life or the transfer of responsibility to instances above the individual himself – fate, God, power (Diligensky 1997, pp. 12–13, cited in Belokurova 2001, pp. 36–7). It is easy to find other examples of this line of thought (e.g. Basina 1997, pp. 92, 102).

In this approach especially those elements are emphasized as typically Russian that make sense negatively. Much stress is put on the ability of individuals to act autonomously as a characteristic of a genuine civil society (Grigoriev 2000, pp. 89–90, 94; Gavra and Gomosova 2000, p. 35). The alleged absence of autonomous individuals in Russia highlights the difference (or even otherness) vis-à-vis the West. Hence the strong emphasis on the culturally determined type of the 'Russian personality' as the main 'psychological and cultural' obstacle to the development of civil society, or the opposition found between the Russian 'psychology of state-dominated paternalism' or the 'archetype of domination–submission' (*arkhetip gospodstva–podchineniia*) (Khlopin 1997a, cited in Belokurova 2001, p. 39) and Western 'individualist life strategies', in a number of reflections (e.g. Gadzhiev 1994, p. 62, cited in Belokurova 2001, p. 33; Diligensky 1997, pp. 10, 13, 15, 17, 20). This theme, a kind of cultural-psychological view of a (national) mentality, common in Russian accounts, cannot be found in the Western discussion.

A possible solution in this perspective is to propose an important role for the state in line with an idea profoundly entrenched in Russian political culture, and in Russian politics and thinking today (see for instance Pursiainen and Patomäki 2004, pp. 60–5; Hale 2002). The state may be considered instrumental in defending people's rights and promoting civil society 'from above', in the absence of the middle class as a necessary base, or the state is needed even in opposition to society that vacillates between passivity, order and destructive tendencies (Belokurova 2001, pp. 35, 37; Gavra and Gomosova 2000, pp. 36–7; Grigoriev 2000, pp. 87–8).

An ultimate conclusion of what Hale (2002) has called the 'statist' approach is that not only are the prospects of achieving a civil society poor but there is no soil for it to take root. Consequently, it is erroneous to think that civil society should be promoted in Russia at all. Many scholars representing this view are 'traditionalists', who have connections with the Slavophile tradition in Russian social thought (Belokurova 2001, pp. 40–1, 44; cf. Pursiainen and Patomäki 2004, pp. 77–86). Those taking this extreme view do not speak of the civilizing nature of civil society but consider it as an epitome of an alien Western culture.

A different view emerges from those texts that stress voluntary organizations and associational activity as the core of civil society (the 'M-tradition'), that is, organizational and institutional factors that enable people to act jointly for common objectives and to lay claims to the state. This conception may imply an explicitly active or even contentious relationship vis-à-vis the state, in contrast to the former view. As a rule the scholarly representatives of this perspective are 'modernizers' (Belokurova 2001, p. 44). Many of them were close to the mass movements in the late 1980s and the early 1990s, and unlike the 'traditionalists', they may have studied associations empirically. Moreover, they often also have links with the organizations of the 'third sector'. In several cases these organizations and their publications promoting civil society are financially supported by Western donors; usually the publications have a limited circulation only. There seem to be links between some intellectuals and the third sector, which can marshal resources for them and offer them a mode of action corresponding to their theoretical and ideological orientations (Belokurova 2001, pp. 42–3). In this context 'civil society' is usually a term utilized because of its ideological proximity to those notions of Western origin that imply associational activity, such as 'non-profit organizations' (*nekommercheskie organizatsii*) and 'non-governmental organizations' (*negosudarstvennye organizatsii*), which were adopted at the beginning of the 1990s in Russia to mark a break with the organizations of the Soviet period (Belokurova 2001, p. 44).

'Modernizers' are generally optimists, or at least they are less pessimistic than 'traditionalists'. They not only find elements of civil society in the Russian past, but they also see in the present process of organization a basis for the development of civil society in contemporary Russia (Belokurova 2001, p. 44).

An issue in this approach are the mechanisms mediating between the state and civil society. One term that characterizes this relationship is 'social partnership' (*sotsial'noe partnerstvo*), originally used to describe relations between the state, the labour unions, and the employers' organizations. The term retains this meaning (see e.g. Crowley 2002; Krivosheev 2004), but in the mid-1990s it was also redefined to cover the regulated relationship of the third sector to the state and the economic sector, especially in relieving social problems (Model' and Model' 2000). In third-sector organizations social scientists meet other people and provide knowledge and practical skills necessary for joint activity with authorities and enterprises on supposedly equal terms (see Liborakina et al. 1996), even though in practice the leading partner in this relationship is usually the state (Pursiainen and Patomäki 2004, pp. 63–5).

Finally, there is a perspective that appears in Belokurova's overview (2001, pp. 40, 44–5) but is not identified as a distinct approach, separate from others. It strives through conceptual work to escape from the dilemma of either denying the applicability of the Western-type concept of civil society in present-day Russia (as many 'traditionalists' do), or identifying its existence there as well (as some 'modernizers' do). Oleg Kharkhordin (1997; 2005) and Vadim Volkov (1997) have worked out, albeit in different ways, a theory-based perspective to people's autonomous activity vis-à-vis the state in Russian history, by relating it to Western traditions. Kharkhordin distinguishes an Orthodox Christian tradition as the basis of a conception of civil society, alongside Protestant and Catholic visions, while Volkov sees the functional equivalent for civil society in the Russian idea and practice of *obshchestvennost'*. Kharkhordin's interpretation leads him to stress friendship networks as the basis of civil society, while Volkov's view of the birth of civil society entails that the Russian tradition of social solidarity and civic virtues is incorporated into it.

All in all, then, at least three different approaches can be discerned in the scholarly discussion that has adopted 'civil society' as a conceptual tool to break with the Soviet past. Those who see civil society as a civilized society usually stress the disparity between the Russian and the Western cultural tradition. They are at pains to show the gravity of the incivility that hampers the evolution of civil society in Russia. In this view the state may seem necessary for positive development. Ultimately, by applying the same framework but changing the perspective, one can also argue that civil society is in fact incompatible with Russian conditions and undesirable. Those, instead, who consider civil society as one having an organized capacity to lay claims to the state adopt more or less deliberately the Western view, which opposes civil society both to the Soviet period and the 'statist' tradition in Russia in general. Third, an approach stressing 'constructively' the domestic basis can be observed as well. Instead of emphasizing the distance between the Russian tradition and the concept of civil society, or adopting the notion in its Western guise, Kharkhordin and Volkov have turned to historically conditioned Russian sociability in search of a Russian solution that could functionally correspond to civil society in the Western sense.

The three alternative modes of 'purposive adoption' summarize the main views on civil society in the scholarly literature. They give an idea of the nature of Russian civil society discourse that facilitates comparisons with the corresponding phenomenon in Estonia.

The Estonian civil society discourse

As in Russia, 'civil society' became a catchword and a concept in Estonian scholarly discourse in the wake of the disintegration of the Soviet Union. However, not only the context for imitation and modification was different, but also the timing and the usage of the concept. In post-Soviet Russia the context was a new round in the struggle to resolve the problem of Russia's relation to the West: how to learn from the West in order to defend Russia against Western challenge, to catch up with it, or to supersede it, a challenge familiar from the reforms of Peter the Great as well as from the adoption of Bolshevism as the Russian variant of Marxism. In post-Soviet Estonia the context was provided by the regaining of its independence and a perceived 'return to the Western world', now substantiated not only by Estonia's membership of NATO and the European Union, but also, secondarily, by the recognizable emergence of a home-grown associational tradition.

Unlike in Russia, the term 'civil society' did not play a prominent role in Estonian public discussion until the middle of the 1990s, or even later. It did not belong to the vocabulary of the 'Singing Revolution' of the late 1980s or to that of the re-establishment of the independent state in 1991. In the process of dissociation from the Soviet Union, priority was given to the terminology of mobilization of the 'people' and of state- and nation-building (Ruutsoo 2001, cited in Raik 2003, p. 201; Ruutsoo 2002a, pp. 189–226). Symptomatic of the secondary role of the notion during the early period of change is that originally no established word corresponded to it (see Aarelaid 1996, p. 9). Civil society was often called *tsiviiliühiskond*, and only later was this term supplanted by *kodanikuühiskond* (Ruutsoo 2001; Lagerspetz 2000, pp. 1–2). Even today the form of the term is not fully fixed.[5]

One major impulse to the introduction and then even to the predominance of the term in the public discussion came, first, from the diffusion of the ideology of the 'open society' through projects funded by Western foundations since the early 1990s,[6] and second, a little later, from a mainly EU-based 'democracy promotion', in which 'Western' concepts and models were introduced into or imposed on Estonia (Raik 2003, pp. 42, 62, 214–15). Usually, at issue were projects designed to increase the participation of interest groups and other NGOs and civic organizations in the political process (ibid., pp. 202–23). Thus, whereas in Russia the concept emerged in opposition to the Soviet system in the late 1980s, in Estonia it was rather adopted in the process of integration with the West.

Notably, the importance of Western project funding increased the sensitivity of the Estonian academic community in the 1990s to civil society as an issue and to the concept itself – in an atmosphere in which the image of the Estonian transition as a 'return to the West' dominated much of the politically relevant social science discussion and research. Yet still in 1997, when social scientists published a major anthology under the title *Return to the Western World: Cultural and Political Perspectives on the Estonian Post-Communist Transition* (edited by Marju Lauristin and Peeter Vihalemm), the concept appeared only marginally. Although an English-language collection of articles published four years earlier by some of the same scholars (Høyer, Lauk and Vihalemm (eds) 1993) had the term 'civic society' (!) in its title, the notion was only occasionally used and in a vague sense, denoting a civilized society in general.[7]

One of the most determined proponents of the term in the late 1990s and later has been Rein Ruutsoo. In his book *Civil Society and Nation Building in Estonia and the Baltic States* (2002a) Ruutsoo considers civil society, in accordance with the 'M-tradition' above, as the 'arena of the polity where self-organizing groups, movements, and individuals, relatively autonomous from the state, attempt to articulate values, create associations and solidarity, and advance their interests' (2002a, p. 40).[8] The concept is being utilized as a critical tool in the analysis of Estonian society. Ruutsoo contrasts the mobilization of the late 1980s – which he portrays as the (re)birth of civil society, based on organizational phenomena like the Song Festival and the existence of various networks and other organizations – to the situation at the beginning of the 2000s, when political groups were indifferent to the development of civic activism and civil society (Ruutsoo 2002a, pp. 157, 174–6, 215, 387, 364, 366).

It is nevertheless significant that the term itself did not gain importance in structuring the popular movement of the late 1980s, along with the terminology of national self-determination and independence.

Ruutsoo has also used the notion in a critical tone in opposing the 'ethnic nation-state idea' to that of civil society, which is an 'essential concept capable of challenging' it (2002b, pp. 38, 41; cf. Ruutsoo 2002a, pp. 224, 231). This distinction seems important, if one wishes to conceptualize the position of the Russian-speaking minority. If the frame of reference in studying democracy in Estonia is the 'ethnic nation-state', those who are not citizens do not necessarily appear in the analysis at all, whereas if civil society is the starting point, they will appear because they are members of it even though they are not members of the state. But other than in passing, the concept has apparently not been seriously used in Estonian research in this sense.[9]

Most frequently the notion has appeared in the scholarly discussion since the late 1990s in the study of democracy, notably of participatory democracy (Lagerspetz, Rikmann and Ruutsoo 2002, p. 75). Western-based international funding and EU-based pressures may have promoted this work, but the initiative of social scientists themselves has clearly been instrumental. Those involved are interested in developing civil society in the sense of the proliferation of NGOs and other forms of popular self-organization, that is, in a definitely empirical sense. The volume and composition of associational activity were examined in 1998 and 2005, first with pessimistic conclusions (Lagerspetz, Rikmann and Ruutsoo 2002), and then with a moderately optimistic outlook (Rikmann et al. 2005).

In this research activity, a close relationship was created between social scientists and the representatives of the state institutions. The most striking indication of the involvement of scientists, both as scholars and as partners of the state organs, is a framework document for regulating the relationships between the NGOs and the Estonian government called the Estonian Civil Society Development Concept, which was approved by the Estonian Parliament in 2002. That efforts to promote democracy played a role in the preparation of the document is evident from the fact that the initial impulse for it came from a project in the UN Development Programme (Lagerspetz 2001, pp. 3, 13; Rikmann 2003, p. 12). It defines the mutual tasks of the public sector and citizens' initiatives as well as the principles of their cooperation in politics, public administration, and the 'construction of an Estonian civil society',[10] in order to develop participatory democracy in Estonia. The framework document has resulted in organized connections between the two partners, and these have stated a need to develop their cooperation further, thanks to the increase in the number of their mutual contacts (Rikmann et al. 2005, p. 85; cf. Kivirähk 2004). Among social scientists the document has generally been welcomed as a constructive measure.

Social science expertise was involved in the process in two ways. First and most importantly, given that the current debate on civil society and the NGOs in Estonia was inspired by Western, mainly Anglo-Saxon models, social scientists were used as experts capable of mediating these models and ideas and of facilitating their adaptation and introduction in Estonia. Second, in connection with the preparation of the document, some of the social scientists involved in it carried out a series of interviews with academic specialists, civil servants, politicians, local government officials, business people, and NGO activists, asking them about their conceptions of civil society (Lagerspetz 2001, pp. 9, 14; Ruutsoo, Rikmann and Lagerspetz 2003). Along the way, some social scientists have made a kind of pedagogical contribution in the process by helping to solidify relevant Estonian terminology and by trying to familiarize the broader public with the idea of civil society (Lagerspetz 2004; Lagerspetz et al. 2003).

Thus the introduction of the concept has clearly been an integral part of the modernizing and Westernizing project of the Estonian state and society. The application was advocated by social scientists who provided a terminology for the advancement of participatory forms of democracy, and helped the voluntary associations, their mutual cooperation, and their cooperation with the state to flourish. That this variant of purposive adoption has a specific modernizing and Westernizing hue is shown by the opposition it has met on the part of an older domestic and German-influenced associational tradition that goes back to the pre-World War I past and the interwar period (see Aarelaid-Tart and Siisiäinen 1993, and Aarelaid (ed.) 1996). This orientation has many strongholds in organizations of traditional Estonian popular culture and education. During the preparation and approval of the Estonian Civil Society Development Concept its representatives felt themselves neglected and some of them have vehemently criticized the new conception as an American import that ignores the genuinely Estonian associational tradition. Their criticism has a terminological dimension. The new terms current in the civil society vocabulary, terms such as the 'third sector' (*kolmas sektor*) and 'non-profit association' (*mittetulundusühing*), have been opposed to the traditional term 'society' (*selts*), used already in the nineteenth century (Haamer 2003, p. 3).[11]

In sum, the Estonian discourse on civil society has been intimately connected with the promotion of democracy in the Estonian state, including above all participatory democracy. The approach that stresses associational activity (the 'M-tradition') has predominated in accordance with the general approval of a practically oriented Western conceptualization and the belief that a civil society is both needed and realizable in Estonia.

Conclusion: civil society discourses and scholars-intellectuals in Russia and Estonia

The civil society discourse in both Russia and Estonia resulted from the crisis and downfall of the Soviet Union and from the subsequent turn to the West in a search for the model of democracy. In both cases an opportunity presented itself rapidly, without a long-standing organized challenge. Civil society had to be created, and models were available. 'Civil society' became a *project*, an element in a framing strategy. It became an object of reflection for scholars and a catchword for those seeking to promote democratization.

Nevertheless, the differences between the two countries are remarkable as well. It was not only the huge difference in size, which has made it much simpler to establish connections between state organs and scholarly experts in Estonia than in Russia. Russia is an old state, in which society has throughout history 'proven unable to impose on political authority any kind of effective restraints' (Pipes 1974, p. xvii), and in which associational life has comparatively weak roots. No consensus relating the idea and the concept of civil society to the past has emerged in Russian social science. Some scholars have expressed scepticism or pessimism due to the 'statist' tradition and the concomitant passivity of the population, others have engaged in a search for elements of civil society in the pre-Soviet and Soviet past, and still others have reconceptualized it in order to link it to the emancipatory elements in Russian sociability. We are witnessing a new round in the complex process of adoption of Western influence, a process in whose background looms the division between Westernizers and Slavophiles.

Estonia is a new state, or a state under reconstruction. It proclaims continuity with the Republic of Estonia of the interwar period, and despite disagreement over how democratic its political system was from 1934 onwards, the distinction between state and (civil) society was certainly much more established and associational activity much stronger than in the Russian tradition. Hence a relatively straightforward adoption of the civil society vocabulary, in line with the 'return to the West', or with integration into Western Europe politically, economically, and culturally, and hence the mainly empirical interest in the scholarly discussion and work.

If civil society is a project and therefore needs to be created or adopted purposively, it must be carried out by a specific group of actors. Here we encounter yet another common element in the Russian and the Estonian situation. The scholars who are at the forefront in the discussion about civil society have difficulty in avoiding political involvement of some sort, even if they would prefer to do so. However, the role of intellectuals is not the same in the two cases.

In Russia it has happened before that the adoption of concepts developed elsewhere as guides for future development has led to elitism and utopianism. A number of commentators fear that something similar might happen again. The 'construction of civil society' has been compared to the once celebratory 'construction of communism' (Maksimenko 1999, p. 120, cited in Belokurova 2001, p. 46). There is a risk of normative bias, as Vladimir Gel'man (2002, p. 20) has put it, when one applies a concept from a different social science culture unreflectively to a transition in Russia. The analysis of civil society is not only diagnostic; it is 'diagnostic-prognostic' (Belokurova 2001, p. 40). Those better informed are obliged to provide 'democratic enlightenment' in this issue to their disoriented co-citizens (Diligensky 1997, p. 21; cf. Alapuro 1993, pp. 211–13; Belokurova 2001, pp. 34, 35, 41; Diligensky 1997, p. 11; Zubov 1997, p. 35) – many of whom have no idea at all of what civil society in the Western sense means. It is in line with this problem that of those employed in Russian NGOs, 60 per cent have a higher education; such organizations are prone to become resource pools for an active minority (Zdravomyslova 2005; Henry 2002, pp. 188, 193, 201; cf. Grigoriev 2000, pp. 90–1).

In Russia, scholars advocating the notion of civil society have not been closely affiliated with centres of power. The situation is different in Estonia. Their relative prominence has been made possible by the perceived needs of statemaking. In fact, they continue a long tradition in that country, as scholars-intellectuals have been politically relevant actors from the days of nationalism and national consolidation in the nineteenth century to the elaboration of minority policy by the Estonian government in the 1990s and the 2000s.[12] The present role of social scientists in proposing models for civil society and providing expertise and new terminology for its development continues this tradition, as does the recent portrayal of Estonia's historical trajectory as a simple return to Western civilization (on this, see Alapuro 2003). Moreover, a number of scholars were prominent actors in the transition itself in the late 1980s and the beginning of the 1990s. But the most important and interesting aspect of the combined role of Estonian scholar-intellectuals is their ability to participate in the nation- and state-building process as *scholars*. The most telling example is the Estonian Civil Society Development Concept. Its cooperative spirit and the unproblematic role of social scientists as scholarly experts in its preparation are in a striking contrast with the ambivalence of the most spectacular Russian attempt to regulate the relationship between the NGOs and the state, the Kremlin's Civic Forum in 2001 (see Nikitin and Buchanan 2002, and e.g. Kharichev 2001).

All in all, the discourses on civil society seem to display, on the one hand, yet another example of the ambivalence of the Russian intelligentsia in relation both to the state and the West, and on the other hand the state- and nation-building role of Estonian intellectuals, a role that is not unfamiliar in other small European latecomer countries.

Notes

1. This chapter is a revised version of a paper presented in the VII World Congress of ICCEES, Berlin, 25–30 July 2005. I thank Mikko Lagerspetz for his comments on the paper and Elena Belokurova, Suvi Salmenniemi, and Anna-Maria Salmi for their comments on the section about the Russian civil society discourse.
2. Pursiainen and Patomäki (2004) have recently reviewed the use of the notion of civil society in contemporary Russian political thought. See also the literature cited in Evans, Henry and Sundstrom (eds) 2006 and Pursiainen 2008. Elena Belokurova and Natal'ia Iargomskaia (2005) have interestingly analysed the use of the term civil society in the discourse of social organizations and local authorities in different regions of Russia.
3. The quotations come, respectively, from the programmatic declaration of the XXVIII congress of the CPSU in 1990 (*Rossiia segodnia* [1991], p. 39); from the programme of the Free Democratic Party of Russia (*Informatsionnyi biulleten'*, no. 1, 1992 [of the St Petersburg regional section of the movement 'Demokraticheskaia Rossiia'], p. 7); from the programme proposal of the Social Democratic Party of the Russian Federation (Kofanova 1991, p. 208); and from the annual report of the Institute of Sociology of the Academy of Sciences of the USSR (*Otchet* [1990], pp. 31–2).
4. Kharkhordin draws the distinction from Charles Taylor (1990, pp. 104–15), but it seems much more complex than the form in which it has been introduced in the Russian discussion.
5. Along with the form *kodanikuühiskond* (literally: citizen's society), the form *kodanikeühiskond* (literally: citizens' society) has been favoured by some social scientists. See Lagerspetz 2000, p. 2; 2001, p. 14.
6. I thank Mikko Lagerspetz for stressing this aspect in the (scholarly) adoption process.

7. I thank Mikko Lagerspetz for drawing my attention to this work.
8. The definition is drawn from Juan J. Linz and Alfred Stepan (1996, p. 7).
9. Non-citizens have the right to vote in local elections, which makes their empowerment an aspect of democratization in the framework of the existing polity and the use of the concept of civil society potentially fruitful at that level. However, other conceptual tools have apparently been found more appropriate in empirical local studies (see Berg 1999; Berg and Sikk 2004). In the anthology *The Challenge of the Russian Minority* (Lauristin & Heidmets [eds] 2002), the term 'civil society' appears only occasionally in connection with the Russian minority. The editors make use of it in a cultural perspective in analysing integration through learning and individual success as a part of the democratic construction of the Estonian state: 'integration is viewed rather as a *cultural process*, stressing the opportunities for members of the minority to learn Estonian, to participate in civil society, to get a good education, etc.' (Lauristin and Heidmets 2002, p. 29; emphasis added).
10. Rikmann 2003, p. 12. See, in more detail, http://www.ngo.ee/kodanikeyhiskond/ekak.html
11. See also other commentaries in the proceedings of the Estonian parliament in 2000–2003 (http://www.riikikogu.ee/rva/toimetised/). I thank Mikko Lagerspetz for reminding me of the importance of the associational tradition in Estonia, Marju Lauristin for the information about the recent debate and Daimar Liiv for the information about how to locate it.
12. On the latter role, Lauristin and Heidmets 2002, p. 25; cf. Heidmets and Lauristin 2002, p. 322.

References

Aarelaid, Airi. 1996. 'Kodanikualgatus, seltsid ja tsiviiliühiskond', in Airi Aarelaid (ed.), pp. 9–16.
Aarelaid, Airi (ed.), 1996. *Kodanikualgatus ja seltsid Eesti muutuval kultuurimaastikul*. Tallinn: Jaan Tõnissoni Instituuti Kirjastus.
Aarelaid-Tart, Airi and Martti Siisiäinen. 1993. 'Voluntary Associations in Estonia and in Finland from the Nineteenth Century to the Present Time'. *Proceedings of the Estonian Academy of Sciences. Humanities and Social Sciences* 42(2): 215–31.
Alapuro, Risto. 1993. 'Civil Society in Russia?'. In *The Future of the Nation State in Europe*, ed. Jyrki Iivonen. Aldershot: Edward Elgar, pp. 194–218.
Alapuro, Risto. 2003. 'Estonian Views of Collective Action and Democracy'. *Journal of Baltic Studies* 34: 457–69.
Basina, Elena. 1997. 'Krivoe zerkalo Evropy'. *Pro et Contra* 2(4): 92–112.
Belokurova, E.V. 2001. 'Kontseptsiia grazhdanskogo obshchestva v rossiiskom prochtenii: obzor publikatsii poslednikh let'. In *Grazhdane i vlast': problemy i podkhody*, ed. G. M. Mikhaileva and S. I. Ryzhenkov. Studia Politica 5. Moscow and St Petersburg, pp. 28–47.
Belokurova, Elena and Natal'ia Iargomskaia. 2005. 'Do i posle Grazhdanskogo foruma: grazhdanskoe obshchestvo v regionakh Severo-Zapada'. In *Grazhdanskoe obshchestvo i politicheskie protsessy v regionakh*. Moscow: Moskovskii tsentr Karnegi, pp. 23–37.

Berg, Eiki. 1999. *Estonia's Northeastern Periphery in Politics: Socio-economic and Ethnic Dimensions.* Dissertationes Geographicae Universitatis Tartuensis 7. Tartu:
Tartu University Press.

Berg, Eiki and Allan Sikk. 2004. 'Ethnic Claims and Local Politics in Northeast-
ern Estonia'. In *Beyond Post-Soviet Transition: Micro perspectives on Challenge and
Survival in Russia and Estonia*, ed. Risto Alapuro, Ilkka Liikanen and Markku
Lonkila. Helsinki: Kikimora, pp. 165–87.

Cefaï, Daniel. 2001. 'Expérience, culture et politique'. *Cultures politiques*, sous la
direction de Daniel Cefaï. Paris: Presses Universitaires de France, pp. 93–116.

Cohen, Jean and Andrew Arato. 1992. *Civil Society and Political Theory.* Cambridge
MA: Harvard University Press.

Crowley, Stephen. 2002. 'Comprehending the Weakness of Russia's Unions'.
Demokratizatsiya 10: 230–55.

Diligensky, German. 1997. 'Chto my znaem o demokratii i grazhdanskom
obshchestve?' *Pro et Contra* 2(4): 5–21.

Evans, Alfred B. Jr., Laura A. Henry and Lisa McIntosh Sundstrom (eds), 2006.
Russian Civil Society: A Critical Assessment. Armonk NY: M. E. Sharpe.

Gadzhiev, K. 1994. *Politicheskaia nauka.* Moscow: Soros-Mezhdunarodnye
otnosheniia.

Gavra, Dimitri and Anna Gomosova. 2000. 'Zivilgesellschaft in Russland – Das
Beispiel St Petersburg: Erste Schritte in Theorie und Praxis'. In *Russland auf
dem Weg zur Zivilgesellschaft? Studien zur gesellschaftlichen Selbstorganisation in
St Petersburg*, ed. Heiko Schrader, Manfred Glagow, Dimitri Gavra and Michael
Kleineberg. *Osteuropa*, vol. 26, pp. 32–49.

Gel'man, Vladimir. 2002. 'Vvedenie'. In Gel'man, Sergei Ryzhenkov, Elena
Belokurova and Nadezhda Borisova, *Avtonomiia ili kontrol'? Reforma mest-
noi vlasti v gorodakh Rossii, 1991–2001.* St Petersburg/Moscow: Evropeiskii
universitet v Sankt-Peterburge, pp. 13–34.

Golenkova, Zinaida T. 1999. 'Civil Society in Russia'. *Russian Social Science Review*
40(1): 4–18.

Grigoriev, Vitaliy. 2000. 'The Russian Approach to Civil Society'. In *Russland auf
dem Weg zur Zivilgesellschaft? Studien zur gesellschaftlichen Selbstorganisation in
St Petersburg*, ed. Heiko Schrader, Manfred Glagow, Dimitri Gavra and Michael
Kleineberg. *Osteuropa*, vol. 26, pp. 86–97.

Haamer, Valter. 2003. 'Kodanikuühiskond: kellele, milleks'. *Riigikogu toimetised* 8
(http://www.riikikogu.ee/rva/toimetised/rito8/artiklid/25haamer.htm)

Hale, Henry E. 2002. 'Civil Society from Above? Statist and Liberal Models of
State-Building in Russia'. *Demokratizatsiya* 10: 306–21.

Heidmets, Mati and Marju Lauristin. 2002. 'Learning from the Estonian Case', in
Marju Lauristin and Mati Heidmets (eds), pp. 319–32.

Henry, Laura A. 2002. 'Two Paths to a Greener Future: Environmentalism and
Civil Society Development in Russia'. *Demokratizatsiya* 10: 184–206.

Howard, Marc Morjé. 2003. *The Weakness of Civil Society in Post-Communist Europe.*
Cambridge: Cambridge University Press.

Høyer, Svennik, Epp Lauk and Peeter Vihalemm (eds), 1993. *Towards Civic Society:
The Baltic Media's Long Road to Freedom. Perspectives on History, Ethnicity and
Journalism.* Tartu: Nota Baltica.

Informatsionnyi biulleten', no. 1, 1992 [of the St Petersburg regional
section of the movement 'Demokraticheskaia Rossiia']. St Petersburg:

Dvizhenie 'Demokraticheskaia Rossiia', Sankt-Peterburgskoe regional'noe otdelenie.

Keane, John, (ed.), 1988. *Civil Society and the State.* London: Verso.

Kharichev, Igor'. 2001. 'Grazhdanskoe obshchestvo v podarok'. *Nezavisimaia gazeta*, 13 September.

Kharkhordin, Oleg. 1997. 'Proekt Dostoevskogo'. *Pro et Contra* 2(4): 38–59.

Kharkhordin, Oleg. 2005. 'Civil Society'. In Kharkhordin, *Main Concepts of Russian Politics*. Lanham MD: University Press of America, pp. 41–65.

Khlopin, Aleksandr. 1997a. 'Grazhdanskoe obshchestvo ili sotsium klik: rossiiskaia dilemma'. *Politiia* 1: 7–27.

Khlopin, Aleksandr. 1997b. 'Stanovlenie grazhdanskogo obshchestva v Rossii: institutsional'naia perspektiva'. *Pro et Contra* 2(4): 60–76.

Kivirähk, Juhan. 2004. 'Kas kodanikuühiskond on moes?' *Postimees*, 19 February.

Kocka, Jürgen. 2000. 'Zivilgesellschaft als historisches Problem und Versprechen'. In *Europäische Zivilgesellschaft in Ost und West. Begriff, Geschichte, Chancen*, ed. Manfred Hildermeier, Jürgen Kocka and Christoph Conrad. Frankfurt/New York: Campus Verlag, pp. 13–39.

Kocka, Jürgen. 2004. 'Civil Society from a Historical Perspective'. *European Review* 12(1): 65–79.

Kofanova. E. 1991. 'O proekte programmy SDPR'. *Politicheskie issledovaniia* 1(1): 208–10.

Krivosheev, V. T. 2004. 'Sotsial'noe partnerstvo i korporativizm: rossiiskaia spetsifika'. *Sotsiologicheskie issledovaniia* 31(6): 38–44.

Lagerspetz, Mikko. 2000. 'Kodanikeühiskonna rollid tänases Eestis'. *Riigikogu Toimetised* 2.

Lagerspetz, Mikko. 2001. 'Estonian NGOs as Civil Society?' Paper presented to the Fifth Conference of the European Sociological Association, August 28–September 1, 2001, Helsinki, Finland.

Lagerspetz, Mikko. 2004. *Kodanikuühiskonna lühisõnastik*. Tallinn: Eesti Mittetulundusühenduste Ümarlaud.

Lagerspetz, Mikko, Erle Rikmann and Rein Ruutsoo. 2002. 'The Structure and Resources of NGOs in Estonia'. *Voluntas* 13: 73–87.

Lagerspetz, Mikko, Aire Trummal, Rein Ruutsoo, Erle Rikmann and Daimar Liiv. 2003. *Tuntud ja tundmatu kodanikeühiskond*. Tallinn: Avatud Eesti Fond.

Lauristin, Marju and Mati Heidmets. 2002. 'Introduction: The Russian Minority in Estonia as a Theoretical and Political Issue', in Marju Lauristin and Mati Heidmets (eds), pp. 19–29.

Lauristin, Marju and Mati Heidmets (eds), 2002. *The Challenge of the Russian Minority: Emerging Multicultural Democracy in Estonia*. Tartu: Tartu University Press.

Lauristin, Marju and Peeter Vihalemm. 1993. 'The Balts – West of the East, East of the West', in Høyer, Lauk and Vihalemm (eds), pp. 13–40.

Lauristin, Marju and Peeter Vihalemm with Karl Erik Rosengren and Lennart Weibull (eds), 1997. *Return to the Western World: Cultural and Political Perspectives on the Estonian Post-Communist Transition*. Tartu: Tartu University Press.

Liborakina, Marina, Mikhail Fliamer and Vladimir Yakimets. 1996. *Sotsial'noe partnerstvo. Zametki o formirovanii grazhdanskogo obshchestva v Rossii*. Moscow: Izdatel'stvo 'Shkola kul'turnoi politiki'.

Linz, Juan J. and Alfred Stepan. 1996. *Problems of Democratic Transition and Consolidation: Southern Europe, South America, and Post-Communist Europe.* Baltimore MD: Johns Hopkins University Press.

Maksimenko, V. 1999. 'Ideologema civil society i grazhdanskaia kul'tura'. *Pro et Contra* 4(1): 113–28.

Model', I. M. and B. S. Model'. 2000. 'Sotsial'noe partnerstvo v Rossii'. *Sotsiologicheskie issledovaniia* 27(9): 42–9.

Nikitin, Alexander and Jane Buchanan. 2002. 'The Kremlin's Civic Forum: Cooperation or Co-optation for Civil Society in Russia?' *Demokratizatsiya* 10: 147–65.

Offe, Claus. 1995. 'Some Skeptical Considerations on the Malleability of Representative Institutions'. In *Associations and Democracy*, ed. Erik Olin Wright. London: Verso, pp. 114–32.

Offerlé, Michel. 2003. 'Avant-propos'. *La société civile en question*, dossier réalisé par Michel Offerlé. Paris: La Documentation Française, pp. 5–12.

Otchet o rezul'tatakh vypolneniia nauchno-issledovatel'skikh rabot i nauchno-organizatsionnoi deiatel'nosti instituta za 1990 god. 1990. Moscow: Akademiia Nauk SSSR, Institut Sotsiologii, pp. 31–2.

Petrov, Nikolai. 2005. 'Vstupitel'noe slovo'. In *Grazhdanskoe obshchestvo i politicheskie protsessy v regionakh*. Moscow: Moskovskii tsentr Karnegi, pp. 5–8.

Pipes, Richard. 1974. *Russia under the Old Regime*. London: Weidenfeld and Nicolson.

Politicheskaia sotsiologiia dlia studentov vyzov, ed. G. P. Sopov. 2001. Rostov-on-Don: Feniks.

Pursiainen, Christer. Forthcoming 2008. 'The Development of Civil Society–State Relations in Russia'. In *Good Governance and the Administrative Reform: Towards a New Contract of the State, Business, and Civil Society in Russia*, ed. S. Medvedev. Moscow: RECEP.

Pursiainen, Christer and Heikki Patomäki. 2004. 'The State and Society in Russia'. In *Contemporary Change in Russia: In from the Margins?*, ed. Egle Rindzeviciute. Huddinge: Baltic and East European Graduate School, Södertörns högskola, pp. 55–93.

Raik, Kristi. 2003. *Democratic Politics or the Implementation of Inevitabilities? Estonia's Democracy and Integration into the European Union.* Tartu: Tartu University Press.

Rikmann, Erle. 2003. 'Kansalaisosallistumisen kulttuuri Virossa'. *Idäntutkimus* 10(1): 3–14.

Rikmann, Erle, Meril Ümarik, Sofia Joons and Mikko Lagerspetz. 2005. *Kodanikualgatuse institutsionaliseerumine Eestis: organiseerumise struktuur ja ressursid.* Tallinn: Tallinna Ülikooli Eesti Humanitaarinstituut.

Rossiia segodnia. Politicheskii portret v dokumentakh 1985–1991. 1991. Moscow: Mezhdunarodnye otnosheniia.

Ruutsoo, Rein. 2001. 'Kodaniku taassünd'. *Eesti Päevaleht*, 21 August.

Ruutsoo, Rein. 2002a. *Civil Society and Nation Building in Estonia and the Baltic States: Impact of Traditions on Mobilization and Transition 1986–2000: Historical and Sociological Study.* Rovaniemi: University of Lapland.

Ruutsoo, Rein. 2002b. 'Discursive Conflict and Estonian Post-Communist Nation-Building', in Marju Lauristin and Mati Heidmets (eds), pp. 31–54.

Ruutsoo, Rein, Erle Rikmann and Mikko Lagerspetz. 2003. 'Süvenev keskustelu: Eesti ühiskonna valmisolek kodanikualgatuse arendamiseks'. In Mikko Lagerspetz, Aire Trummal, Rein Ruutsoo, Erle Rikmann and Daimar Liiv. 2003. *Tuntud ja tundmatu kodanikeühiskond*. Tallinn: Avatud Eesti Fond, pp. 46–81.

Taylor, Charles. 1990. 'Modes of Civil Society'. *Public Culture* 3(1): 95–118.

Tilly, Charles. 1975. 'Western State-Making and Theories of Political Transformation'. In *The Formation of National States in Western Europe*, ed. Charles Tilly. Princeton NJ: Princeton University Press, pp. 601–38.

Volkov, Vadim. 1997. 'Obshchestvennost': zabytaia praktika grazhdanskogo obshchestva'. *Pro et Contra* 2(4): 77–91.

Zdravomyslova, Jelena. 2005. 'Venäjän kansalaisjärjestöt ja kansalaisaktiivisuus Venäjällä'. In *Kansalaisyhteiskunta liikkeessä yli rajojen*, ed. Airi Leppänen. Helsinki: Palmenia-kustannus, pp. 204–14.

Zubov, Andrei. 1997. 'Sovremennoe russkoe obshchestvo i civil society: granitsy nalozheniia'. *Pro et Contra* 2(4): 22–37.

Part 2
Media and Society

Part 2

Media and Society

4
Journalistic Source Practices in Russian Business Dailies

Katja Koikkalainen

The basic task of the financial press is to provide useful and interesting information for businessmen and others who are interested in financial and economic questions. In Russia, economic reforms and structural changes have meant a boom in the popularity of business publications since the early 1990s. When Russia took its first steps towards a market economy, there was a huge need for reliable information about the economy, markets and business. The Soviet press did not offer a suitable model for informing its readers about the rising market economy. One of the first tasks for the new financial press was teaching how to behave in a market economy. While the mass-circulation national dailies have since then lost their unique position for television (Vartanova 2001, pp. 24, 27), the demand for specialized information such as business information has been increasing. Besides the printed press – newspapers and journals – there are a number of internet sites and television programmes devoted to financial information, and a television channel RBK-TV, devoted to economic news, is also available. The financial press market is, like the magazines market, one of the media sectors with the most considerable foreign ownership and investment as compared with other segments of the media market.

The financial printed press market in Russia is particularly numerous in terms of titles: there were over 700 periodical business publications in 2004 (Kolesnikov and Cherkasov 2005, p. 24). However, the concept of the 'economic press' is broad and includes quality newspapers and specialized magazines as well as weekly free advertisement papers (see Kulev 1996, pp. 13–14; Mordovskaia 1998, pp. 75–6). The quality papers not only write about business life, they also serve it (Kulev 1996, pp. 6–7). They publish economic and financial information to provide a basis for decision making in industry, banking, finance and the trading sector for readers who need precise, useful and operational information. The functions of the business press can also include formation of information infrastructure, satisfying the needs of entrepreneurs, disseminating information on legislative issues and declaring the ideas and principles of market economy (Grabel'nikov 1999, p. 31).

This chapter focuses on source practices in two quality general financial dailies, both of which are important for the Russian business community: *Kommersant* and *Vedomosti*. *Kommersant* (Businessman) is today more like a general quality newspaper than just a financial newspaper, but it was the first financially orientated newspaper in the new Russia after the collapse of Soviet Union. According to Kolesnikov and Cherkasov (2005, p. 26), adding various sections like sports, culture and entertaining contents is a current trend among Russian business publications. *Vedomosti* (Gazette) is more purely a financial newspaper. *Kommersant* and *Vedomosti* are among the best known central daily newspapers, and *Kommersant* in particular is the oldest of Russia's quality financial newspapers. It was founded in 1989, even before Soviet Union collapsed. In 2006 its daily print run was approaching 120,000.[1] The paper was independent at first until it was sold to businessman Boris Berezovsky in 1999, then in 2006 the whole publishing house ended up in the hands of businessman and general director of Gazprominvest Alisher Usmanov (Dolgosheeva 2006; Kulikova and Cherkasova 2006). *Kommersant* has 14 regional editions and a sister publication in Ukraine, launched in July 2005. As they say in *Kommersant*, the financial section, not the whole paper, is competing with its new rival, *Vedomosti*. Founded in 1999, *Vedomosti* has gained and is currently displaying a good level of respect in the financial newspaper market. Its average daily print run is also rising and was nearly 70,000 in 2006.[2] *Vedomosti* has seven regional editions.

Other business publications in Russia at the federal level include, for example, weekly newspapers like *Ekonomika i zhizn'*, weekly magazines like *Ekspert* and *Den'gi*, and a large number of regional papers and magazines. In the internet, the RBC news service is devoted to economic and financial news; the business-oriented TV channel RBC belongs to the same company.

Although *Kommersant* and *Vedomosti* are competitors, both have their strong sides and their particular 'niches'. Nowadays, *Kommersant* focuses on social questions and politics, but the financial section still is an essential part of the paper. *Vedomosti* is more purely a financial paper. For both, precise and accurate information is of prime importance. As the editors say, news and the latest information is what they are hunting for, and their own, exclusive contacts with newsmakers is the way in which they prefer to gather their information.

My study sought to examine the position of the Russian financial press in a global context. There are both similarities and difference between the Russian and international financial press standards and practices. The study examines aspects of professionalization, including the objectivity norm that 'guides journalists to separate facts from values and to report only the facts' (Schudson 2001, p. 150). The models and ideals are, however, heterogeneous and not unchangeable. The systems tend to change over time, but the models help to identify features of different systems and compare them with each other (Hallin and Mancini 2004, p. 12). Media systems may not be homogenous even inside one country – for example, in Britain, three different journalistic cultures have existed: the tabloid press, the quality press, and broadcasting (Hallin and Mancini 2004, p. 12). According to Hallin and Mancini (ibid., p. 13), national differentiation is diminishing and convergence is advancing. There are also a number of studies around the world that report a shift towards more informal, intimate, critical and cynically detached news reporting styles (Schudson 2005, p. 191). When speaking about foreign role models in this study, the most important ones for the financial press in Russia are the *Wall Street Journal* and the *Financial Times*. Both represent the so-called liberal media model that prevails in North America and Britain, and which emphasizes journalistic professionalism based on political neutrality and 'objectivity' (Hallin and Mancini 2004, pp. 11, 253). Characteristic of the liberal model is the 'relative dominance of market mechanisms and of commercial media' (ibid., p. 11). The liberal model differs from the polarized pluralism system, also identified by Hallin and Mancini, which is predominant in the Mediterranean area and Southern Europe and has also points of contact with the Russian media system. The polarized pluralism model is characterized by 'integration of the media into party politics, weaker historical development of commercial media, and a strong role of the state', and it places more emphasis on analysis and commentary than the liberal model (ibid., pp. 11, 29). The third model identified by Hallin and Mancini is called the democratic corporatist model, and it encompasses Northern Europe.

Differences between media systems have significantly diminished over time because of the diffusion of global media models (ibid., p. 251). It is, however, generally believed that globalization means adaptation more than invasion, and that it is taking place via localization. The process where media maintain both a global and culturally specific orientation is defined as domestication (Gurevitch et al. 1991, p. 206).

There are numerous examples of, for example, a mix of foreign influences and national tradition in television programming (for an overview, see Chadha and Kavoori 2005). The export of discursive practices has been found to be less visible than the export of concrete media products (Chalaby 1996, p. 323); the diffusion of Anglo-American journalism practices in France is an example. When discussing East European media systems, it is very likely that there are emerging new and indigenous media models instead of a simple replacement of socialist models directly with Western ones (de Smaele 1999). There are similar results in the Russian regional press: regional papers have been affected to some extent by foreign influences, but have not adopted them wholesale (Pietiläinen 2002).

There are several ways in which foreign influence reaches a Russian newspaper. Among them are reading foreign newspapers, visiting foreign editorial offices, working in a foreign newspaper, having foreign counterparts, and foreign news sources. When asking editors and reporters of *Kommersant* and *Vedomosti*, I found that it was not a question of copying models as such, but of creating new ones of one's own. The flow of ideas is certainly not one-sided: *Financial Times* and *The Wall Street Journal* draw their views about what is happening in Russia from their Russian counterparts. Perhaps they can use this experience somewhere else.

My research concentrated on Moscow-based editorial offices and the central editions of both newspapers. That is mainly because Moscow is the country's financial centre and the locus of federal decision-making. The results cannot necessarily be generalized to all business media in Russia, but it is likely that the routines and practices I have identified are also familiar in other newspaper offices.

Journalistic source practices

Value of sources

In this study I focused on journalistic source practices in *Kommersant* and *Vedomosti*. I have drawn my examples from research interviews conducted in 2002–2006 with 17 journalists in these two newspapers; some of them work as editors. In the coding of the extracts, 'VM01' is the code of the interviewee, and '40' represents the number of the speech act in the interview. The letters before the numeral code indicate present or past occupation (*Kommersant/Vedomosti*) and gender (female/male).

In European and North American context the relationship between sources and journalists can be seen as a field of power relations or of constant struggle over the preferred meanings in the community (Berkowitz and TerKeurst 1999, p. 125). Many journalists are aware of this struggle, including the drive towards positive self-portrayal by companies, so the journalists constantly evaluate the information they get (see, for example, Doyle 2006, p. 439). In source practices, there are both similarities and differences between the Russian media and the media in other countries. Personal sources are as highly ranked as they are everywhere else, while press releases are of minor importance. In Germany, for example, press releases have become very important information sources. German researchers argue that journalism depends on the information disseminated by public relations. More than half of the interviewed German journalists believed that press releases were important, generated themes, and saved time in reporting and investigation. At the same time, they suspected that the releases were too uncritical (Weischenberg, Löffelholz and Scholl 1998, pp. 249–50).

Connections with particular sources are connected to the position of a journalist and media organization in the media field. The main sources are personal contacts, politicians, and official reports and releases (this may be compared with the results that are reported in Randall 1996, pp. 60–5). In Russia, there are less visible and active non-governmental organizations (NGOs), which make them a less important source than in Western Europe and the USA; and police and rescue services are not common sources in the business press unless the story is about crime. Most of the interviewed journalists named 'newsmakers' as the best source. A 'newsmaker' is a person (or institution) from a company or government who can provide first-hand information on a news event. The information flow is sometimes bidirectional: journalists occasionally share information with their source.

The journalists have a kind of rank order, at least an implicit one, for their sources. Some statements are generally preferred to others: this kind of importance might be attached, for instance, to a source with a high position in an organization. It is understandable that journalists should make a particular effort to reach first-hand sources and get comments from the highest level of an organization:

> The most important information source is always the person who has made the decision and taken part in the process. If, for example, Gazprom buys from [Vladimir] Gusinsky a part of MediaMost's shares, it is understandable that there are two information sources, or sources of final information – Gazprom preferably in the person of [Alexei] Miller and Gusinsky. (VF12, 42)

Business journalists have access to a wide range of sources; some of them are open to all, others are personal. For routine news, several open-access sources are used: press releases or contacts with a company, online news services and news agencies, and press conferences. On the other hand, personal networks can also produce items for the daily news. When it comes to news agencies, journalists appreciate them for giving the signals: providing information on possibly newsworthy events (VM06, 42; compare also with Doyle's (2006, pp. 436–7) findings on *Financial Times* journalists). Besides domestic news, news agencies are used for international news: 'An understandable reason for that is that we do not have so many people there [abroad] with whom to discuss' (KM04, 40). In Russia, business periodicals do not make extensive research databases like, for example, the *Economist* in Britain; undertaking ratings and expert enquiries is, however, present (Kulikov and Cherkasov 2005, p. 26).

According to some of the interviewees, corporations whose shares are quoted on the stock exchange are regarded as cautious with reporters, and it is often hard to find a first-hand source inside the company itself. In closed companies this is easier (KF14, 32). Companies that use Western standards are more likely to be regarded as reliable because they are assumed to avoid lying:

> The easiest is, probably, with those companies who aim at raising capital and entering Western markets. It is good to work with companies whose shares are already quoted in the West. They use Western standards of information handling. But, of course, there are also some difficulties. They do not tell us anything before the official opening, since that is not allowed ... And what is nice is that they avoid lying ... It is also very important to us that if the company does not want to tell us something, at least it does not lie. (VF03, 60)

In both papers, a variety of sources is promoted: if there are two opposite views on an event, both sides should be covered in the news item (the *Kommersant* code in such matters is presented in Davydov and Dzialoshinskaia 1999, p. 131). The practices of Moscow business journalists show similarities with those of the 'younger generation' of St Petersburg journalists (Pasti 2004, pp. 179–80): for them, personal contacts are among the most important sources together with public authorities and the Internet. For St Petersburg practitioners who had begun their journalistic careers in the Soviet period, the most important news source was other media (ibid.). None of the Moscow journalists in my research spontaneously mentioned another medium as an important source.

There were no signs of differences in source preferences as between the two newspapers, although at the personal level there were some differences. Sources were valued for various reasons. For example, politicians are widely regarded as unnecessary sources; at the same time, they can be easily reached. According to one of the interviewees (KM04, 60), it is easiest to work with representatives of the legislative branch because there are a lot of them and all of them want to make a good impression on journalists.

Forming networks

Many of the interviewees emphasize the importance of a wide range of sources and of personal contacts. First-hand information is highly valued:

> The most important information sources are the market players. The more 'one's own' the article, the more important are one's 'own' sources. Reading a report from a business news agency and writing an article on it is not complicated at all. So the most important sources are the parties that are actually engaged in the markets. With them, as I've already said, you have to be in contact all the time to find news. To understand what's happening. (VM07, 28)

Or in another formulation:

> The most important sources are, of course, people, the parties that are in the marketplace, the newsmakers. Open information comes from news listings, naturally; we have newsgathering from all kinds of listings, but the most interesting news ... you get only when discussing with people. (KM10, 34)

However, it takes time to form a good source network. *Kommersant* had started building its network before the Soviet Union collapsed and before the shift to a market economy had taken place. As a *Kommersant* journalist put it, the market rose side by side with the paper itself:

> *Kommersant* was launched slightly before the market was launched. The market rose together with us, and there are a lot of people, we simply do know a lot of people and they do know us, in many enterprises, now already big ones. Simply [that is why] we get information in there. (KM04, 38)

This example illustrates how the source network forms. As long as personal sources are essential, the networks of a journalists and a newspaper are of extreme importance. Discussions and continuous contacts to companies form a steady base for source networks:

> The correspondent or the journalist has got a theme, and he/she contacts his/her own newsmakers, their competitors, turns to experts, analysts, market participants. And, of course, keeps an eye on the news agencies, and internet in the first hand. Of course nobody can demand that the journalist should go to the scientists or spend a lot of time in libraries, but particularly the presence in markets, and keeping an eye on its development, [brings] news. (KM02, 92)

Journalists not only get information from their sources but also form a network of information sharing. The sources themselves get something in exchange for the information they provide to the newspaper. The paper obtains news from the sources, and the sources get PR (KM04, 62). Most personal sources belong to the readers of the paper; about some developments in their own field even officials and businessmen do not know before it is published in a newspaper with exclusive rights (VM07, 46). One of the interviewed journalists explained that they are partly like allies with the officials in the field she reports on: the officials have to keep themselves informed of how the field is developing, and the articles in newspapers may have an influence on its development (KF14, 56). Sometimes information may be transferred from the news office to a source already during the writing process:

> We get from them, on the first hand, information and, on the second hand, comments ... They get from us a possibility to express their point of view and bring it out for a big target audience. And sometimes also information; it happens that you call somebody and tell that the ministry of economy and development has drafted a bill. And they say: How interesting, we did not know about that. (VF12, 64)

To work with such sources is not always easy, but neither is it always difficult. According to the 'ranking list' of an interviewee, it is the easiest to work with analysts, and in the second place with PR people. Sometimes consulting companies and other companies that provide information services, as well as computer companies, are even easier to work with than analysts. The next ones are companies and businesses in the provinces and after them companies in big cities. The most difficult is cooperation with state companies and officials (VM08, 55). However, many of the journalists interviewed found PR persons unhelpful and distant; this attitude is common also in the USA and Western Europe (see, for example, Hoge 1985, p. 297; Cameron, Sallot and Curtin 1997).

Anonymous sources

Anonymity of sources raises issues among Russian journalists; it is thought to be common and unavoidable, although our interviewees would generally to reduce its incidence. Although some of the interviewed journalists saw the wide usage of anonymous sources as a special Russian phenomenon, the practice is also common in the West, especially in investigative journalism. Kuutti (2002, p. 135) has suggested that if there was no possibility of using anomymous sources, there was less or not at all critical journalism: personal sources would not reveal any sensitive matters to a journalist if they were afraid of being reported. This is the picture also in Russian journalism. In business journalism, anonymous sources are also used for news on ongoing business transactions or other sensitive matters, including insider information. Anonymous sources are used not only for judging the government or criticizing it, but also for revealing unverified information.

Source reliability depends on the situation. Reliability is evaluated using several criteria: a source's position, the price of information (non-paid information is normally the most reliable), and the reasons for anonymity. A boss is a preferable source to a press service or anonymous source. One of the interviewees from *Vedomosti* explained that access to information heavily relies on the position of the journalist and the paper:

> I would like to specify right away that we never pay anyone for information. It is given to us because of the professionalism of our journalists. They are respected, trusted and considered to be honourable. (VF03, 31)

According to the interviewed journalists, in the editorial offices there were quite often situations with non-verified information, and both newspapers work cautiously with it. In *Vedomosti*, information from anonymous sources is treated as reliable enough for publication if three independent sources verify it. In unclear cases, the news item is reported in a cautious style; one of the basic tasks of a newspaper is said to be to publish information and keep the reader informed at as early stage as possible although official verification is missing (VF03, 31).

Norms of objectivity

Getting first-hand information and bringing 'talking heads' to the newspaper columns seems to be one of the methods used to achieve objectivity in journalism (see Schudson 2001 for a discussion of the objectivity norm in American journalism). Interviews are often used ritually, putting uncertain statements into the text – this way they look more 'objective' than texts written by the journalist him/herself. Tuchman (1978) calls this the strategic ritual of objectivity. She discusses the ways in which news journalists see objectivity and comes to the conclusion that it is a strategic ritual for journalists. In practice, a journalist puts a statement in quotes if she or he is not sure of its validity. When putting a statement in quotes the journalist avoids taking a stand on the issue and shifts responsibility onto the source. The factual basis of a journalistic text is highlighted in the same way in the Russian economic press. The routine use of personal sources and their quotation underlines the difference from the Soviet and conventional Russian journalistic practice. According to McNair (2000, p. 91), 'journalistic objectivity has not yet emerged as the dominant professional ethic in Russia' and 'there is still relatively little accumulated experience of objective or independent journalism'.

Fact-based information journalism is used especially in news agencies. In spite of the increasing worldwide influence of information journalism, some scholars believe the newspaper still remains the primary medium of partisanship, political commentary and analysis, and that the boundary between 'news' and 'opinion' is an area of constant movement (Boyd-Barrett and Rantanen 1998, p. 6). The boundary has more to do with the appearance of credibility than with the elimination of ideology from news texts. This supports the view that in the Russian economic press, the news agency style with fact-based journalism is preferred as a means of highlighting the reliability of the printed press and its difference in this respect from other media.

In *Kommersant* it seems that some of the journalists find that showing one's opinion is accepted, while in *Vedomosti* opinions are restricted to opinion pages. According to a readership survey by the Russian Union of Managers (AMR), showing one's own opinion in an article was widely considered a positive thing, and readers of business publications did not find that it excluded objectivity (*Reiting kachestva* 2004). In the survey, *Kommersant* got extra points from respondents for showing its opinion in its written materials. *Kommersant* and *Vedomosti* were voted the most respected daily business papers; third place went to *Izvestiia*. The AMR survey was undertaken among over 300 managers and business union representatives and it included also general newspapers with a financial section. In the rating, trustworthiness, informativeness, impartiality and topicality were crucial aspects when Russian managers selected what to read.

Among business journalists, however, the objectivity norm is widely accepted. Some of the business journalists found all kinds of interpretative writing useless; they took the view that no analysts or university-based scholars were needed on newspaper pages. In the next quotation a *Kommersant* practitioner shares his view:

> We understand very well that a journalist can never beat the parties in the market if we look at their expertise on the issue ... It is very important to understand what is happening. That is why a journalist does not have the right to his or her own opinion. That is why we try to get to the newspaper pages opinions, comments, assessments by respected people, highly esteemed specialists. That is why we do not need analysts. And we miss academic specialists even less. The representatives of the scholarly world are, in our opinion, boring; we seldom discuss with them. (KM02, 155)

The excerpt shows us that in *Kommersant*, some journalists did not receive analysts very warmly. This is the largest difference I found between *Kommersant* and *Vedomosti* in source practices: in *Vedomosti*, analysts were thought to be an essential part of business reporting. One of the journalists who were interviewed stressed their initiative regarding this issue:

> I could say that nowadays we, *Vedomosti*, are a model for other media. You can notice it well. Now, after three years [since *Vedomosti* was launched] I look at other newspapers: they also cite analysts; we brought analysts to the stage. Before us nobody turned to them apart from the Western media, the *Moscow Times* or Reuters. Now analysts are there almost in all articles about business, they are cited by *Izvestiia*, *Vremia novostei*, *Kommersant* ... From us more things are taken than we take from others. We do orientate, although more to the *Wall Street Journal* and the *Financial Times*. (VF03, 24)

Although analysts are seen as interesting and useful sources by many interviewees, the validity of a statement has to be evaluated by the same criteria as all the information that sources provide. One must consider that an analyst can have ties with companies or be involved in different businesses. An analyst always represents her or his employer company, too. Here Russian business journalists share the concern of their British colleagues (see Doyle 2006, pp. 441–2).

Conclusion

Journalistic source practices in the Russian business newspapers, *Kommersant* and *Vedomosti*, seem to have something in common with their Western counterparts while other features differ. According to my interviews with Russian business journalists, at least three kinds of source criteria can be found: (i) Relationship between the source and the information. If the relationship is remote, the source is not as valued as a source that is closer to the information. (ii) Position of the source. A boss is a preferable source to a press service or an anonymous source. (iii) Situation. For standard news different criteria are used as compared with one's own news, or 'scoops'.

Personal sources are very common in Russia, just as in the West, while press releases are of less significance. There was no big difference between the opinions of *Vedomosti* and *Kommersant* journalists or between men and women. In this respect, the most valued sources are first-hand ones inside companies themselves; accordingly, forming good contact networks is of major importance for a journalist. An ideal news source could be a top manager in a big company. Politicians are not very valued sources among business journalists – maybe journalists are looking for a clear distinction between politics and economics? In the West, politicians are also valued sources (see Randall 1996, pp. 60–5). Some journalists see that analysts are good sources, but others hold the opposite view. *Vedomosti* journalists have a generally positive attitude. Research centres and universities are not among everyday sources. PR offices are among less valued sources because journalists want first-hand information. Some of the journalists interviewed said that PR officers were as much concerned to prevent as to provide access to information. PR officers may often provide general information when journalists prefer to uncover their own news and employ a wide variety of sources.

It seems that in their source practices, business journalists in *Kommersant* and *Vedomosti* have a lot of common with Western counterparts. These publications are among the first media enterprises when introducing international styles or practices. For a reader, the clearest signs of similarity are found in the introduction of fact-based journalism and the presence of 'talking heads' instead of a journalist-interpreter. The march of financial analysts into the press has broadened the selection of news sources in Russian business dailies. It seems that *Vedomosti*'s working standards are closer to the standards of the *The Wall Street Journal* and *Financial Times* than those of *Kommersant*, and that the impact of the Western press is mainly through foreign ownership.

Notes

1. *Gazeta Kommersant*, 2006, available at: www.media-atlas.ru/editions, accessed 20 February 2007.
2. *Srednegodovye tirazhi*, 2007, available at: www.vedomosti.ru/about/performance.shtml, accessed 20 February 2007.

References

Berkowitz, D. and J. V. TerKeurst. 1999. 'Community as interpretive community: Rethinking the journalist–source relationship', *Journal of Communication* 49(3): 125–36.
Boyd-Barrett, O. and T. Rantanen (eds), 1998. *The Globalization of News*. London: Sage.
Cameron, G. T., L. M. Sallot and P. A. Curtin. 1997. 'Public relations and the production of news: A critical review and theoretical framework', in B. R. Burleton (ed.), *Communication Yearbook 20*, Thousand Oaks, London and New Delhi: Sage, pp. 111–55.
Chadha, K. and A. Kavoori. 2005. 'Globalization and national media systems: Mapping interactions in policies, markets and formats', in J. Curran and M. Gurevitch (eds), *Mass Media and Society*, 4th edn. London: Hodder Arnold, pp. 84–103.
Chalaby, J. K. 1996. 'Journalism as an Anglo-American invention: A comparison of the development of French and Anglo-American journalism, 1830s–1920s', *European Journal of Communication* 11(3): 303–26.
Davydov, V. and M. Dzialoshinskaia (eds), 1999. *Delovaia pressa Rossii: Nastoiashchee i budushchee*. Moscow: Globus.
de Smaele, H. 1999. 'The applicability of Western media models on the Russian media system', *European Journal of Communication* 14(2): 173–89.
Dolgosheeva, E. 2006. 'Slovo dlia investora', *Vedomosti*, 29 December.
Doyle, G. 2006. 'Financial news journalism. A post-Enron analysis of approaches towards economic and financial news production in the UK', *Journalism* 7(4): 433–52.
Grabel'nikov, A. 1999. 'Vidy delovoi pressy Rossii', in Davydov and Dzialoshinskaia 1999, pp. 30–48.
Gurevich, S. M. 2001. *Ekonomika sredstv massovoi informatsii*, 2nd edn. Moscow: RIP-Kholding.
Gurevitch, M., M. Levy and I. Roeh. 1991. 'The global newsroom: Convergences and diversities in the globalization of television news', in P. Dahlgren and C. Sparks (eds), *Communication and Citizenship: Journalism and the Public Sphere in the New Media Age*, London: Routledge, pp. 195–216.
Hallin, D. C. and P. Mancini. 2004. *Comparing Media Systems. Three Models of Media and Politics*. Cambridge: Cambridge University Press.

Hoge, J. 1985. 'Business and the media: Stereotyping each other', in R. E. Hiebert and C. Reuss (eds), *Impact of Mass Media. Current Issues*, New York and London: Longman, pp. 296–99.

Koikkalainen, K. 2004. 'Russian Financial Press in a Global Context', in E. Vartanova and Y. N. Zassoursky (eds), *Shaping Tomorrow's Media Systems*, Moscow: UNESCO Chair in Journalism and Mass Communication, Faculty of Journalism, Moscow State University, pp. 172–9.

Kolesnikov, A. N. and N. V. Cherkasov. 2005. '12 tendentsii razvitia mediabiznesa v Rossii (na primere sektora delovoi zhurnalistiki)', in E. L. Vartanova (ed.), *Ekonomika i menedzhment SMI. Ezhegodnik 2005*, Moscow: VK.

Kulev, V. S. 1996. *Delovaia pressa Rossii*. Moscow: Moskovskii gosudarstvennyi universitet, Fakul'tet zhurnalistiki.

Kulikova, Iu. and M. Cherkasova. 2006. 'Na "Kommersant" nashelsia pokupatel'', *Kommersant*, 31 August.

Kuutti, H. 2002. *Tutkittu juttu. Johdatus tutkivaan journalismiin* [Introduction to investigative journalism], Jyväskylä: Atena Kustannus.

McNair, B. 2000. 'Power, profit, corruption, and lies: The Russian media in the 1990s', in J. Curran and M. -J. Park (eds), *De-Westernizing Media Studies*, London and New York: Routledge, pp. 79–94.

Mordovskaia, Ye. I. 1998. *Delovye izdaniia v sisteme periodicheskoi pechati: Tipoo-brazuiushchie faktory, kharakter stanovleniia i razvitiia*. Candidate's dissertation, Journalism Faculty, Moscow State University.

Pasti, S. 2004. *Rossiiskii zhurnalist v kontekste peremen. Media Sankt-Peterburga*, Tampere: Tampere University Press.

Pietiläinen, J. 2002. *The Regional Newspaper in Post-Soviet Russia: Society, Press and Journalism in the Republic of Karelia 1985–2001*, Tampere: Tampere University Press.

Randall, D. 1996. *The Universal Journalist*, London: Pluto Press.

Reiting kachestva i populiarnosti delovykh pechatnykh SMI Rossii. 2004. Assotsiat-siia menedzherov Rossii. Moscow. Available from: http://www.amr.ru/upload/iblock/c7e/reyting_SMI.pdf (accessed 30 March 2007).

Schudson, M. 2001. 'The objectivity norm in American journalism', *Journalism* 2(2): 149–70.

Schudson, M. 2005. 'Four approaches to the sociology of news', in J. Curran and M. Gurevitch (eds), *Mass Media and Society*, 4th edn., London: Hodder Arnold, pp. 172–97.

Tuchman, G. 1978. *Making News. A Study in the Construction of Reality*, New York: Free Press.

Vartanova, E. 2001. 'Media structures: changed and unchanged', in K. Nordenstreng, E. Vartanova and Y. Zassoursky (eds), *Russian Media Challenge*, Helsinki: Aleksanteri Institute, Kikimora Publications, pp. 21–72.

Weischenberg, S., M. Löffelholz and A. Scholl. 1998. 'Journalism in Germany', in D. H. Weaver (ed.), *The Global Journalist. News People around the World*, Cresskill, NJ: Hampton Press, pp. 229–56.

5
Journalists in the Russian Regions: How Different Generations View their Professional Roles

Svetlana Pasti and Jukka Pietiläinen[1]

The history of the post-Soviet media offers abundant material for research on the transformation from an authoritarian and closed society to a democratic and open one. The post-Soviet media, as its sixteen-year history shows, have in principle been kept on the leash of the political authorities – it is possible to let go of the leash, or to shorten it. During the *perestroika* era and in the early 1990s Russian journalists' understanding of the 'fourth estate' had a real sense of political efficacy and empowerment. Yeltsin's government, fascinated by the spirit of freedom of speech, had given the green light to liberal laws and reforms, and its inability to control the political situation left space for freedom, even anarchy.

A decade later, at the start of the 2000s, the new government of Vladimir Putin adopted a course of strengthening political authority which, according to the General Secretary of the Union of Journalists of Russia, Igor Yakovenko, has resulted in systematic 'purges' of the political, media and financial fields and drastically changed the conditions of media freedom and elections in the country. Yakovenko points out that after the fall of Vladimir Gusinsky's media holding and its core, NTV, there was not a single non-government national channel left in Russia. The Russian media was taught a lesson after which most media outlets introduced a form of self-censorship (Yakovenko and Pasti 2004, p. 7).

Analyses of media developments in Russia have generally divided the post-Soviet period into three stages: up to 1995; the later Yeltsin period, 1996–1999; and a third period after Putin came to power in 2000 (I. Zassoursky 2001; Y. Zassoursky 2001).

In recent years Russian and Western experts have noted a reactionary tendency and have described the present political course in such terms as 'quasi-democracy', 'guided democracy', 'pseudo-elections', 'pseudo-referendums', 'no free media' (Shevtsova 2007; Petrov 2005; Furman

2005; Yavlinsky 2004; Lipman and McFaul 2001; Oates and Roselle 2000). The Freedom House Annual Survey of Freedom Country Ratings from 1972 to 2000 indicate that the state of political rights and civil liberties do not show a positive dynamic over the last decade (Rukavishnikov 2003, p. 32). For two years running Russia has been in the group of not-free countries; in 2006 it was grouped with Burma, Zimbabwe and China (Freedom House 2006). Reporters without Borders (RSF) regularly set a low index of freedom of journalists and media in Russia: the 121st place (139 countries) in 2002, the 148th place (166) in 2003, the 140th place (167) in 2004, the 138th place (167) in 2005, the 147th place (168) in 2006. The experts of RSF point to increasing state control over media, limitation of information about the situation in Chechnya and an absence of different points of view on television (Reporters without Borders 2006; Moscow Media Law and Policy Institute 2005).

The British newspaper the *Guardian* (11 April 2005) sounded the alarm about the collapse of the liberal press with the closure of the critical to the Kremlin daily *Russkii Kur'er*, difficulties in *Moskovskie novosti* and *Gazeta*, and problems in *Izvestiia* because of its coverage of the Beslan school siege, all of which 'in part mimics the demise of its political equivalent – the liberal and libertarian parties virtually extinct in parliament and facing annihilation at the ballot box from new left and rightwing alternatives crafted by the Kremlin'. The *Guardian* cites Alexei Simonov of the Glasnost Defence Foundation: 'Our state does not defend the press, it defends its citizens from the press.'

On the other hand, some researchers see post-Soviet Russia as a normal country among middle-income countries in which state intervention in the media is almost universal. In 2000–2001, while Putin's government was hounding the tycoons Berezovsky and Gusinsky out of the media business, a similar campaign was unfolding in South Korea, categorized as not even partly free but free by Freedom House (Schleifer 2005, pp. 173–6). As is the case in poor or middle-income countries, there is little public demand for alternative, non-government media. The Russian media have matured as businesses, but they have not created better journalism. Reporting is too muffled, and too bland as far as political coverage is concerned (*Media Sustainability Index 2004*, p. 191).

Another comment on the present situation in Russia suggests that there is no turning back because the majority of transformations are irreversible, while there is an appearance of *sovietism*, the core of the political culture that is evident in the common process 'of *sovietization* of the political and social spheres' (Blum 2005). The Levada Centre in its numerous opinion polls confirms the strong adherence of the people to Soviet habits and values (Levada 2003, 2004). One of the most recent studies revealed that the Soviet model of political system remains the most attractive in comparison with Western democracy and the present post-Soviet system, and its popularity among ordinary people increases every year (Dubin 2005, p. 14), whereas Russian support for the adoption of a democratic political system based on the Western model has been in decline since 1996 (EU–Russia Centre/Levada Centre 2007, p. 14).

The aim of this chapter is to find out what kind of differences exist in professional values among Russian journalists on the basis of their background in terms of age, gender, education, income, professional position and type of media. A central background feature was also belonging to the older or newer generation of journalists, whose importance has been noted by Sosnovskaya (2000) and Pasti (2004, 2005a, 2005b) and was also suggested on the basis of journalistic texts and practices (Geisslinger 1997; Voltmer 2000). We shall also consider whether the values of journalists in Russia are similar to those of journalists in Third World countries which have until recently been ruled by authoritarian or one-party systems, and in which journalists are poorly paid and subject to conflicting pressures.

Earlier research

In the United States, research on the professional values of journalists has a long tradition. Johnstone, Slawski and Bowman (1972, 1976) used eight variables, and distinguished by factor analysis a *neutral orientation* and a *participating orientation*. They classified functions like 'investigate government claims', 'provide analysis and interpretation of complex problems', 'discuss national policy while it is still being developed' and 'develop intellectual and cultural interests of the public' as a participant orientation to journalism, while 'get information to the public quickly', 'importance of verified information', 'concentration on the widest possible public' and 'provide entertainment and relaxation' were classified as a neutral orientation.

Weaver and Wilhoit (1986, pp. 112–17) called the orientations identified by Johnstone et al. an *information disseminator* role (neutral orientation) and an *interpretive/investigative* role (participant orientation). They also added a third, *adversarial* role, which has a sceptical orientation both to public officials and to business. Both Johnstone et al. and Weaver and Wilhoit found that the organizational environment was most predictive of journalistic role orientation. First, star reporters with higher salaries had the strongest leanings toward the interpretive role. Second, journalists working in print media were more likely to subscribe to an interpretive orientation than their colleagues working in other media. Third, persons with supervisory editorial authority tended to lean toward the disseminator role. Values also had an impact: journalists who valued autonomy highly favoured the interpreter role while journalists who placed greater importance on job security tended to be disseminators (Weaver and Wilhoit 1986, pp. 117–21). In their follow-up study, Weaver and Wilhoit (1996) added a fourth role, *populist mobilizer*, now with a battery of 12 questions. The new populist mobilizer function consists of four elements: 'developing the interests of the public', 'providing entertainment', 'setting the political agenda' and 'letting ordinary people express views'.

The questionnaire was developed further by Ramaprasad (2001, 2003), who included six additional questions on media roles for her survey of Tanzanian journalists in order make it sensitive to the specific political and press dynamics in a developing country. Similar surveys have also been conducted in Spain (Canel and Sánchez-Aranda 1999), Nepal (Ramaprasad and Kelly 2003), Uganda (Mwesige 2004), and Brazil (Herscovitz 2004). Weawer's global survey (1998) also included other countries.

A comparative study of American and Russian journalists was made by a team of researchers from both countries based on material collected in 1992 (Kolesnik, Svitich and Shiryaeva 1995; Wu, Weaver and Johnson 1996). Wu, Weaver and Johnson reported that they had tried to employ the same factor analysis as Weaver and Wilthoit (1986), but 'failed to produce similar composite measures in either the Russian or US surveys'. Therefore they used individual variables to define disseminator and interpretive roles. It was possible, in this study, to discern the traits of the role of agitator in Russian journalists. They believed 'more in such active roles as setting the political agenda and developing the interest of the public, but not in investigating government claims'. This suggested that 'Russian journalists see themselves playing a role as creative, independent agents in the Russian political and social context', as members of the intelligentsia of that time (Wu, Weaver and Johnson 1996, p. 544).

It seems that a change in values occurred rather quickly among Russian journalists in the first half of the 1990s. While in 1992 journalists could be divided into three equal groups (authoritarian-technocratic, humanistic and informative-cognitive) on the basis of their professional ideologies, by 1995 over two-thirds supported the informative-cognitive model while the authoritarian-technocratic approach had almost completely lost its support, although in practice this approach still seemed to have quite a lot of backing (Dzialoshinsky 1996, pp. 156–7). Roudakova (2004) points out that in the first half of the 1990s Russian journalists engaged fervently in public battles and therefore became indistinguishable from politicians and other players on the field of power, instead of becoming a guild that maintains a certain distance from the state. In this respect Russian journalism is very similar to the political journalism era in the history of Western journalism.

Most Russian journalists now reject the political role of journalists, while they support the idea that a journalist is 'an objective observer and analyst who is not supposed to take somebody's side'. Nonetheless only seldom do they see journalism as a fourth estate (Glasnost Defence Foundation 1995, pp. 37–40). Voltmer (2000) has observed that despite the news becoming more factual and timely, a high degree of subjective evaluations has remained in Russian journalism. Sosnovskaya (2000, p. 194) has pointed out differences between Soviet, *perestroika*-era and post-Soviet journalists. While *perestroika*-era journalists were primarily interested in public relations and to some extent fulfilled the function of a civil society, the post-*perestroika* journalists are primarily concerned with the commercial sphere. According to journalists of the old school, the public needs journalistic opinions. They also think that opinionated journalism demands greater literary mastery than factual journalism (ibid., p. 178). Sosnovskaya (2005, p. 146) continues that in the Soviet era the cognitive component of professional identity was dominant, during *perestroika* the affective component dominated, while in the post-*perestroika* period practical knowledge is the dominant component.

Koltsova (2001, 2006) has pointed out that Russian journalists are aware of political control and consider it inevitable. This seems to be due to the sudden collapse of old power relations, 'while "new" ones are still not routinized and thus have become highly visible to the actors' (Koltsova 2001, p. 333). According to her, Russian journalists are more controlled than their Western colleagues but less dominated. Pasti (2004, 2005a) argues that Russian journalism of the 1990s has been formed by two types of professional roles, representing two types of professional subcultures: the old generation (practitioners entering the profession in the Soviet era) and the new generation (practitioners who entered the profession after 1990). The old professionals perform the role of social organizers with the inherent functions of upbringing, educating and punishing, whereas the young generation of the 1990s is orientated to the new role of entertainers of the masses. Despite their differences, both accept the political function of journalism as a propaganda machine during elections and other important events.

The present study

The European Union together with other international organizations continues to initiate and invest in programmes for the support of democracy in Russia in different fields, including the media. One of the recent TACIS projects was titled 'Promoting Independence of Regional Mass Media in Russia' and implemented in 2002–2004 with the participation of the University of Tampere Department of Journalism and Mass Communication by the Internews-Europe Consortium and the Union of Journalists of Russia, with the support of the professional journalistic associations and the schools of journalism of the universities in selected regions. The project provided three cycles of seminars for journalists on the problems of journalistic ethics in nine regions of the North-West, the Volga, the Urals, Siberia, the Central and Southern parts of Russia. In total about 1,200 media professionals took part in the programme (Glasnost Defence Foundation 2004).

The profession of a journalist has a low status in contemporary Russia, while it typically functions as an appendage of the political system. The seminars were aimed at raising this status by strengthening the self-regulation of the professional community on the basis of ethical norms. A new round of seminars on journalistic ethics started in spring 2005 for journalists in the same regions (Glasnost Defence Foundation 2005).

For the authors of this chapter, a fortunate opportunity arose to combine their work as invited experts in the seminars with the collection of primary data. As experts we had been involved in the elaboration of the training curriculum, preparation of books for journalists and schools of journalism and delivery of lectures. As researchers we had an opportunity to observe the journalists' seminars aimed at generating discussions on questions of journalistic ethics and professionalism and current problems of professional practice focused on conditions for the media and journalists in the given region, and on efforts to elaborate suggestions for strengthening journalistic autonomy and independence.

In the course of the seminars we carried out a survey of journalists aimed at gathering information about the social profile of regional journalists, their professional values and attitudes to their work. The research task was to clarify to what professional roles regional journalists are inclined and what contents fill those roles. How have the concepts of the professional role been patterned, and what kind of belief systems have emerged? How is the professional consciousness of Russian journalists developing in comparison with journalists of other countries? How much do Russian journalist generations differ from each other in their perceptions of the profession? And what implications for the further development of journalism in Russia can be derived from a better understanding of the views and attitudes of younger generations?

The survey was carried out during the third cycle of the regional seminars held for journalists, editors and other media professionals in October–December 2003 in the cities of Yekaterinburg, Kazan', Nizhnii Novgorod, Novosibirsk, Petrozavodsk, Rostov-on-Don, Samara, Tomsk and Yaroslavl'. Participants were invited to the seminars by local trainers, among whom were teachers of schools of journalism in universities and members of the Union of Journalists of Russia. The participants, in total approximately 400 persons, represented different types of media of their own and neighbouring regions. A total of 237 questionnaires were returned. The study does not claim any generalizability of its findings for the whole journalistic population. It is possible that the sample is biased toward those who are more conscious of ethical questions and interested in developing their skills. However, the sample is varied and represents Russian regional journalists widely and can be used to identify differences.

A questionnaire comprising 35 questions was based on earlier studies by Weaver (1998), Weaver and Wilhoit (1996), Ramaprasad and Kelly (2003) and Ramaprasad (2001) on journalists in the United States, Tanzania and Nepal. Added were some questions topical for the study of Russian journalists such as second job, attitudes to and the practice of producing stories paid by political or economic interests, and as well as support for censorship. Professional functions were elicited with a battery of 19 questions. Respondents were asked if they agreed or disagreed with statements on a five-point scale. Factor analysis was used to process the questionnaires. Additionally, comparative analysis of the responses was conducted on the basis of age in the profession (the journalist's generation), gender, type of media and region as well crosstabulation of the variables.

Findings

Journalistic generations

The sample was divided into three groups labelled 'journalistic generations' on the basis of the year in which they started in journalism.

The first generation, the Soviet one, had started in journalism before 1990, the second generation, the transitional one, had started in journalism in 1991–1999, and the third, the post-2000 generation, had started in 2000 or later. Some differences were apparent between these three generations of Russian journalists; they are summed up in Table 5.1.

Age

The mean age was 38 years, a third were less than 23 years old while a quarter were over 50 years. A quarter had started in journalism before 1980 while more than half had started in journalism only after the collapse of the Soviet Union. One third had started in journalism after 1999; the most common starting year was 2001. The age group difference between the old and the new generations was as much as 57 years: the oldest respondent had been born in 1928 and the youngest respondent in 1985, whereas the age difference in professional experience between the generations amounted to 51 years: some Soviet journalists had started journalistic work in 1952 in the era of Stalin, whereas the young journalists had started their work at late as 2003. The number of Soviet journalists was reasonably large in the journalistic population of regional Russia. Thus, the sample included 99 Soviet journalists, 75 transitional journalists and 61 journalists who had started their career after 2000.

Gender

Of the sample of 237 respondents, one third were males. The gender analysis showed an increasing intake of women into the profession in our sample: 40 per cent of the Soviet generation were males, 30 per cent of the transitional generation were males and only 15 per cent of the new generation were males. That is, the rising generation of males already did not perceive journalism as a masculine occupation and a worthy business although in the Soviet time it had traditionally been a male profession. For example, in the 1970s only a third of journalists were women (Svitich 2003, p. 84). In this respect, Russia is similar to some other countries, like Finland, in which journalists are increasingly women, although the 'feminization' of the profession may be happening more rapidly in contemporary Russia. One of the reasons for the decrease in the number of male journalists can be found in new educational requirements that have recently reappeared in the media, preferring to employ graduates of the schools of journalism at universities. In comparison with the transition period, the number of journalists with a journalistic education is increasing. Thus, the profession is becoming closed to those without a formal education. In order to attract more men into higher education

Table 5.1: Differences on the basis of three generations of Russian journalists (percentages)

	Soviet	Transitional	Post-2000
Gender, male	40.9	29.2	14.8
Salary level, average on scale 1–5	3.60	3.04	2.27
Education in journalism (full or part)	62.5	36.0	63.0
Work in several media	41.3	27.9	24.5
Second job	44.3	41.7	47.2
Union membership	86.4	35.2	3.7
Critical attitude to materials paid for/by political and economic interests	34.1	16.4	11.1
Has published articles paid for political and economic interests	55.2	62.0	50.0
Supports control of entertainment	65.5	75.4	67.9
Supports control of political materials	45.3	54.3	66.0
Portraying regional leaders in a positive manner very important	0	0	0
Portraying a head of regional government positively very important	2.7	1.4	1.9
Portraying a positive image of the region very important	6.3	2.9	5.7
Propagating regional government policy very important	1.3	0	0
Portraying a positive image of the community very important	3.8	0	3.8
Actively supporting regional government development programmes very important	12.5	4.5	7.7
Discussing regional policy when it is still being developed very important	73.4	58.6	58.5
Informing voters about local politicians' viewpoints very important	61.4	40.8	61.1
Reporting objectively on regional development programmes very important	83.1	73.2	74.1
Providing analysis and commentary of complex problems very important	78.3	70.0	68.5
Promoting the strength and unity of communities very important	65.4	47.8	44.2
Developing intellectual and cultural interests of the public very important	73.2	71.4	69.8
Keeping voters informed about the work of regional government very important	70.7	70.4	57.4
Giving ordinary people a chance to express views on public affairs very important	72.3	58.6	49.1
Investigating claims and statements made by local government very important	45.7	32.4	34.6
Criticizing actions of authorities very important	41.4	13.4	5.7
Providing accurate information in a timely manner very important	89.2	81.7	87.0
Working with letters to the editor very important	58.8	59.4	51.9
Providing entertainment and relaxation very important	22.5	17.4	34.0

some state universities have started to enrol males after military service through an easier examination, which is in a certain sense a return to the Soviet practice of recruiting males for higher education. The other reason for the lack of attractiveness of journalism is the low salaries. Thus, in the media young journalists begin earning about 2,000 roubles a month (about 57 Euros), whereas in the PR service of a big company or bank a graduate of a school of journalism begins at about 40–50,000 roubles (1,400 Euros) a month. The old generation has an opportunity to stay in the profession by getting a pension as well as a salary, and its income on average is higher than the income of the transitional (middle) generation and the young generation of the 2000s.

Income

Income was elicited on a five-point scale in roubles. One third of the journalists earned between 6,000 and 10,000 roubles, which was equivalent to 170–300 Euros (on an average exchange rate of 35 roubles to 1 Euro in May 2005). One third of the journalists earned less than 6,000 roubles (less than 170 Euros) and one third earned more than 10,000 roubles (more than 300 Euros).

Education

Approximately half had an education in journalism (completed or not) and most of the others had higher education in some other field.

Second job

Nearly half of the respondents had some other job besides the main job and one third worked in several media. Approximately one fifth of the respondents were not journalists working in any media; most of these were PR specialists and teachers of journalism. However, the results of the analysis did not differ much even when the non-journalists were excluded from the analysis. The new generation demonstrated less mobility than the Soviet generation in getting a second job. Half of them had a second job outside journalism, as was also the case among the Soviet generation, but only every fourth worked in several media.

Interestingly, some questions on the questionnaire were omitted by the respondents. For instance, the question on their posts (*dolzhnost'*) was missed by every fourth. They were those journalists who worked in one or several media, who combined work in the media and PR sectors, pensioners who received a pension and continued to work in the media and other organizations, and also students of schools of journalism whether or not they were working in the media. It was assumed that some of the respondents probably did not know – or were not interested to know – how their post was defined in their contracts (if indeed any contracts had been signed), whereas those combining work in different media and PR sections felt confused as to what post should be selected for the questionnaire response. This calls to mind the former lack of clearly defined labour agreements between journalists and employers, a system of keeping work and payment officially and non-officially (paid under the table) and a weakly developed professional identity, since journalists revealed confusion in their self-identification.

Union in membership

The Union of Journalists meant nothing to the post-2000 generation. Whereas a vast majority of the Soviet generation continued their membership, only a third of the transitional generation of the 1990s were members and very few of the new generation.

Attitudes to materials paid by political and economic interests

Approximately half of the journalists surveyed produced hidden advertisements – stories favourable to and paid for by a particular source, but presented as news. There was a major difference in attitudes between those who produced paid materials and those who did not. Many of those who saw paid materials as normal, or normal but not part of journalism, also produced them, while 80 per cent of those who thought they should not exist did not produce them. Soviet journalists most often considered these materials should not exist while transitional and post-2000 journalists considered them a private matter even if they did not personally produce any. Table 5.2 shows the relationship between the practice of producing paid materials and attitudes towards them. One third of the Soviet generation believed that articles paid by outsiders but presented as news should not exist. The post-2000 generation saw them increasingly as a private matter. On the other hand, the number of

Table 5.2: Attitudes to articles paid for political and economic interests (number of respondents)

Attitude to paid materials	Had produced paid materials (regularly or occasionally)	Had not produced paid materials
A normal phenomenon	20	4
Normal but not journalism	29	11
Private issue of every journalist	56	47
They should not exist	11	41

those who saw these materials as 'normal' or 'normal but not journalism' remained stable at around one third in each group.

Professional roles

Respondents were asked to rate the importance of a number of professional functions on a five-point scale as shown in Table 5.3. Of 19 tasks, seven were the same as in the study by Weaver and Wilhoit (1996) while most of the others were taken from Ramaprasad and Kelly (2003). The journalists perceived accurate and timely information, objective reporting, development of intellectual and cultural interests of the public, and analysis of complex problems as the most important functions. The least important were all functions related to support for the authorities

Table 5.3: Support of professional functions (percentages)

Professional functions	% very important	% not important at all
Providing accurate information in a timely manner	85.8	1.3
Reporting objectively on regional development programmes	77.3	0.4
Developing intellectual and cultural interests of the public	72.2	1.8
Providing analysis and commentary of complex problems	71.9	0.4
Keeping voters informed about the work of the regional govt.	67.0	0.5
Discussing the regional policy when it is still being developed	63.3	0.4
Giving people a chance to express views on public affairs	61.9	0.4
Working with letters to the editor	56.8	1.4
Informing voters about local politicians' viewpoints	55.6	0
Promoting the strength and unity of communities	54.6	2.3
Investigating claims and statements made by the local govt.	38.2	0.9
Providing entertainment and relaxation	24.1	6.8
Criticizing actions of authorities	21.4	2.7
Actively supporting regional government development programmes	6.2	14.4
Portraying a positive image of the region	6.0	20.2
Portraying a positive image of the community	3.0	22.0
Portraying a head of the regional government positively	1.7	35.6
Propagating regional government policy	0.9	32.9
Portraying regional leaders positively	0.0	34.3

(the last six tasks on the list in Table 5.3) as well as criticism of the authorities and entertainment. As was the case with the earlier study by Wu, Weaver and Johnson (1996), Russian journalists tended to give higher scores to these professional functions than American journalists.[2] Possibly because of the selected sample (participants in professional training seminars), in this study support for some tasks (providing analysis and commentary on complex problems, giving ordinary people a chance to express views on public affairs) received significantly stronger support than in the Wu, Weaver and Johnson study, while some others (investigating government claims, criticizing the actions of authorities or opposing government officials) were supported at the same level as in the earlier study.

Analysing the rating of professional functions, these 19 variables were subjected to factor analysis.[3] The results are summed up in Table 5.4. There five factors emerged, but it was decided that four factors were sufficient since the fifth had a heavy loading on only one variable. These four factors together explained 43 per cent of the variance and were only slightly correlated. The strongest correlation (.17) was between the third and fourth factors.

The first factor was composed most clearly of six variables: portraying regional leaders positively; portraying the head of the regional government positively; portraying a positive image of the region; propagating the regional government policy; portraying a positive image of the community; and actively supporting regional development programmes. This cluster could be called 'development journalism' in line with Ramaprasad and Kelly (2003) but in the Russian case it would be better to call it a *propagandist* role. A majority reject this role rather than supporting it. Yet there is a minority of nearly 20 per cent who support an open propagandist role.

The second factor was composed of five variables: discussing regional policy when it is still being developed; informing voters about local politicians' viewpoints; reporting objectively on regional development programmes; keeping voters informed about the work of the regional government; and providing an analysis of complex problems. It comes close to the *informer* role, although it also includes one function, discussing policy while being developed, classified as participant by Johnstone, Slawski and Bowman (1976).

The third factor was composed of four variables: promoting the strength and unity of communities; developing the intellectual and cultural interests of the public; working with letters to the editor; and giving ordinary people a chance to express views on public affairs. These

Table 5.4:   Factor analysis of professional functions

	I	II	III	IV
Propagandist				
Portraying regional leaders positively	.82			
Portraying the head of the regional government positively	.77			
Portraying a positive image of the region	.77			
Propagating regional government policy	.75			−.23
Portraying a positive image of the community	.72			.20
Actively supporting regional government development programmes	.51		.28	
Providing entertainment and relaxation	.25		.22	.21
Informer				
Discussing regional policy when it is still being developed		.71		
Informing voters about local politicians' viewpoints		.71		
Reporting objectively on regional development programmes		.58	.30	
Keeping voters informed about the work of the regional govt.		.45	.33	
Providing analysis of and commentary on complex problems		.44		.26
Organizer				
Promoting the strength and unity of communities	.23		.73	
Developing intellectual and cultural interests of the public	.26		.67	
Working with letters to the editor			.38	
Giving people a chance to express views on public affairs		.25	.33	
Investigator				
Investigating claims and statements made by the local govt.		.36		.46
Providing accurate information in a timely manner		.25	.22	.46
Criticizing the actions of the authorities				.30
% of variance explained	21.1	14.4	4.7	2.9

Principal axis analysis; varimax rotation. Factor loadings below .20 not included.

functions establish an *organizer* role – well in conformity with the Soviet tradition of journalism.

The fourth factor was composed of three variables: investigating claims and statements made by local government; providing accurate information in a timely manner; and criticizing actions of authorities. This was a somewhat strange combination: investigative and critical functions together with accurate information. However, those journalists who emphasized criticism and investigation also emphasized accurate informing as the grounds for criticism. In fact, over 95 per cent of those who considered criticism or investigation to be very important also perceived accurate and timely reporting as very important. We call this role *investigator*, although it has also strong elements of both the adversary and informer roles as defined by earlier research.

Russian journalists differed from journalists in both Tanzania and Nepal, on the one hand (Ramaprasad and Kelly 2003), and from journalists in the United States (Weaver and Wilhoit 1996, 1986) and Spain (Canel and Sánchez-Aranda 1999), on the other. American journalists displayed functions belonging to three or four groups: (i) neutral or information disseminating, (ii) interpretive or investigative, (iii) adversary and (iv) populist mobilizer. The Spanish survey also included an advocating value. In the Nepal study, the functions were grouped around development journalism (support for national leaders and their policies), citizen education (educating people about how government operates), public advocacy, and culture. In Tanzania the value groups were very similar to those in Nepal: national development (support for national leaders and their policies), educating about government, information/analysis and entertainment (Ramaprasad and Kelly 2003). In Brazil three value groups – interpretive, adversary and disseminator – were discovered, but these factors had different loadings than in the US survey (Herscovitz 2004, p. 79).

In Russia the most interesting difference was the close connection between the adversary role and factual information. In other words, there was no distinction between the neutral and participant roles. Russian journalists rather made the distinction between various forms of participation: (i) supporter of the public good (informer), (ii) supporter of the community (organizer), or (iii) supporter or opponent of the authorities (propagandist and investigator). Russian journalists perceive journalistic functions in a somewhat similar way as Brazilian journalists, who also connect factual information and the adversary role. Moreover, the same connection between the adversary function and factual information was found in public opinion towards the media in Russia (Pietiläinen 2005, p. 113).

In this study further correlations were made between background variables and types of roles identified on the basis of the factor analysis. The results are shown in Table 5.5. The *informer* and *investigator* roles were

Table 5.5: Correlations between the background variables and roles identified by factors (correlations with significance over 0.1)

	Propagandist	Informer	Organizer	Investigator
Age		.20		
Salary		.21	−.18	
Working in several media		−.15		
Supporting political censorship	.31			−.14
Education in journalism	−.20		.15	.20
Years in journalism		.17		
Starting age	.19	.15		
Has produced paid materials			−.25	−.19
Positive attitude to paid materials	.14	−.21		
Union member		.19		
Rank and file journalist	−.19			
Working in press service	.19	.21	.15	
Soviet		.15		.15
Old post-Soviet	.20			
Young post-Soviet	−.13	−.18		
Transitional		−.13		

supported more among Soviet journalists while the *propagandist* role was supported more often among those journalists who had started in the post-Soviet era but were older and had earlier worked in some other profession. Younger post-Soviet journalists supported the *propagandist* and *informer* roles less than others. The *organizer* role did not depend on journalistic generations, while the post-2000 generation was not significantly correlated with any of the roles. In general, younger respondents tended to respond more 'in the middle', while older journalists tended to give a lot of support to most of the statements.

The *propagandist* role was characterized by supporting political censorship, lack of education in journalism, an older starting age in journalism and a positive attitude to articles paid by political and economic interests. Support for this role was linked with working in the press service. It was opposed by those working as rank and file journalists.

The *informer* role was characteristic of older journalists with high salaries and long experience in the profession. They also had a negative attitude to paid articles and were often members of the Union of Journalists. They worked in several media less often than other journalists. Those working in the press service also supported this role.

The *organizer* role was characteristic of journalists with lower salaries, who did not produce articles paid by outsiders. They also had education

Table 5.6: Significant (p < 0.05) correlations of professional roles and background variables in three generations (+ means more support for that role, − means less support for that role)

	Soviet generation	Transitional generation	Post-2000 generation
Age		+ informer + propagandist	
Education in journalism		− informer	− propagandist + investigator + organizer
Salary	− propagandist − organizer	+ informer	
Union membership		+ informer	
Has published paid articles	− organizer		+ propagandist − investigator
Support political censorship	+ propagandist	+ propagandist	− investigator

in journalism more often than others. Many workers in the press services also supported this role.

The *investigator* role was supported by journalists with an education in journalism. They did not produce articles paid by outsiders and they opposed political censorship. The correlations between support for four professional roles and other variables suggest interesting differences between the three generations as summarized in Table 5.6.

Age caused significant variance only in the transitional generation, in which older journalists rather supported the informer and propagandist roles. Among this generation, lack of education in journalism, high salaries and union membership increased support for the informer role. The practice of articles paid by outsiders reduced support for the organizer role among the Soviet journalists, whereas among the post-2000 journalists it increased their support for the propagandist role and reduced support for the investigator role. Support of political censorship led to support for the propagandist role among the Soviet and transitional generations, while it reduced support for the investigator role among the post-2000 generation. Education in journalism had a significant impact on the post-2000 journalists, reducing their support for the propagandist role and increasing their support for the investigator and organizer roles.

Discussion

This study of regional journalists in Russia focused on differences between three generations of practitioners in order to identify breaks and continuities among older and newer journalists in their attitudes and values. Three generations of Russian journalists entered the profession in different political epochs: before 1990, in the epoch of socialism – the Soviet generation; in the 1990s, the crisis decade of the dismantling of the Soviet system with simultaneous introduction of the capitalist patterns – the transitional generation; and in the 2000s, heading for the stabilization of society and its consolidation which can be seen also as a return to Soviet traditions and values – the post-2000 generation.

The present situation differs from the previous stage of the 1990s when journalism as well as other institutions experienced a crucial transformation in all respects. It ceased to implement official instructions for ideological campaigns because after the collapse of communism the media became free from state and party control. Journalism became an open field for anybody caring to try his/her hand in an increasingly popular profession. Two utterly different generations began to form journalism: on the one hand, the homogeneous and disciplined professionals of the Soviet school of journalism, and newer and more heterogeneous practitioners, often lacking education and experience in journalism, who rejected some elements of Soviet journalism and searched for new models, also from the West, on the other. The two generations were in a professional and ethical conflict with each other, with different understandings of the profession and of the journalist's role in society. Whereas the old generation retained 'a cultivated view of journalism as an important societal task' with the advocacy, organizer and educator functions, the new generation gravitated towards a newer and more fashionable genre of entertainment 'aiming at a sensationalist media agenda. Many of them perceived journalism as a type of PR, working for the interests of influential groups and persons in politics and business' (Pasti 2005a, p. 89). However, both conducted propaganda during elections because the media remained political instruments of the state and big capital (ibid., p. 108). The information wars, full of lies and scandals paid for by competing interest groups, became an attribute of Russian journalism of the 1990s (Zassoursky 2004).

The present situation in journalism reflects the direction in which the entire society has been moving under the leadership of President Putin towards a stabilization in which some elements of a return to Soviet traditions can be seen. The dependence of the media on state and private sponsors differs little from its previous dependence on the state in Soviet times as federal structures or private investors subsidize up to 90 per cent of Russia's newspapers. Sponsors generally see their publications as a political resource and do not expect the projects to cover their costs. Nearly every serious national daily today has either a financial and industrial group behind it or the state itself, while regional authorities support most of the leading newspapers in the regions (*The Russian Periodical Press Market* 2005, p. 11). The Russian government report of 2006 notes, on the one hand, the dynamic growth of advertising, retail and subscriptions, and on the other hand a lack of development of media measurement, the low trustworthiness of statistics on the media market, and the economic and political dependence of some editions, especially regional and local newspapers, on government bodies at different levels (*The Russian Periodical Press Market* 2006, pp. 8–9).

Television is almost completely under state control. According to Mikhail Fedotov (2005), establishing state control over previously private or formally private media began in 2001, and included control over the advertising media market through the 'Media Committee' under government officials. The journalism of the 2000s received reinforcement from the post-2000 generation which had time to graduate from schools of journalism and came to work in the media. The economically dependent media as well as journalists working in them have to adjust to the agenda and policy of their financiers, especially at election times. Before the parliamentary elections of 1999, journalists did not show much understanding of the norms of fair and impartial broadcasting (White, McAllister and Oates 2002, p. 30). The familiar Soviet approach to the media as instruments of propaganda and manipulation still is inherent in the mentality of government officials and emerging capitalists.

This study did not reveal as large a gap between generations in their perceptions of professional roles as found by the study of St Petersburg journalists of the 1990s (Pasti 2005a). On the contrary, this study points to the continuity in professional values across three generations. Thus, the *organizer* role, which includes feedback to the audience, finds support in all three generations. A decade earlier, in the middle of the 1990s, this work with letters to the editor was practically rejected by the young generation, not least because of that the media were freed from their duty to respond to letters to the editor and the letters rooms were eliminated in the editorial offices (Pasti 2004).

Although the *propagandist* role finds the least support in all three generations, in practice journalists have to perform in this role by promoting a positive image of the authorities. Interestingly, the transitional and post-2000 generations mostly support political control of the media. The *informer* role of a journalist who objectively informs and discusses regional development and local politics has the strongest support across all three generations. However, combining functions of neutral (dissemination of information) and participant (interpretation, investigation and criticizing) orientations in the journalists' minds testifies to a lack of neutrality in conformity with the Russian tradition in journalism. This study also confirms the finding in the previous study of St Petersburg media (Pasti 2004) concerning the lack of a neutral orientation among journalists. Moreover, the new generations have little interest in investigative journalism and only a few young journalists support criticizing the government. Thus, since 1992 (Wu, Weaver and Johnson 1996) Russian journalists have not changed their professional values but rather remain the collaborators of the state than its investigators and critics.

The results also suggest that the oppositional role of journalism which was part of a professional self-identity in the period of *perestroika* and *glasnost'* is decreasing, since a clearly adversarial function (criticizing the authorities) does not elicit much support among the new generations. On the other hand, a paternalistic relationship to the audience has retained its position. The clearly declining functions are those linked with the idea of 'public journalism' such as 'a chance for ordinary people to express their views', 'keeping voters informed about the work of regional government' and 'promoting the strength and unity of the community'. This could be interpreted as a distancing from the Soviet past, in which the journalist was typically a representative of ordinary people and journalism functioned somewhat in the role of public control. On the other hand, it reveals that the journalists have little respect for their audience.

The clearest break between the older and younger generations emerges in their attitudes to the writing of stories paid for by political or economic interests. Many journalists look at venal journalism as an essentially private matter. Viktor Loshak (2005), a reputable and experienced journalist and editor, recently published an article in the newspaper *Izvestiya* entitled 'The plastic boys'. This article became the public protest of an older generation against the 'plastic journalism' that had emerged with the coming of those younger journalists who had grown up with the internet and came to journalism primarily to receive thousands of dollars and have a good time. In general, Russian journalists have preserved many Soviet-era values, of which the most important is the willingness to exert influence in society, one way or another, and a moral conviction that a journalist should not be indifferent to what s/he writes about. The young generation also supports the political tradition of paternalism which results in the arbitrariness of political authority on the one hand and servility in journalists, on the other.

Notes

1. The authors of the article would like to thank Professor Kaarle Nordenstreng, Dept. of Journalism and Mass Communication at the University of Tampere and Yury V. Kazakov, the coordinator of the Tacis project 'Promoting Independence of Regional Mass Media in Russia' (2002–2004) for their support of this study.
2. Weaver, Wilthoit and Johnson used a four-point scale, while this study used a five-point scale.
3. The statements were analysed using principal axis factoring with varimax rotation. Principal component analysis and maximum likelihood analyses were also conducted, but they did not give as easily interpretable solutions.

References

Blum, Alain, 2005. 'Politicheskaia sistema Rossii posle putinskikh reform', *Polit.ru, Issledovaniia*, http://www.polit.ru/research/2005/01/27/polit_system.html.

Canel, María José & José Javier, Sánchez-Aranda, 1999. 'La influencia de las actitudes profesionales del periodista español en las noticias', *Anàlisi* 23: 151–70.

Dubin, Boris, 2005. 'Rossiia i sosedi: problemy vzaimoponimaniia', *Vestnik obshchestvennogo mneniia* 1: http://www.polit.ru/research/2005/04/14/neighbours.html.

Dzialoshinsky, Iosif, 1996. *Rossiiskii zhurnalist v posttotalitarnuiu epokhu*, Moscow: Vostok.

EU-Russia Centre, 2007. *Voices from Russia: Society, Democracy, Europe*. EU–Russia Centre/Levada Centre Research, February 2007, http://www.eu-russiacentre. org/assets/files/Eu-RC%Levada%Research%Commentary.pdf.

Fedotov, Mikhail A., 2005. 'Media in Modern Russia: Between Love and Hate'. Paper presented at the International Conference *Perestroika 20 Years Later: Glasnost and Journalism Development*, Moscow, 24–25 June 2005.

Freedom House, 2006. *Nations in Transit 2006 Countries Summaries by Region*: http://www.freedomhouse.hu/nitransit/2006/CountrySummariesNIT06.pdf.

Furman, Dmitry, 2005. 'Politicheskaia sistema Rossii posle putinskikh reform', *Polit.ru, Issledovaniya*, http://www.polit.ru/research/2005/01/27/polit_system. html.

Geisslinger, Esther, 1997. 'Zwischen Putsch und Preissteigerung. Russische Medien auf dem Weg vom "alten" zum "neuen" Journalismus', *Publizistik* 42(3): 346–60.

Glasnost Defence Foundation, 1995. *Journalists and Journalism of Russian Province. Survey.* Moscow.

Glasnost Defence Foundation, 2004, 2005. Projects, consulted at http://www. gdf.ru.

Herscovitz, Heloiza G., 2004. 'Brazilian Journalists' Perceptions of Media Roles, Ethics and Foreign Influences on Brazilian Journalism', *Journalism Studies* 5(1): 71–86.

Johnstone, John W. C., Edward J. Slawski and William W. Bowman, 1972. 'The Professional Values of American Newsmen', *Public Opinion Quarterly* 36(4): 522–40.

Johnstone, John W. C., Edward J. Slawski & William W. Bowman, 1976. *The News People. A Sociological Portrait of American Journalists and Their Work*, Urbana IL: University of Illinois Press.

Kolesnik, Svetlana, Lyubov', Svitich and Anna, Shiriaeva, 1995. 'Rossiiskii i amerikanskii zhurnalist', *Vestnik Moskovskogo Universiteta, Seriia 10 Zhurnalistika* 2: 20–7.

Koltsova, Olessia, 2001. 'News Production in Contemporary Russia. Practices of Power', *European Journal of Communication* 16(3): 315–35.

Koltsova, Olessia, 2006. *News Media and Power in Russia*, London and New York: Routledge.

Levada, Yuri, 2003. 'Limits and Options of Historical Choice: Some Remarks on the Course of the Russian Transformation', *Social Sciences* 34(4): 19–26.

Levada, Yuri, 2004. 'Chelovek sovetskii', *Polit.ru, Public lectures*, http://www.polit. ru/lectures/2004/04/15/levada.html.

Lipman, Masha and Michael, McFaul, 2001. ' "Managed Democracy" in Russia. Putin and Press', *Harvard Journal of Press/Politics* 6(3): 116–27.

Loshak, Viktor, 2005. 'Plastmassovye mal'chiki', *Izvestiya*, 16 February.

Media Sustainability Index 2004. The Development of Sustainable Media in Europe and Eurasia, Washington DC: IREX, consulted at www.irex.org.

Moscow Media Law and Policy Institute, 2005. 'The ratings of freedom of press: a place of Russia', *Telecom-Law*. 8 December, http://www.medialaw.ru.

Mwesige, Peter G., 2004. 'Disseminators, Advocates and Watchdogs. A Profile of Ugandan Journalists in the New Millennium', *Journalism* 5(1): 69–96.

Oates, Sarah & Laura, Roselle, 2000. 'Russian Elections and TV News Comparison of Campaign News on State-Controlled and Commercial Television Channels', *Harvard Journal of Press/Politics* 5(2): 30–51.

Pasti, Svetlana, 2004. *Rossiiskii zhurnalist v kontekste peremen. Media Sankt-Peterburga*, Tampere: Tampere University Press [English publication under the author's earlier surname: Svetlana Juskevits, 2002. *Professional Roles of Russian Journalists at the End of the 1990s. A Case Study of St Petersburg Media*, University of Tampere, http://tutkielmat.uta.fi/pdf/lisuri00006.pdf].

Pasti, Svetlana, 2005a. 'Two Generations of Contemporary Russian Journalists', *European Journal of Communication* 20(1): 89–115.

Pasti, Svetlana, 2005b. 'Return to Media Serving the State: Journalists in Karelia', in Harri Melin (ed.), *Social Structure, Public Space and Civil Society in Karelia*, Helsinki: Kikimora, pp. 117–44.

Petrov, Nikolai, 2005. 'Politicheskaia sistema Rossii posle putinskikh reform', *Polit.ru, Issledovaniia*, http://www.polit.ru/research/2005/01/27/polit_system. html.

Pietiläinen, Jukka, 2005. 'Media in the Life of Russians', in Harri Melin (ed.), *Social Structure, Public Space and Civil Society in Karelia*, Helsinki: Kikimora, pp. 99–116.

Ramaprasad, Jyotika, 2001. 'A Profile of Journalists in Post-Independence Tanzania', *Gazette* 63(6): 539–55.

Ramaprasad, Jyotika, 2003. 'The Private and Government Sides of Tanzanian Journalists', *Harvard International Journal of Press/Politics* 8(1): 8–26.

Ramaprasad, Jyotika and James D. Kelly, 2003. 'Reporting The News From The World's Rooftop', *Gazette* 65(3): 291–315.

Reporters without Borders, 2006. *Worldwide Press Freedom Index 2006*, http://www.rsf.org/article.php3?id_article=19388.

Roudakova, Natalia, 2004. 'Journalists as Politicians: "Independent" Media and the Privatization of Politics in Russia in the 1990s', Paper presented at the Fourth Annual International Young Researchers' Conference 'The Problems of the Post-communist State', Miami University, The Havighurst Center for Russian and Post-Soviet Studies, 4–6 November.

Rukavishnikov, Vladimir O., 2003. 'Kachestvo rossiiskoi demokratii v sravni-tel'nom izmerenii', *Sotsiologicheskie issledovaniia* 5: 30–41.

The Russian Periodical Press Market: 2005. Situation, Trends, Prospects, 2005. Federal Agency for the Press and Mass Communication of the Russian Federation. May Report, http://www.fapmc.ru/.

The Russian Periodical Press Market: 2006. Condition, Trends, Prospects, 2006. Federal Agency for the Press and Mass Communication of the Russian Federation, May Report, http://www.fapmc.ru/.

Schleifer, Andrei, 2005. *A Normal Country. Russia after Communism*, Cambridge MA: Harvard University Press.

Shevtsova, Lilia, 2007. 'Imitation Russia' http://www.eu-russiacentre.org/assets/files/shevzova.pdf.

Sosnovskaia, Anna, 2005. *Zhurnalist: lichnost' i professional (psikhologiia identich-nosti)*, St Petersburg: St Petersburg University.

Sosnovskaya, Anna, 2000. 'Social Portrait and Identity of Today's Journalist: St Petersburg, A Case Study', in Jan Ekecrantz and Kerstin Olofsson (eds), *Russian Reports: Studies in Postcommunist Transformation of Media and Journalism*, Stockholm: Almqvist & Wiksell International, pp. 139–96.

Svitich, Lyubov', 2003. *Professiya: zhurnalist*, Moscow: Aspekt Press.

Voltmer, Katrin, 2000. 'Constructing Political Reality in Russia. *Izvestiya* – Between Old and New Journalistic Practices', *European Journal of Communication* 15(4): 469–500.

Weaver, David & G. Cleveland Wilhoit, 1986. *The American Journalist. A Portrait of U.S. News People and Their Work*, Bloomington IN: Indiana University Press.

Weaver, David & G. Cleveland Wilhoit, 1996. *The American Journalist in the 1990s. U.S. News People at the End of an Era*, Mahwah NJ: Lawrence Erlbaum.

Weaver, David (ed.), 1998. *The Global Journalist: News People Around the World*, Cresskill: Hampton Press.

White, Stephen, Ian, McAllister and Sarah, Oates, 2002. 'Was It Russian Public Television That Won It?', *Harvard Journal of Press/Politics* 7(2): 17–33.

Wu, Wei, David, Weaver and V. Owen Johnson, 1996. 'Professional Roles of Russian and U.S. Journalists: A Comparative Study', *Journalism & Mass Communication Quarterly* 73(3): 534–48.

Yakovenko, Igor and Svetlana Pasti, 2004. 'Political Situation', in *Monitoring the Media: Coverage of the December 2003 Parliamentary Elections in Russia*, Moscow: The Union of Journalists of Russia, pp. 7–17.

Yavlinsky, Grigory, 2004. 'What has Happened to Russia', *International Herald Tribune*, 27 September.

Zassoursky, Ivan, 2001. 'Media and Power: Russia in the Nineties', in Kaarle Nordenstreng, Elena Vartanova and Yassen Zassoursky (eds), *Russian Media Challenge*, Helsinki: Kikimora, pp. 73–92.

Zassoursky, Ivan, 2004. *Media and Power in Post-Soviet Russia*, Armonk NY: M. E. Sharpe.

Zassoursky, Yassen N., 2001. 'Media and the Public Interest: Balancing between the State, Business and the Public Sphere', in Kaarle Nordenstreng, Elena Vartanova and Yassen Zassoursky (eds), *Russian Media Challenge*, Helsinki: Kikimora, pp. 155–88.

6
Debating Kyoto: Soviet Networks and New Perplexities

Marie-Hélène Mandrillon

The announcement made in September, and confirmed in November 2004, of Russia's decision to ratify the Kyoto Protocol put an end to three long years of prevarication by the Russian authorities in various international fora. It did not, however, lay to rest the controversy on the subject among the Russian elite, splitting the political leadership and the economic and scientific communities. The opposition in each of the three groups between Kyoto opponents and supporters gave rise to some strange alliances.

What was at stake? The Protocol to the United Nations Framework Convention on Climate Change, drawn up in Kyoto in 1997, represented the first attempt by world governments to implement a concerted set of regulations for making economically tolerable a jointly conceived effort to meet the risks of global climate change.[1] The goal is for the industrialized countries to reduce their greenhouse gas emissions, responsible for global warming, over the period 2008–2012 by roughly 6 per cent as compared with 1990 levels. Russia's commitment was to not exceed the volume of emissions registered in 1990, that is, just before the collapse of the USSR and the deep recession which followed.

Under the rules, the Protocol, to come into force, must be ratified by 55 countries accounting for 55 per cent of the industrialized countries' CO_2 emissions. But after the United States, which is responsible for 36 per cent of global emissions but which had excluded itself from the scheme in 2001, the agreement's implementation – awaited by Japan and especially the European Union – depended completely on what Russia might decide. Russia being responsible for 17 per cent of total emissions, its agreement was needed for the crucial 55 per cent threshold to be attained. This gave it a virtual *de facto* veto over the Protocol's application.[2]

Since 2001, the Russian government had sent out mixed signals, sowing doubts as to its real intentions. When opening a G8-sponsored conference of scientists, political and economic leaders, representatives of the UN agencies and NGO heads from around the world,[3] the Russian President caused bafflement among the audience when he bantered about Russia being 'a cold country where a few extra degrees would provide savings in heating and clothing ...' (Associated Press 2003).

Before the conference, the debate had been the narrow preserve of specialists. It took an openly political turn when Vladimir Putin gave the ministries and agencies concerned, as well as the Russian Academy of Sciences, until 20 May 2004 to deliver their opinion on the advisability of ratifying the Protocol, letting it be known that the decision would be made 'in accordance with Russia's national interests'. This was the context for the conflict of opinion which propelled the environmental issues that had been obscured since the collapse of the USSR in 1991 to the forefront of the Russian domestic scene.

The purpose of this chapter is to examine what was at stake in the debate: on the one hand, strategic considerations concerning a post-communist Russia's place in the world, its choice of alliances, possible WTO membership, and a multilateral approach to international conflicts and global risks; on the other, domestic policy considerations concerning energy policy, development choices and the power structure, often closely entwined with strategic issues.

The way the debate developed shows that the issues took shape and acquired definition according to the players involved and their manner of confrontation.[4] In following the players' moves, we shall discover a tangled web of financial competition, administrative turf battles and personal rivalries. Special attention will be paid to how the confrontation unfolded in scientific circles. Their present division provides a clue to the survival of networks of scientists established during earlier environmental controversies dating from the 1970s and 1980s. The description of each camp and its constituent alliances will explain how the dispute's virulence drew its energy from a surprising compact between neoliberal ultras and old-guard technocrats.

Friends and foes of Kyoto

Two men were at the origin of the public altercation concerning ratification. Their portraits could not be more dissimilar, and their association was an odd mix. On the one hand we had Andrei Illarionov, Vladimir

Putin's economic adviser, and a highly-placed member of the Presidential administration, which acts as a sort of super-cabinet. A young (40 year old) economist, educated at the University of St Petersburg, he started his political career in the President's home city. Viewed as an ultra-liberal and critic of the government's economic record, he is celebrated for his unbridled verbal attacks, which the Russians call *skandal*. A fluent English speaker, he is a sought-after guest in liberal circles and the Anglo-Saxon press. Kremlin-watchers speculate endlessly on whether his public declarations reflect the President's opinions and on how much influence he really wields over the head of state. Their doubts have accumulated since the announcement early in January 2005 that he had been relieved of his functions as Putin's G8 sherpa. His involvement in the Kyoto Protocol's ratification dossier was however very real, and his interlocutors in other European governments spheres readily acknowledge his mastery of the intricate details of the subject.

Illarionov sees 'Kyotoism' as a 'new totalitarianism' (Singleton 2004), and has said that its implementation would be an 'Auschwitz for civilization' (Rosbalt 2004). Behind these extravagant tirades, he holds the solid conviction that there is no scientific basis for claiming that climate change is anthropogenic: he attributes it rather to solar activity. Emission reductions are in these circumstances far too costly for results that would be uncertain at best. American political leaders on all sides agree that the world's foremost economy cannot afford them. So what can poor struggling Russia be expected to do? It would amount to imposing pointless restrictions on its growth. Not only that, but the limits imposed on Russia would be unfair, since China, treated as an emerging economy, does not have to make the slightest effort. Lastly, meeting the Kyoto commitments runs counter to the Russian policy goal of doubling GDP by the year 2010. The domestic proponents of ratification are therefore the enemies of growth, while the 'Socialist' European leaders who exert pressure on Russia are waging an 'undeclared war'. The President's 'coerced' decision changes none of this. In future, care must be taken to minimize the harmful effects of the Kyoto provisions.

No paths could be more different than those of Andrei Illarionov and Yuri Izrael, sometimes portrayed as Vladimir Putin's science adviser, although he does not appear in the Presidential administration's organization chart. Described by his enemies as a 'Soviet fossil coming to the rescue of fossil energies' (Schiermeier and MacWilliams 2004), he was born in 1930 in a Tashkent academic family. After joining the Party in 1955 he made his way steadily to the top of university geophysics, and the *nomenklatura*. Head without interruption from 1970 to 1993 of Gidromet, the powerful half-civilian half-military hydrometeorology service, holding ministerial rank under both Brezhnev and Gorbachev, he is said to have declined the new post of environment minister created in the late 1980s, preferring to reinforce his service's position by giving it administrative authority over environment matters. In 1990 he created his own research institute, the Institute for Global Change and Ecology, under the broad umbrella of the hydrometeorology service and the Academy of Sciences. He pursued a double career which led him in Russia to the Presidium of the Academy and, within the United Nations, first to the World Meteorological Organization (WMO) and then to the post of Vice-President of the Intergovernmental Panel on Climate Change (IPCC)[5] where he has represented the USSR from the moment of the Panel's inception in 1988, and of which he was still Vice-President in 2004 (Agrawala 1998).

Yuri Izrael, on the strength of his scientific laurels in the field of climate change, based his position on the aims of the UN Framework Convention. In his view, the Kyoto Protocol was a step in the wrong direction. There were two points to his reasoning. First, its effects would be too limited for it to have a significant impact on global climate change, despite the huge expense entailed. The effort needed would therefore be misguided (Viktorova 2001). Second, insufficient study had been devoted to the regional effects of global climate change, and the money would be better spent on study of this aspect of the subject (Izrael 2004). Taking Russia as an example, he declared that, contrary to the consensus position expressed in the IPCC reports that he himself had signed, climate change would be beneficial to central regions at intermediate latitudes, and would greatly extend Russia's arable area. He asked for more resources to be made available to the research under his command (Izrael 2003).

He furthermore opined that such undesirable consequences as the melting of the permafrost in the North could be countered technically, and that extreme phenomena, like droughts and typhoons, could be addressed by geophysical technology. The latter should be developed and applied so as eventually to control climate or, at least, adjust to climate as it evolved. He was confident that Russian science and technology were capable of meeting this challenge, for the benefit of humanity and the planet's future (Leskov 2003). So it was that a meeting of minds occurred between Illarionov, with his laissez-faire attitude towards the new players in the Russian economy, the oil sector in particular, and Izrael, the champion of Soviet technocratic intervention and of the belief that a technical solution could be found for every problem.[6] Both men were led to reject both the formulation of state preventive policies and any kind of global regulation, regarded as foreign interference (Jurkov 2003).

The dispute's development owed much to these two characters who, despite their contrasting biographies, found that they had many purposes in common. Yuri Izrael was scientific organizer of an international conference that was held in Moscow in September 2003. Its main conclusion was to contest the scientific justification for combatting climate change. One result of the ensuing official consultations was the task entrusted to Yuri Izrael of organizing a consultative 'Seminar' at Academy of Sciences Presidium level. The Seminar pronounced against the desirability of ratifying the Protocol. This angle of the controversy will be treated in more detail below.

The anti-Protocol camp drew support not only officially from the Academy, but also from business and industry – mainly the petroleum and heavy chemicals industries and the Siberian and Far Eastern regions connected with them.[7] When the issue of rejection came to a vote in the Duma,[8] it received backing from the Nationalists and the Communists (Granik 2004). Abroad, it won approval from European 'Kyotosceptics' such as the Danish scientist Bjorn Lomborg (2004) and, in no uncertain fashion, the American Global Climate Coalition interest group, which had helped to craft the United States' withdrawal from the Kyoto Protocol in 2001.[9]

Turning now to the advocates of ratification, we find chief among them Viktor Danilov-Danilian, Russia's only post-USSR environment minister. He held this post from its creation at the end of the Soviet era until the ministry was abolished in 2000 (Larin et al. 2003). As minister, he was one of the key players involved in the UN Climate Convention and Russia's signing of the Kyoto Protocol. Born in 1938, he received his training at the school of mathematical economics attached to the Academy of Sciences' Central Institute of Mathematical Economics in Moscow. The Institute successfully liberated the subject from its ideological trappings, and counselled the use of mathematical methods as an instrument in reforming the post-Stalinist Soviet economy. Danilov-Danilian, as a member of this reform movement, was a pioneer in applying economic mathematics to the environment. He trained regional managers along these lines, and contributed his expertise to drafting official policy. A corresponding member of the Academy of Sciences, he today directs one of Russia's primary environmental research centres, the Institute for Water Problems.

In his opinion, the Kyoto Protocol is merely a modest first step in a long and arduous struggle, conceived as a series of stages negotiated at world level, against climate risk. The economic machinery laid down in the Protocol should be used as a tool for restructuring the Russian economy, so as to lessen its dependence on petroleum and modernize its ageing, energy-voracious and inefficient industrial sector. This is the price for achieving sustainable growth. Kyoto can help in this by attracting the necessary foreign investment (Danilov-Danilian and Losev 2000).

On the side of Danilov-Danilian we have other members of the defunct Environment Ministry, former Climate Convention negotiators, and scientists taking part in the IPCC's work. Like the ex-minister, they often hold posts in the Academy of Sciences, sometimes as heads of Institutes, or direct environmental NGOs.

These 'fathers' of the Protocol are not alone in preaching its implementation. Also very active are representatives of the energy sector standing to benefit from it. These are principally the two public operators which hold a monopoly over gas, Gazprom, and electricity, the Unified Energy System, run by Boris Yeltsin's one-time chief of staff, Anatolii Chubais.[10] To them may be added, at government level, the ministry of foreign affairs, which took part in the international negotiations on climate from the outset and has never wavered in its support for ratification, even though it maintained a low profile in the public debate.

Splits and alliances

The vehemence of the Kyoto controversy derived from the fact that it carried echoes of other disputes or gave them focus by presenting them in a new form. Here are some of them taken in turn, although it should be remembered that they were, in fact, intermeshed.

International issues

With the untidy emergence of a multipolar world and trade globalization at the end of the Cold War, two major currents of thought opposed each other in Gorbachev's USSR and then post-Soviet Russia. While the common goal was to restore Russia's standing in the world after the loss of the USSR's superpower status, one school recommended respect for multilateral principles and alignment with the positions of the European Union, while the other preferred an alliance with the old American partner-cum-enemy. In this view of things, Russia's two big neighbours – China flexing its might and the enlarged 25-member European Union – were regarded as rivals.

'Green diplomacy' was, in this context, considered as an instrument for increasing Russia's clout in the UN system, where the United States was isolated, pending the Organization's reform. This throws a revealing light on Russia's willingness to participate in the Kyoto process, from which the Americans were absent.

The same could be said of the negotiations over Russia's membership in the World Trade Organization (WTO), which had dragged on since Gorbachev's reforms in the late 1980s (Roche 2003). After China, as well as former Soviet republics like Ukraine and Kazakhstan, had joined the WTO, Russia and the European Union became engaged in a giant game of give and take. The latter traded its support for Russia against the implementation of a string of reforms at home and espousal of multilateralism abroad. Ratification of the Kyoto Protocol was to be the litmus test. According to observers, the lifting of the EU's reservations and a declaration of its support for Russia in May 2003 swung the balance (Aslund 2004; Kempf 2004).

The setting of conditions was a red rag to the opponents of ratification. Yuri Izrael, for one, assumed an ideological stance reminiscent of the 'besieged fortress' syndrome. Labelling the European attitude inadmissible outside interference, he exclaimed, 'Our conference is purely scientific in nature and there they are imposing conditions on us' (Timoshenko 2003). On a different tack, Andrei Illarionov opined that the linkage between Kyoto and the WTO amounted to discriminatory pressure against Russia, since China had not been subjected to the same treatment during its negotiations for WTO membership. He pointed out that the question of human rights could have been raised at that time (Illarionov 2003).

More broadly, he argued that the underlying principle of the Kyoto agreement was in itself discriminatory. The Protocol divides countries into two groups: the industrialized countries, including Russia as well as the whole of Eastern Europe, deemed historically responsible for greenhouse gas emissions, and the developing countries. Their share in emissions is bound to increase on account of their predicted growth. But, for the sake of fairness as recognized by the 1997 negotiators, they were exempted from any restrictions precisely in order not to impede their development. The provisions are valid only for the period covered by the Protocol, that is, until 2012. Negotiations for the following period are due to open in 2005. The European Union's and Japan's proclaimed objective is to implicate such emerging countries as China, India and Brazil to a greater extent so that they will accept binding commitments.[11]

The intrusion of the Russo-Chinese relations issue is good proof that the whole question of Russia's place in the world was inflamed by the Kyoto debate. One other area that sprang into relief was the way domestic and bilateral problems correlated. This was particularly well illustrated by the reaction against pressures exerted by the British government on the occasion of a visit to Moscow in July 2004. The reason almost certainly lay in London's decision to give refuge to a former Chechnyan leader, accused by Moscow of being a terrorist, and Tony Blair's refusal to extradite him.

For these reasons, the Kyoto ratification go-ahead should not too quickly be interpreted as a final choice of strategic alliances, with a tilt towards the European Union and a turning away from a prestigious duel with the United States. At the same time, the signal conveyed by ratification could reasonably betoken a refusal by Russian diplomacy to follow an opt-out policy. It could also be regarded as a comfort for all those in Russia who feel that their country's loss of its past role as leader should not translate into its isolation on the world scene and who prefer to go down the difficult path of negotiated integration.

Competing forces within a fast-changing energy sector

Discussing the Russian energy sector is, given the tangle of strategic, economic, financial and political interests it embodies, a hazardous enterprise. Since the 2003 arrest of the director of Yukos, the largest Russian oil conglomerate and the fourth biggest in the world, we know that Vladimir Putin has personally taken this dossier under his wing. The inner workings of Russian energy policy are particularly obscure. We can, however, try to give a broad outline of some of the questions posed by ratification, at least as they concern our subject.

Since the 1998 financial crisis, the Russian economy's recovery has depended to a very large extent on the activity of the energy, mining, drilling and commodities trading sectors, owing partly to their share in GDP and partly to their export role. This is what economists call a rent economy. The Russian government's target of doubling GDP by the year 2010 relies on the continued growth of these sectors. Their problem is that their industrial plant, which dates back to the Soviet era, is obsolescent and their administration is often governed by Stalin-style commandist principles. This does not give them a competitive edge on the world market. Their modernization depends on the country's ability to attract foreign investment (Leskov 2004).

The Kyoto ratification dispute was thus fuelled by a first subject of contention, which was this: Would implementing the Protocol work as an instrument in favour of urgently needed modernization or would it, on the contrary, constitute an additional handicap in a situation where the energy sector could otherwise keep on growing without any kind of environmental constraint?

The Russian elite was split on this question. As we have seen, the economists were divided between supporters of the first option, like Danilov-Danilian, and those of the second, like Illarionov. A further divide existed among the players on the operating side. On the one hand were those, such as Gazprom and UES (accounting for a full 38 per cent of emissions), who thought they could benefit from joint 'decarbonization' programmes; on the other were those, like the oil drilling and ore mining companies (such as Norilsk Nickel), who stood to suffer on account of their excessive emissions (*Russia in Global Affairs* 2003).[12]

The Kremlin's reassertion of control introduced a new factor, of a more political nature. Would the benefits of a practical implementation in the field of the joint projects accrue equally to all the operators concerned, or would they go solely to the state enterprises – or enterprises liable to come under more subtle state influence in the future and thus be regarded as 'friendly'? We enter here into the confrontation between 'politicians' and 'oligarchs', power games within the Kremlin, and personal rivalries such as that between Andrei Illarionov and Anatolii Chubais, head of UES (Walters 2004).

Amid all these uncertainties, it is worth noting Gazprom's and UES's creation of a lobby and interest group on both the home front and in Brussels. They have set up specialized consultancies, scouted for foreign partners, prepared projects, grouped themselves within the employers' union, and instituted a National Carbon Agreement.[13] Despite this somewhat confusing situation, it is clear that the opponents of ratification have not succeeded, notwithstanding the Presidential adviser's efforts, in getting themselves organized, whereas the pro-Kyoto industrialists have rallied together and formed the requisite alliances. Their action receives publicity from the press owned by private financial interests. The pro-Kyoto camp has also attracted support from international ecology groups and environmentalist NGOs, more particularly the Russian branches of Greenpeace and the WWF.

It is true that the association movements and the few independent media have a negligible impact on both the Russian authorities and public opinion. The important fact is the pro-Kyoto industrial and financial circles' ability to assemble a coalition that can not only gain attention from foreign investors and policymakers, in Europe especially, but also exert pressure on the Russian government and bureaucracy. The fact that these official institutions are neither impermeable nor monolithic makes them accessible to outside influences.[14]

Institutional antagonisms

With the exception of the Foreign Ministry, whose pro-ratification stance has been unwavering, the position of the different ministerial departments has vacillated during the course of the debate. Even after the decision was taken, hesitancy was more often the rule than enthusiasm. For example, in May 2004, the offices of the Ministry of Industry and Energy issued a report on the economic and financial consequences of observing the Kyoto commitments. Its conclusion was that, no matter which growth scenario was envisaged, the CO_2 emission volume ceiling would not be reached before 2017. This contradicted the assertion by the President's adviser that Kyoto would impose artificial limits on GDP growth, and bolstered the position of the supporters of ratification (Kuraev 2004). It is interesting to note that neither the senior officials of the ministry who had contributed to writing the report nor the minister himself, Viktor Khristenko, was willing to endorse the conclusions reached by their own experts.

A similar intra-ministry flip-flop occurred in the Ministry for Economic Development and Trade. The Deputy Minister in charge of the matter, Mukhamed Tsikanov, a highly active negotiator in the annual conferences of the UN Climate Convention, voiced a multitude of contradictory statements none of which could be understood as indicating a real shift in the Ministry's official position.

Some observers have interpreted this cacophony as a symptom of competition between the two economic ministries – as well as among their internal directorates – to be given charge of the system for implementing the Protocol and have the responsibility for running it (Walters 2004). The situation as regards the public services dealing with the environment is not quite the same.

Since the ministry was disbanded in 2000, its tasks have been assumed by the Ministry for Natural Resources. Climate change being, however, a global issue, the centre of authority lies mostly with the federal Hydrometeorology Service. It is indeed the Service's Director, Alexander Bedritsky, who is regularly appointed to head the Russian Federation's delegation to the United Nations.

In May 2004, an administrative overhaul boosted the Service's status by attaching it directly to the Cabinet and substantially increased its budget (RIA Novosti 2004). In September 2004 Vladimir Putin entrusted Alexander Bedritsky with speaking for the Ratification Bill before the two houses of Parliament. Bedritsky had until then expressed himself in favour of the principle of ratification but had been extremely cautious as to its date and practical details. His reservations appear to have been overcome by the various signs of presidential approval. The Ministry for Natural Resources, for its part, finally issued a terse go-ahead for the ratification process.

The process has to be accompanied by a series of measures setting out the modus operandi for putting the different Protocol mechanisms into effect. The quarrel over who in Russia should be responsible for operating the Kyoto Protocol is therefore far from over (Zaslavsky 2004). Whereas in the economic and political spheres positions seem to be governed by considerations of interest or opportunistic motives, in scientific circles they have old and deep-seated origins.

The argument among scientists: the persistence of Soviet-era networks

In industrialized countries, the scientific community puts pressure on governments to take action against the dangers of climate change. In Russia, the situation is quite different. Scientists have not only failed to issue any warnings but, when their opinion has officially been sought, they have expressed opposition to the Kyoto Protocol. Not surprisingly, this has had a very broad impact.

The reasons for this singular situation are many. Ideology is the first explanation. The old Stalinist view whereby political problems were met with technical solutions is still alive and well. It lasted beyond Stalin's totalitarianism and continued to prevail under Khrushchev and Brezhnev, prolonging the domination of single party rule. Yuri Izrael's career is a fine example of this.

When the first environmental issues began to emerge in the USSR at the time of the thaw in the 1960s, the regime's reaction consisted in blocking any political questioning of the communist system and endeavouring to channel criticisms by submitting them to experts for them to debate in the form of technical alternatives. Yuri Izrael, as Head of the Hydrometeorological and Environmental Supervision Service, was given the job of drafting options for remedying the most blatant cases. First on the agenda was the pollution of Lake Baikal caused by the cellulose complex set up on its shores. Second was the drop in water-levels in the Caspian and Aral Seas. Another task for Izrael was to supervise the schemes for diverting rivers in North Russia and Siberia in the 1970s, dubbed the 'project of the century'. It was natural, then, that he and the Academicians of his generation should tackle the question of global warming in the same way.

Gidromet had also the tasks of compiling air and water quality data, monitoring industrial plants and construction sites, with power to halt them temporarily or permanently, and ensuring their compliance with the standards in force. Consequently, Yuri Izrael had control over what was done in research centres and planning offices under Gidromet's command or attached to specialized ministries and enterprises. He was in close touch with the government departments responsible for producing and enforcing standards (Pryde 1991). Even though Gorbachev's policies finally ended the runaway technological spiral, more particularly the river-diversion scheme, and clipped Gidromet's wings by creating an environmental ministry in 1988, Izrael was able to preserve his networks in and around his own research centre, the Institute for Global Climate and Ecology (IGCE), which worked on behalf not only of Gidromet but also of the Academy of Sciences, and which was founded in 1990.[15]

When draconian budget cuts from 1992 onwards led to the collapse of the Soviet research system, the climate science colony managed to become even more concentrated. Climate change studies went on uninterrupted in Russia as part of the IGCE's activities. The Institute's Director was able to garner international support for them, whereas international funding had dwindled or dried up in the case of other research institutes. Meanwhile, in 1988, Izrael, as USSR representative, had been appointed Vice-President of the Intergovernmental Panel on Climate Change (IPCC), and was so able to graft his domestic networks on to the international ones of this nascent experiment in world governance.

The second factor explaining Russia's unusual position on the world climate research scene lies precisely in Yuri Izrael's preponderant role in Russian research, coupled with his rank in the world science hierarchy. Numerous parties to the controversy, whether for or against the Kyoto Protocol, were trained – or worked at some time or another – in the IGCE. This was the case with V. Kokorin, who runs WWF-Russia's climate programme and is one of ratification's most ardent supporters. This meant that he was one of his erstwhile Director's adversaries in the debate.

Another consequence of Izrael's pivotal role is that most of the Russian specialists doing work for the IPCC, like the scientists and engineers who are regular members of the Russian delegation at UN Climate Convention meetings, are 'alumni' of the IGCE or other Gidromet research bodies – even though this allows no automatic conclusions to be drawn as regards their opinions. Even so, this web of scientific, professional or personal relations, which facilitates access to information or international postings, is typical of a powerful network, centred on a single person (Degenne and Forsé 2004). Yet another factor which may explain the Russian scientific community's attitude is the continued existence of Soviet-style practices where its internal debates are concerned.

Orchestration and stifling of debates

Foreign scientists invited to the World Conference on Climate Change in Moscow in September 2003 were dismayed, already at the preparatory meeting stage, by the way it was being organized, to the point where some of them considered not attending it, and *Nature* carried a report of the possibility of a boycott (Schiermeier 2003). A Berlin researcher told the journal, 'I refuse to let myself be manipulated for purposes of which I don't approve' as a reason for not attending. Others ended by going, while deploring the 'autocratic behaviour' of the Science Committee President, Yuri Izrael, suspected of 'orchestrating' the choice of speakers and the programme, for the sake of favouring anti-Kyoto Protocol papers. This, in spite of repeated professions by its organizer that the Conference was to be a 'purely scientific' gathering (Timoshenko 2003).

Putin's opening address with its joking remark that ratification was still under study, and back-room manoeuvres to prevent Russian environmental movements having their programmed say, helped to discredit the Conference, which had been intended as a showcase, as well as an opportunity to restore the reputation of Russian science in the eyes of the international community and the political leaders present.[16] The criticism by Western scientists does show, however, a curious mixture of justifiable condemnation of practices running counter to the rules of free discussion and slightly ingenuous surprise at the 'politicization' of scientific discourse – as though, in post-Soviet Russia as everywhere else, science and politics were not intertwined.

Science and politics: experts and counter-experts

The major victory[17] obtained by Treaty opponents was the official stand against ratification taken by the main scientific institution, the Russian Academy of Sciences. There was nothing surprising about this situation. The Academy had undergone severe cuts in funding; it had lost half its staff; it had suffered from science's declining public respect; and it no longer enjoyed its Soviet-era status of justifier of authority. Despite this, it managed to thwart all attempts by the government to reform it. Because of a lack of resources and standing, it failed to continue as a driving force in science. Yet it was more than a mere club of greying Academicians. Thanks to the sponsorship it exercised over its research institutes, it retained substantial property, budget and bureaucratic resources.

The Academy of Sciences thus offers an example of institutional continuity over and beyond political changes (Mandrillon 1998). The request it received to provide a scientific opinion on the advisability of ratifying the Kyoto Protocol gave it the chance to get back into politics and play a role commensurate with its ambitions. When Illarionov made known Putin's demand, the Academy President, Yuri Osipov, decided to set up a consultative 'Seminar' on 'Possible anthopogenic climate change and on the issue of the Kyoto Protocol', whose chairmanship he entrusted to Yuri Izrael.[18] The Seminar was composed of twenty-six members, Academicians, corresponding members and specialists in geophysics, energy and economics. From 16 January to 14 May 2004 it held eight sessions, which produced eighteen papers.

After four months of deliberations, the participants adopted a two-page statement professing to be the opinion of the Academy of Sciences for transmission to the President and government. It advised against ratifying the Treaty. The findings were summed up in eight points, the first of which stated, 'The Kyoto Protocol is scientifically unfounded'.[19] Of course, this conclusion, presented by the press as the scientists' rejection of a treaty deemed by the highest scientific authority to be 'harmful' to the country's interests, had some domestic impact in Russia. But the debate left public sentiment largely indifferent, seeing that only specialists were aware of the Ministry of Energy's contrary opinion.

On the other hand, the effect upon the international scientific community was profound. The 'veto' by Russian science was immediately hailed by Kyoto-sceptics as the ringing endorsement for which they had so long been waiting. The journal *Nature*, for its part, devoted a critical editorial to the event, saying that the Russian Academy had been held hostage by Protocol opponents.[20]

In Russian society, dissenting voices take a long time to make themselves publicly heard. Here, they took the form of an open letter addressed on 30 June 2004 to the President of the Academy and the Minister of Energy by members of a workshop organized by the Academy's Economics Section. The signers included specialists who had taken part in the consultative Seminar but who cast doubt on the impartiality of its opinion and the extent to which it reflected the view of the Russian scientific community regarding the Kyoto Protocol. They believed that the Protocol was 'beneficial' to Russia (Mnenie uchenykh 2004). Open letters to the government are a traditional method among the Russian and Soviet intelligentsia for letting dissent be publicly known. What is striking in this case is that a group of five eminent scientists who had taken part in the Academy Seminar refused to endorse the Seminar's conclusions (Danilov-Danilian 2004).

Two other economists besides Viktor Danilov-Danilian, an atmo-spheric physicist and a geochemist, signed the letter. Common to all of them was the fact that each in his own specialism had sounded a warning against environmental danger as early as the 1960s or 1970s and that each had risen to posts of high responsibility in Russia or inter-nationally in the post-Soviet period (Larin et al. 2003). Dimitri L'vov (born in 1930) is a theorist of innovation-based economic growth. For-merly an adviser to Mikhail Gorbachev, he today heads the Academy of Sciences' Economics Section. Aleksandr Granberg (born in 1936), a specialist in regional economics, has directed the Economics Institute and been editor of the journal *EKO* in Novosibirsk (Josephson 1997). Now in charge of the Council on Productive Forces, the famous SOPS, heir to the institution founded in the early 20th century by the 'father' of Russian scientific ecology, Vladimir Vernadsky, he is the author of a sustainable development strategy for Russia.[21] Georgii Golitsyn (born in 1935) won international renown for his contribution in the 1980s to the nuclear winter theory. Director of the Atmospheric Physics Institute, he was one of the authors of the latest IPCC report, published in 2001. He directs studies on the effects of warming in high latitudes. The youngest of these scientists, the only one to be born after the war (in 1946), is Nikita Glazovsky. A specialist in geochemistry, he studied at the Faculty of Geography of Moscow University, where he still teaches. Very early on, he took an interest in the desertification resulting from Soviet pol-icy in the Aral Sea basin in Central Asia. Vice-Minister for Environment in the early 1990s, he is Vice-President of the International Geographic Union and regional director for the ex-USSR of the NGO 'Leadership for Environment and Development'.

This brief inspection of their career profiles is enough to show that, during the Soviet era, they were led to take public – if not explicitly political – stands, in keeping with their scientific convictions. Some of them have longstanding close personal relations; others simply met at meetings of the Academy's specialist committees or Gosplan exper-tise institutions. The group shares similar attitudes, working methods, frames of reference and even values. This explains why their personal ties have endured through the sweeping political changes in society and why they were able to rally together on the occasion of the Kyoto ratifi-cation debate. The group's unity was naturally reinforced by the fact that each of its members had at some point in their careers crossed paths with Yuri Izrael and his entourage. In Granberg's case, it had happened when Siberian economists campaigned to preserve Lake Baikal; Glazovsky's occasion concerned the protection of the Aral Sea; and all of them had been in contact in the 1980s through their involvement in the 'project of the century' for diverting the rivers of North Russia and Siberia to the Caspian Sea and Central Asia (Raviot 1995; Mandrillon 1989).

These decades-old links among the different groups of experts, whether they were based on like-mindedness or disagreement, may be seen as the bonding material that built them into a public action community concerned with the use of natural resources for the USSR's and post-Soviet Russia's economic development.

Conclusion

Since the ratification of the Kyoto Protocol in 2004 and its entry into force in 2005, Russian climate politics have moved very slowly and the discussion of the country's post-Kyoto policy has not yet concluded. Therefore, it is still very difficult to understand why Russia decided to subscribe to a general agreement to limit the impact of global warming and what dictated the timing of the decision. The main problem is the obscurity surrounding the decision-making process within a divided Russian leadership. Much the same situation prevails in post-Soviet Russia scholarly circles.

Another obstacle to comprehension lies in the intense competition among the various players to be the 'operator', read 'beneficiary', in charge of implementing the Protocol mechanisms. It is still an open field. Who will be the industrial operative in an energy sector undergoing change? Who, it may also be wondered, will be the administrative operator? Gidromet was given the task of preparing ratification but it is hardly likely, given its institutional weakness, that it will be made responsible for actually managing the quota market mechanisms or setting up joint decarbonization projects. The real struggle will probably be between the Ministry of the Economy and the Ministry of Energy and their respective industrial and financial allies. It is the same in the scientific arena, where each party is trying to snare resources for its particular institute, even though no one can be sure whether climate research will be supported or where the funds might come from: the Russian national budget, private and public international cooperation, or R & D investment by Russian industrial and financial groups.

In this connection, a field for study will open when Russia drafts its still non-existent regulatory framework, required for implementing the Protocol's economic mechanisms. This will give some idea of the costs and benefits involved and perhaps tell us whether Kyoto will bring the 'shower of gold' anticipated by some or whether, as predicted by other

Protocol advocates, it will require intensive efforts. On the environment front, it remains to be seen how much effect the pro-Kyoto camp's victory will have. Does it signal a revival of civic responsibility? Or does the resuscitation of a river diversion scheme as suggested by the powerful Mayor of Moscow, Yuri Luzhkov,[22] betoken a still active Communist legacy? The fate in store for this latest manifestation of Soviet 'gigantomania' will provide an excellent test.

Now that we are at the end of this preliminary, 'close to the events' examination of the controversy, a supposition may be advanced. Its corroboration will require comparison with empirical studies on other areas of official action by Russia.[23] What is disconcerting in this analysis of divisions and alliances is how far removed we are from the expected picture of a battle between two Russias – one directly descended from Soviet rule, state-oriented, hermetic, aggressive towards the outside world, in opposition to a new liberal Russia at home in a globalized world and open to co-operation. This is not at all the case. What we see are 'fault-lines' that run through the middle of each camp, and unexpected coalitions formed by actors who seem to be taking a part that is out of character. The key is surely to be found in a meticulous study of these people's behaviour both in their own country and in world fora, allowing us to discover what values they carry with them as they move from one stage to the other.

Notes

1. There is an ample supply of literature on climate change and the ways to deal with it. Two recent works are Le Treut and Jancovici (2004) and Hauglustaine, Jouzel and Le Treut (2004).
2. Russia having ratified the Kyoto Protocol on 18 November 2004, it was scheduled to take effect on 15 February 2005. Consult the Climate Convention site: http://www.unfccc.int.
3. The G-8 group of the eight most industrialized countries is made up of the seven major OECD countries and Russia. An annual summit is attended by heads of state and government. The decision to convene an international conference on climate change in Moscow was taken at the Genoa summit in July 2001.
4. Our analysis of the Russian situation is indebted to the approach adopted by Marie-Claude Smouts (2000, p. 115): 'there is no clear distinction between the subject and the debate on the subject, the interests in play and considerations of justice. Everything builds out of the discussion. Everything is interwoven, and forms a system. The climate change negotiation is particularly revealing in this respect.'

5. The IPCC was set up in 1988 to provide scientific expertise at the instigation of the United Nations Environment Programme (UNEP) and the World Meteorological Organization (WMO). Every four years it produces reports based on the work of about two thousand researchers, and a short breakdown intended for policymakers. The last report was published in 2001 (IPCC 2001). For a detailed presentation and analysis of the IPCC's work, see Chevassus-au-Louis 2003 and Weill 2004.

6. Concerning this question, well covered in the historical literature on the USSR, see, for example, the two authoritative studies by Douglas Weiner (1988, 1999).

7. See the list of participants in a conference organized by a Moscow think tank (*Russia in Global Affairs*, 2003).

8. It is worth remembering that, since the parliamentary elections of 7 December 2003, the 'right-wing' parties SPS and Iabloko, in favour of ratification, no longer held seats in Parliament.

9. As regards the activity of this lobby, consisting of oil company and mining region representatives, and its influence on the US position in international negotiations, see Hourcade, 2002; for an analysis of America's energy policy, see Chevalier, 2004.

10. The coalition's existence was highlighted by the publication in September 2003 of a small luxuriously illustrated brochure designed for the general public, under the joint auspices of the WWF, the EU-backed Russian Regional Ecology Centre and the National Carbon Convention which assembles pro-Kyoto enterprises. The text's authors are past or present participants in world climate negotiations (*Kiotskii protokol* 2003).

11. Of the states formed from the ex-USSR, Russia and Ukraine, along with the three Baltic countries which joined the European Union in 2004, are deemed to be industrialized, unlike those in the Caucasus and Central Asia. The latter's only commitment is to make an inventory of their emissions. Would Illarionov approve of a different treatment for Russia?

12. The 'joint implementation' mechanism for greenhouse gas emission reduction projects is a Kyoto Protocol instrument which allows an industrialized country to carry out investment in another industrialized country and benefit from the emission credits generated by the reductions so obtained at lesser cost.

13. Since July 2003 such major public and private industrial and services groups as Rusal and UES, which account for one third of greenhouse gas emissions in Russia, have joined the Agreement organization. Its aim is to associate Russia with the European CO_2 market launched at the beginning of 2005: see http://www.natcarbon.ru.

14. This question has been covered by Jean-Robert Raviot. Here is one example of personal relations: Viktor Danilov-Danilian's son, Anton Viktorovich, holds a senior post in President Putin's economic administration; as such, he represents the state on the governing board of the petroleum group Transneft.

15. See the Institute's site: http://www.igce.comcor.ru/.

16. The official speeches and Conference proceedings may be consulted at http://www.wccc2003.org.

17. The 'Kyoto-sceptic' networks immediately passed on the news of the Russian scientists' *nyet*. See, for example, Murray (2004).

18. The presentation of the Seminar and some of its sessions may be consulted at the site of the Presidium of the Russian Academy of Sciences: http://www.pran.ru/rus/news/Kiotprotokol%20170404.html.
19. The recommendations were adopted on 14 May 2004: http://www.pran.ru/rus/news/Kiotprotokol210504.html.
20. The editorial bore the title *Dragged into the Fray*, vol. 429, 27 May 2004.
21. Along with Danilov-Danilian and Tsikanov, the Ministry of Economy's negotiator at the Climate Convention: see Granberg et al. 2002.
22. While Gorbachev had laid the previous 'project of the century' to rest in 1986 and general impoverishment during the years of transition had strangled other grandiose engineering schemes, *gigantomania* seems to be on the march again, witness a 2,500 km-long diversion scheme running from Siberia to the Aral Sea. 'Russia reviving massive river diversion plan', *New Scientist*, 9 February 2004.
23. For example, Russia's place within the G8, or the negotiations on its joining the WTO. Reference may be made to the work by Gilles Favarel-Garrigues on Russia's cooperation in countering money-laundering. See 'Domestic reformulation of the moral issues at stake in the drive against money laundering: the case of Russia', *International Social Science Journal*, 185, September 2005: 529–41.

References

Agrawala, Shardul. 1998. 'Context and Early Origins of the Intergovernmental Panel on Climate Change,' *Climatic Change* 39, 4 (August): 605–20.

Aslund, Anders. 2004. 'Kyoto could be Russia's ticket to Europe', *International Herald Tribune*, 6 April.

Associated Press. 2003. 'Putin casts doubt on the Kyoto Protocol', 29 September.

Chevalier, Jean-Marie. 2004. 'Énergie et environnement: des paradoxes explosifs', in Chevalier and J. Mistral (eds), *La Raison du plus fort. Les paradoxes de l'économie américaine*, Paris: Laffont, pp. 143–61.

Chevassus-au-Louis, Nicolas. 2003. 'Enquête sur les experts du climat', *La Recherche* 370 (December): 59–63.

Danilov-Danilian, Viktor. 2004. Ekho Moskvy broadcast, interview by Aleksei Vorob'ev, 30 September, consulted at http://www.echo.msk.ru/interview/27134/.

Danilov-Danilian, Viktor and K. S. Losev. 2000. *Ekologicheskii vyzov i ustoichivoe razvitie*, Moscow: Progress-Traditsiia.

Degenne, Alain and Michel Forsé. 2004. *Les réseaux sociaux*, Paris: Armand Colin.

Granberg A. G., V. I. Danilov-Danil'ian, M. M. Cikanov and E. S. Sophoeva (eds), 2002. *Strategiia i problemy ustoichogo razvitiia Rossii v XXI veke*. Moscow: Ekonomika.

Granik, Irina. 2004. 'Gosudarstvennaia Duma vybrala Kioto', *Kommersant*, 23 October.

Hauglustaine Didier, Jean Jouzel and Hervé Le Treut. 2004. *Climat: Chronique d'un bouleversement annoncé*. Paris: Le Pommier/Cité des sciences et de l'industrie.

Hourcade, Jean-Charles. 2002. 'Dans le labyrinthe de verre. La négociation sur l'effet de serre', *Critique internationale* 15 (April): 143–59.

Illarionov, Andrei. 2003. Ekho Moskvy broadcast, interview by Aleksei Benediktov, 16 October, consulted at http://www.echo.msk.ru/interview/23656/.

Intergovernmental Panel for Climate Change (IPCC). 2004. Consulted at http://www.ipcc.ch/.

IPCC. 2001. *Intergovernmental Panel for Climate Change, Third Assessment Report – Climate Change*, 4 vols, consulted at http://www.grida.no/climate/ipcc_tar/.

Izrael, Yuri. 2003. 'Chto zhdet sel'skoe khozyaistvo Rossii v XXI veke ?', *Khimiia i zhizn' – XXI vek*, 5 September.

Izrael, Yuri. 2004. 'Prizrachnaia vygoda', *Nezavisimaia gazeta*, 16 July.

Josephson, Paul R. 1997. *New Atlantis Revisited. Akademgorodok, the Siberian City of Science*. Princeton NJ: Princeton University Press.

Jurkov, Anatolii. 2003. 'Den'gi iz vozdukha', *Rossiiskaia gazeta*, 18 December.

Korpoo, Anna, Jacqueline Karas and Michael Grubb. 2005. *Russia and the Kyoto Protocol: Opportunities and Challenges*. London: Chatham House.

Kempf, Hervé. 2004. 'En décidant de ratifier le protocole de Kyoto, Moscou renforce la position européenne sur le climat', *Le Monde*, 2 October.

Kiotskii protokol. Voprosy i otvety. 2003. Moscow: WWF.

Kuraev, Sergei. 2004. 'Kiotskii protokol: reshenie za Prezidentom', *Opec.ru* 20 May, consulted at http://www.opec.ru/comment_doc.asp?d_no=48468.

Larin, Vladislav et al. 2003. *Okhrana prirody Rossii: ot Gorbacheva do Putina*. Moscow: KMK.

Le Treut, Hervé and Jean-Marc Jancovici. 2004. *L'Effet de serre. Allons-nous changer le climat?* Paris: Flammarion.

Leskov, Sergei. 2003. 'Kiotskii protokol ne vliiaet na klimat', *Izvestiia*, 10 August.

Leskov, Sergei. 2004. 'Ekonomiat na teple tol'ko bogatye', *Izvestiia*, 1 October.

Lomborg, Bjorn. 2004. *L'Ecologiste sceptique. Le véritable état de la planète*. Paris: Le Cherche-Midi.

Mandrillon, Marie-Hélène. 1989. 'Environnement et politique en URSS', *Problèmes Politiques et Sociaux*, Série URSS. Paris: La Documentation française, 15 December.

Mandrillon, Marie-Hélène. 1998. 'Russie: Quel avenir pour la recherche?', *Problèmes politiques et sociaux*, Série Russie, no. 802. Paris: La Documentation française, 1 May.

Mandrillon, Marie-Hélène. 2005. 'Le protocole de Kyoto en Russie: une ratification en trompe-l'œil ?' *Critique Internationale* 29: 37–47.

Mandrillon, Marie-Hélène (ed.) 2005. 'L'Environnement à l'Est. Le modèle européen à l'épreuve', *Revue d'Études Comparatives Est-Ouest*, 36(1), March.

Mnenie uchenykh. 2004. 'Mnenie uchenykh: Kiotskii protokol vygoden dlia Rossii', *Tsentr ekologicheskoi politiki Rossii*, 20 July, consulted at http://www.ecopolicy.ru/?id_rec=161.

Murray, Iain. 2004. 'Russian Academy says Kyoto lacks scientific substantiation', *Cooler Heads Coalition*, 28 May, consulted at http://www.globalwarming.org/article.php?uid=670.

Oldfield, Jonathan. 2005. *Russian Nature: Exploring the Consequence of Societal Environmental Change*. Aldershot: Ashgate.

Pryde, Philip R. 1991. *Environmental Management in the Soviet Union*. Cambridge and New York: Cambridge University Press.

Raviot, Jean-Robert. 1995. *Écologie et pouvoir en URSS. Le rapport à la nature et à l'espace: une source de légitimité politique dans le processus de désoviétisation*. Thèse de doctorat en science politique, Paris: IEP.

RIA Novosti. 2004. 'Rosgidromet to earn \$37 in 2004', 22 May.

Roche, Michel. 2003. 'L'adhésion de la Russie à l'OMC: les causes du retard à la fin de 2003', *Revue d'études comparatives Est–Ouest*, 34(2): 31–52.

Rosbalt. 2004. 'Andrei Illarionov: Kyoto Protocol is economic "Auschwitz" for Russia', Moscow, 24 February.

Russia in Global Affairs. 2003. 'Kyoto Protocol: Pros & Cons', consulted at http://eng.globalaffairs.ru/books/IU8.html.

Schiermeier, Quirin. 2003. 'Researchers rattled as Kyoto Protocol hangs in the balance', *Nature* 423 (792).

Schiermeier, Quirin and Bryon MacWilliams. 2004. 'Climate change: Crunch time for Kyoto', *Nature* 431, 2 September.

Singleton, Alex. 2004. 'Kyoto "a totalitarian ideology", says top Putin advisor', 19 May, consulted at http://www.adamsmith.org/blog/archives/000356.php.

Smouts, Marie-Claude, dir. 2000. 'Politiques de la biosphère', *Critique internationale* 9: 114–76.

Timoshenko, Aleksandr. 2003. 'Akademik Yurii Izrael': "Torgovlia kvotami prosto vozbudila biznesmenov', *Novye izvestiia*, 22 September.

United Nations Framework Convention on Climate Change. 2005. http://unfccc.int/2860.php.

Viktorova, Liubov'. 2001. 'Chto delat' s klimatom?', *Izvestiia*, 26 October.

Walters, Greg. 2004. 'Kyoto Financial Rewards: Who Will Benefit?', *St Petersburg Times*, 16 June.

Weill, Claire (ed.) 2004. *Science du changement climatique. Acquis et controverses*. Paris: IDDRI.

Weiner, Douglas R. 1988. *Models of Nature: Ecology, Conservation, and Cultural Revolution in Soviet Russia*. Bloomington: Indiana University Press.

Weiner, Douglas R. 1999. *A Little Corner of Freedom: Russian Nature Protection from Stalin to Gorbachev*. Berkeley: University of California Press.

Zaslavsky, Il'ia. 2004. 'Na Kiotskom protokole zarabotaiut monopolii i chinovniki', *Gazeta.ru*, 27 October, consulted at http://www.gazeta.ru/print/2004/10/27oa_137792.shtml.

7
Political Capitalism and the Russian Media

Markus Soldner

The Russian media system has changed dramatically over the past twenty years. The changes were already initiated well before the collapse of the Soviet Union. In the course of *perestroika* and *glasnost'*, print media outlets in particular achieved a remarkable degree of freedom. Although the state and Communist Party remained largely in control of the media sector, censorship was reduced drastically. Newspapers and magazines, slowly but surely, began to acquire more and more characteristics and functions of what is usually called the 'fourth estate'.

From the mid-1980s to the collapse of the Soviet Union, the mass media flourished in an unprecedented way, mainly due to the fact that most of them were deeply involved in what one could call to a certain extent 'investigative journalism'. They broadly informed the public about crimes committed under communist rule. And they also served as a forum for debates about the future of Russian society and polity. Many scholars have called this period the 'golden age' (Fossato 2001, p. 344)[1] of Soviet/Russian journalism. But as we shall see, things changed significantly soon after the Russian Federation became an independent state.

This chapter considers national television, radio networks and the so-called central press, that is, Moscow-based newspapers and magazines of national significance, at least among the political and economic elites. It will not focus on the regional media, although they evolved into a field of increasing significance and interest, as parts of the audience increasingly turned to regional and local media outlets, disregarding the national ones. However, it would go well beyond the limited space available to look into a wide range of regional media markets. Knowing well that their economic potential has risen sharply, this paper will not consider entertainment-oriented media either. The focus here is only on outlets with a distinct political profile.

The main thesis of the chapter is that certain peculiarities of the Russian polity and of the political and economic processes that took place during the 1990s together with particular deficits in the sphere of media law created a situation in which big business invested heavily in mass media outlets in order to reap political dividends and economic profits *outside* the media market. So far, the Putin presidency has been marked by continuities and modifications. Above all, the mass media continue to be used as a political resource. 'Political capitalism', understood as the conversion of political into economic power and vice versa, is still alive. But since the 'privatization of the state' under Yeltsin gave way to the 'bureaucratization of the economy', it is no longer big business but state actors for whom control of media outlets is of primary importance.

Mass media in the Independent Russian Federation

After the collapse of the Soviet Union, control over the media by the communist authorities ceased to exist. The state retreated from formerly state-owned media outlets and soon the property conditions of more and more newspapers and magazines were transformed. In many cases, the shares of a certain publication were distributed among the journalists working for it. So it was journalists who, in addition to covering news, managed the media outlets (Pleines 1997, p. 393). At the same time, new outlets were launched by private companies, collectives, and individuals. The process of marketization of the Russian media sector gathered speed, and meanwhile many functions the press served during *perestroika* became less and less important (Belin 2001, pp. 325–6).

At the beginning of the 1990s, a continuing economic and social crisis developed in the Russian Federation. With relatively minor changes in intensity, this crisis characterized Russia's socio-economic situation between 1992 and August 1998. The so-called financial crisis of August 1998 further darkened Russia's prospects of improving social and economic welfare. The rouble was devalued, stocks fell rapidly, inflation rose, ordinary people lost their savings and many banks collapsed, unemployment rose, and often the state and the companies paid wages and salaries several months late.

The continuous economic and financial crisis, even sharpening after August 1998, has steadily worsened the situation of the Russian media market. By and large, it reflected the 'social economic and political developments taking place in Russian society as a whole' (Fossato 1997). Among the most important problems of the Russian media sector at the end of the 1990s were the following (Belin 2002, pp. 139–41; Fossato and Kachkaeva 1998; Vartanova 2001, pp. 30–1):

- newspaper circulation rates have continued to decline since 1992;
- production and distribution costs have continuously risen;
- after August 1998, the advertising market which had begun to flourish in the mid-1990s came under serious strain.

During the 1990s, with only very few exceptions, no newspaper or magazine, no television network or radio station yielded a profit (Fossato and Kachkaeva 1997). After August 1998 many newspapers cut back on their reporting. Some even ceased publication (Goble 1998).

The picture drawn so far has concentrated on the facts that (i) by and large, censorship on the part of the Russian state authorities ceased to exist; and that (ii) during the 1990s, the Russian media sector experienced a deep economic crisis. This picture, however, is incomplete. Up to now, we have not said much about the main forms of media property in the Russian Federation. However, particularly in Russia, the various forms of media property as well as the economic and political goals of the owners have to be taken into consideration.

Big business and the federal mass media market

The development of property relations in the Russian media has to be seen in the wider context of the privatization of state assets. The following developments concerning the course of Russia's privatization efforts are important in our context.

The first signs of economic concentration were already apparent at the beginning of the 1990s. From the mid-1990s the formation of a handful of big economic conglomerates, the so-called Financial-Industrial Groups (FIGs), gathered speed. In most cases, a huge commercial bank was located at the core of such a FIG. As a rule, several huge companies from the industrial sector and in some cases a few companies from the trading sector were also part of a FIG. The overwhelming majority of these industrial companies were operating in strategically important and/or profitable sectors of the Russian economy, such as in the energy or mining sector (Johnson 2000, ch. 6; Pappe 1998; Schröder 1999; Utkin and Eskindarov 1998). This concentration of financial and industrial capital reached a first peak with the second phase of privatization in the mid-1990s. Above all, it was the rigged 'loans-for-shares' auctions that accelerated the process.

At the beginning of the 1990s, the first two emerging economic conglomerates began to build up media empires. In 1995, other FIGs followed. During Boris Yeltsin's tenure, the media market was divided up between various Russian big business interests.[2] There were very few central newspapers and magazines left which did not belong to a larger commercial structure. One national television network (*RTR*) was, and continues to be, fully state-owned; the second one, though partly state-owned, seemed to be under the control of Boris Berezovsky, a well-known political entrepreneur. In addition, there were four privately owned television networks of more or less national significance, in which FIGs had shares.

During the 1990s, there was only one commercial structure which was almost exclusively engaged in media operations. The *MOST* group was built around the *MOST* bank but, unlike most FIGs, it included no important industrial companies. For the other conglomerates the media market seemed to be – in terms of amounts of investment – a less significant part of their economic activity. Likewise, starting around 1997, some of the conglomerates controlling media assets began to transform simple ownership of outlets into organized holding structures (Fossato and Kachkaeva 1998).

Although by and large the Russian media's independence from state control has not been reversed by restricting laws from the end of 1992 to the resignation of Boris Yeltsin as Russian president at the turn of the millennium, economic *and* editorial freedom remained very limited. Russian big business took advantage of the ongoing economic crisis. Cash-strapped media outlets were not in a position to refuse help from 'sponsors' of this kind, since the Russian economy could not support the overwhelming majority of print and electronic media (Belin 2001, p. 341).

Political capitalism

In every political system the mass media play an important political role. And the phenomenon of the owner of a mass media outlet (or another 'connected' actor) trying to influence societal and political processes using his/her newspaper, radio station or TV channel is not unique to Russia. The peculiarity of the situation in the Russian Federation in the 1990s lies in the specific political and economic features that developed after the Russian state gained independence.[3] It is these circumstances that give the mass media such a marked influence on the Russian transition process.

Most importantly, a functional differentiation between the economic and political spheres did not take place. Business and political leadership during the Yeltsin era was closely intertwined. Strictly speaking, the interdependence and collaboration of businessmen and politicians makes it almost impossible to use the terms 'economic actor' or 'political actor', respectively. A second feature is that while the Russian Federation has a constitution which meets the formal criteria of a democracy, political decisions were often reached behind closed doors through informal bargaining and executed by presidential decree rather than parliamentary legislation. In particular, the privatization process was almost exclusively regulated by Yeltsin's presidential decrees (Remington, Smith, and Haspel 1998, p. 314).

The political and economic system that had come into existence in Russia in the 1990s can best be described as 'political capitalism'. Max Weber (1980) contrasted modern 'rational market-oriented capitalism' with 'politically oriented capitalism'. The former system is based on private ownership of the means of production. Economic actors accumulate their profits which they earn in a competitive market environment. Under political capitalism, on the contrary, gains are made exploiting all sorts of political domination and the resulting distortion of the rules of the market, respectively.

Although in his analysis of political capitalism Weber concentrated mainly on ancient, Oriental and Far Eastern societies, his findings can be fruitfully applied to the transition process in Eastern Europe. Two structural elements of Weber's concept of political capitalism are widely seen as particularly applicable to postcommunist transition processes: (i) rent seeking, and (ii) the conversion of political into economic power and wealth.

According to Anders Åslund (1996, p. 13) rent-seeking 'refers to any activity designed to exploit a monopoly position or to gain access to government subsidies, as opposed to profit-seeking in a market with competitive firms'. The economic reform process in Eastern Europe created and often sustained a wide range of market distortions that were eagerly exploited by economically and politically powerful actors. These distortions and subsequent rent-seeking behaviour were exceptionally extensive in Russia. In addition, economic privileges like tax exemptions, exclusive licences and direct and indirect subsidies were and are abundantly granted on the basis of political and personal connections, thereby ignoring the public good (Åslund and Dmitriev 1999, p. 109).

As a consequence, many economic subjects evolving and expanding in Russia during the 1990s had a vital interest in preserving the status quo. They profited from a partly reformed economy, market distortions, highly selective privileges and the resulting rent-seeking opportunities. As we shall see, it was mainly actors from this group that – in parallel to swiftly acquiring economic, and thus political, strength – invested heavily in the Russian media market.

The second structural element of political capitalism is the conversion of political into economic power and wealth. It is visible in all transition countries in Eastern Europe and the former Soviet Union. In an early study, Jadwiga Staniszkis (1991) came to the conclusion that the distinctive feature of the Polish postcommunist transition, at least in its early years, was the direct conversion of political into economic power and wealth, which resulted in novel combinations of political power and capital. Although there is a lively debate whether the conversion of political capital into individual private wealth on a massive scale indeed took place in all countries undergoing economic transition after the fall of the Soviet Union, few doubt that the phenomenon was clearly observable in Russia (Eyal, Szelényi, and Townsley 1998).

To fruitfully apply the 'conversion' feature of political capitalism to the Russian transition during the 1990s, one has to go one step further. In Yeltsin's Russia, the conversion was circular: there was not only the conversion of political into economic power, but the conversion of economic into political power as well. An analysis of Russian politics under Yeltsin reveals an exceptional interdependence and collaboration of economic and political actors.

> In the system of 'political capitalism', the position of entrepreneurs depends on their links to the authorities, and that of bureaucrats on their ability to defend and promote their friends in business. In other words, the struggle for power is perceived as one of the forms of competition. (Kagarlitsky 2002)

As we have seen, where 'political capitalism' dominates, entrepreneurs and members of the political elites enjoy a whole range of opportunities to enrich themselves in financial terms (by for instance rent seeking, arbitrage, asset stripping, and exclusive licences) and/or strengthen their position in the hierarchy of power. They profit from this societal configuration and are not really interested in further economic reform or a comprehensive democratization that would slowly but steadily end this distorted system of economic and political competition.

The post-1989 transition process was characterized by the necessity to transform the fundamental institutions and rules governing as well the political as the economic system. If 'the state' is too weak to define, implement and guard the new institutional environment reasonably autonomously, rules and institutions become objects in non-transparent bargaining processes with low democratic accountability. The consequences, then, are twofold: (i) the state runs the risk of being privatized, in other words, becoming the spoil of influential particular interests; and (ii) strategic actors tend to bend or even annul the mechanisms of the market to further their interests (Christophe 1998, p. 210). This is exactly what happened in Russia in the mid-1990s.

Privatization of the Russian state

One of the most important consequences of 'political capitalism' is that it suppresses the emergence and establishment of alternative societal actors, such as political parties, trade unions, independent mass media and NGOs. As Melanie Tatur has put it, political capitalism

> relativized the newly defined property rights because the exclusive access to markets or to financial resources abrogated the validity of formal property assets. The dynamic of political capitalism as such did found neither a pluralization of social collective actors nor the constitution of new regulating and integrating rules and norms. Instead, it led to the segmenting and anarchizing decomposition of the administrative structures of power. (Tatur 1995, p. 99)

Throughout Eastern Europe, and especially visible in Russia during the Yeltsin presidency, it was the 'earliest and biggest winners in the overall reform process' (Hellman 1998, p. 204) that impeded further economic reform or comprehensive democratization and sought to preserve a distorted economic and political order serving their own narrow interests. Among these 'winners', the most important were:

- banks,
- state managers,
- financial-industrial conglomerates, and
- new entrepreneurs-cum-mafiosi. (Hellman 1998, pp. 232–3)

Not accidentally, the overwhelming majority of entrepreneurs owning mass media outlets in Russia during the 1990s belonged to this group of winners. Joel Hellman's general conclusion in his analysis of the East European transition is especially apt in the case of Russia:

> These net winners did not oppose the initiation of the reform process, nor have they sought a full-scale reversal of reform. Instead, they have frequently attempted to block specific advances in the reform process that threaten to eliminate the special advantages and market distortion upon which their own early reform gains were based. (Hellman 1998, p. 204)

During the Yeltsin presidency, these actors tried to gain and/or preserve a veto position in the Russian political system. For most of the time, their actions did not formally violate the constitution. But they undermined the constitutionally defined rules and norms concerning the political decision-making process. Therefore, they pursued a strategy that mainly concentrated on two elements:

- the 'privatization of the Russian state', and
- massive investment in the Russian mass media market, thereby using outlets as a political resource.

For Michael McFaul, it was big business that had privatized the Russian state, or at least many federal and regional political institutions:

> In a sense, the state has been privatized by this *nouveau riche* and thereby operates in the interests of its new owners rather than society writ large. These small, well-organized, and powerful business groups have crowded out other claimants to the state, particularly with regard to the national executive branch. Equally important, the Russian state enjoys little autonomy from these interest groups. (McFaul 1998a, pp. 192–3)

This 'privatization of the Russian state' in the Yeltsin era therefore yields important consequences for the political process in Russia: 'Rather than representing the sum of interests in society or acting as an autonomous agent, the Russian state functions to defend the interests of a small capitalist class' (McFaul 1998b, p. 198). The consequences are all too obvious:

> Russian banks have grown dependent on the state for inside information, state assets, and money; the intimate relationship between the state and the companies exporting raw materials sustains rent-seeking, not profit-seeking, behavior; the extent of state transfer to

these economic entities, coupled with continued high levels of state ownership in production enterprises, raises serious questions about how 'private' Russia's private sector really is. (McFaul 1998a, p. 318)

It is these specific circumstances that make ownership or control of mass media highly important to a set of actors, conventionally referred to as 'oligarchs'. Whereas formal political institutions were of minor importance in the Yeltsin period, large politicized media holding companies played the role of 'surrogate parties'. The main functions of mass media outlets in these times were:

- to provide informational support;
- to establish communication contacts with voters;
- to mobilize resources; and
- to lobby political decision-makers. (Zasursky 1999, p. 133)

In the context of the Russian Federation during the 1990s, the meaning of the mass media as a political resource is twofold. Media campaigns for the most part were addressed to political decision-makers and/or to rivals in the economic or political sphere. Addressing public opinion in this context mostly was of minor importance, since elections – with the exception of the 1996 national presidential elections[4] – had little impact on public life.

Russian mass media outlets as a political resource

This financial dependence on banking and industrial groups led to biased coverage in many Russian media outlets. Moreover, media investments by financial circles were aimed essentially at securing important financial and political dividends outside media markets. Profits are certainly desirable, but not immediately expected; control over powerful outlets is more important as a means of gaining political influence.[5] To name only the most significant examples of business interests trying to acquire political influence, one can identify four events in which the Russian media have played a crucial role during the past ten years (Belin 2002; Dinello 1998; Zasursky 1999):

(i) The first bankers' war in winter 1995/96

Two major feuding camps, led by economically important and powerful banks, clashed over the ongoing privatization process. In short, one camp consisting of *ONEKSIMbank* and its close partner *MFK Bank* was perceived by the opposing camp as a common enemy who had acquired too much power. Previously, a consortium led by *ONEKSIMbank* had won a considerable number of shares in strategically important industries, thereby invading 'alien' territory. The coalition of opponents of *ONEK-SIMbank* accused leading state officials of favouring *ONEKSIMbank*. First and foremost, this war was led by publishing compromising material (*kompromat*) via media outlets under the control of both groups of actors. Political and economic actors were targeted equally.

(ii) The re-election campaign of President Boris Yeltsin in spring and summer 1996

At the beginning of 1996, President Yeltsin's rating was extremely low. It seemed almost impossible for him to win the next presidential elections. Beginning in spring 1996, despite differing economic interests, leading Russian economic actors began to rally behind Yeltsin in order to prevent Communist candidate Gennadii Zyuganov from becoming President. Following this step, the overwhelming majority of media outlets covered political events and candidates in a strikingly biased manner. Most criticism of the President disappeared; meanwhile, news reporting kept up an incessant anti-Communist drumbeat. With very few exceptions, the media presented Yeltsin and Zyuganov to readers and viewers only as the Kremlin and its big business allies wanted them to be seen. It is widely accepted in Russia that media coverage thus played a crucial role in securing Yeltsin's re-election in July 1996.

(iii) The second bankers' war in summer 1997

The extensive coalition of business interests in support of Yeltsin lasted for about a year after Yeltsin's victory. Already in the summer of 1997, the bankers' second war erupted. The attacks became even more intensive than during the first bankers' war once *ONEKSIMbank* began to win at auctions of state enterprises. Repeating the patterns of the first bankers' war, an avalanche of accusations in several mass media outlets targeting *ONEKSIMbank's* 'empire' and its presumed political allies followed. Remarkably, the culmination point at which this new war was set free was the sale of 25 per cent of the shares of *Sviaz'invest*, Russia's leading telecommunications company. The auction was won by an international consortium (including *ONEKSIMbank*) offering a bid almost 60 per cent above the starting price. The losers in the auction – Boris Berezovsky and Vladimir Gusinsky, among others – had to realize that with this sale of state assets, the executive had changed the rules that had led to the notorious rigged auctions of 1995 and 1996. Henceforth, as government officials claimed, not bargaining behind closed doors and sweetheart deals should determine the winners in privatization auctions, but the highest bid.

(iv) The information war before the Duma election from summer 1999

Unlike the situation in 1996, business interests could not agree on a common party or candidate in the face of the upcoming parliamentary and presidential elections, scheduled for December 1999 and June 2000, respectively. Because the parliamentary elections were widely seen as the primaries to a great degree determining who would be Boris Yeltsin's heir as Russian president, from the summer of 1999 two camps of business interests waged an unprecedented open battle. Each of these camps controlled a television network of national significance – the media resource of greatest importance[6] – and a number of printed media outlets. Again, media coverage followed the patterns described with regard to the two bankers' wars. But with one exception: the structure of the business alliances had changed.

By investing in the media market, Russian business interests in the 1990s aimed to exert influence in order to facilitate short-term and long-term financial gain. But media investment, particularly emerging organized holding structures, was also intended to secure political goals.

Shortcomings in Russian media law

Besides the peculiarities of the Russian political system in the Yeltsin era, shortcomings in Russian media legislation and law enforcement further impeded the democratic development of the mass media. One can find a whole range of contradictions as well as a number of issues to which the law provides no solution at all. This situation gives the executive as well as other actors a great deal of room to manoeuvre. Above all, the great majority of problems relevant to the Russian media were governed not by federal law, but by presidential or governmental decrees. Three examples may serve to illustrate the resulting problems.

The first Russian law 'On the mass media' was passed by the Russian Supreme Soviet already in December 1991. There is a widespread consensus that this law marked a milestone in the transformation towards an independent mass media. Although this judgement cannot fundamentally be contested, the problem lies above all in the fact that many issues and processes – first of all relating to the broadcast media – are not regulated by this law. This holds true despite the many revisions that the law has undergone. The media law uses the term 'founder' of a mass media outlet. This results in opacity and legal ambiguity. According to the law, the 'founder' is the subject registering an outlet with the authorities. The 'founder' can do this irrespective of ownership rights. The term 'owner' is not included in the law. On the one hand, this allows property relations to be obscured, and on the other it encourages ownership disputes.

Unlike the print media, electronic media need not only register with the authorities, but must also possess a broadcasting licence. The procedure by which broadcasting licences are granted is not governed by federal law, but by decree. A whole range of presidential decrees and governmental regulations contain clauses concerning licensing. In the course of time, a variety of – sometimes even competing – executive committees became involved when a broadcasting licence was to be awarded. During the Yeltsin presidency, there was no transparent procedure for granting licences. In the course of the 1990s, 'in the absence of a specific act on broadcasting licensing, the field [was] regulated by several general acts as well as by governmental regulations and presidential decrees' (Sklyarova 2003, p. 2).[7] For example, *MOST*'s TV channel *NTV* was awarded a federal licence shortly after Yeltsin's re-election in 1996 by presidential decree – apparently a reward for supportive coverage during the election campaign by mass media outlets belonging to the *MOST* group.

The third point is the procedure by which licences can be revoked. Among the cases in which a broadcasting licence may be withdrawn, the Russian law 'On the mass media' lists the following reason: 'if licence terms have been repeatedly broken or the rules for disseminating radio and TV programmes provided for by the present law have been violated, in connection with which warnings have been made in written form' ('On the mass media' 1992, Art. 32).[8] Furthermore, as Sklyarova points out, 'One of the main requirements is the broadcaster's strict "adherence to all applicable law"' (2003, p. 8). These obscure requirements, together with the precept that '[t]he licence shall be cancelled by decision of the body that has granted it or by the Federal Television and Radio Broadcasting Commission' ('On the mass media' 1992, Art. 32) and not by decision of a court, 'places broad powers in the hands of the [authorities] to decide the fate of media outlets through administrative measures' (Dunlap 2001, p. 11). In sum, as Jens Deppe puts it, 'The operation of broadcasting media in the Russian Federation is completely dependent on the control of the executive branch, although – or precisely because – appropriate federal legislation [during Yeltsin's presidency was] lacking' (Deppe 2000, ch. 4).[9]

One striking example illustrating the lack of legal transparency, the priority that is given to political considerations and political discretion was media minister Mikhail Lesin's action against the TV channel *TV Tsentr* in the course of the 1999 parliamentary election campaign. The media ministry issued two warnings – the first one for a violation of electoral regulations by a *TV Tsentr* programme, the second one because the company changed its address without formally notifying the licencing authority (Sklyarova 2003, p. 8). Referring to altered licencing procedures, Lesin announced that *TV Tsentr*'s licence would not automatically be renewed after expiring several months later. Although the channel secured a court decision declaring the media ministry's warnings void, Lesin insisted on holding a licence tender. Ultimately, *TV Tsentr* 'retained its licence only after back-room negotiations between Lesin and Luzhkov' (Belin 2002, p. 149).[10] If the media ministry's goal was to demonstrate that the position of each media company was very vulnerable, it entirely succeeded.

Russia under Putin – bringing 'the state' back in?

Summing up the two terms of the Putin presidency, it becomes apparent that many things have changed, but one structural fact has remained the same: Although quite a few media outlets have become profitable since the turn of the millennium, many remain dependent on outside sponsors.

Numerous 'oligarchs' of the Yeltsin era have lost their positions of economic and political power. Three of the most prominent businessmen with considerable media assets which the Putin regime seemed to view as politically dangerous were 'liquidated': Mikhail Khodorkovsky's business empire was confiscated and he is currently serving an eight-year prison term; Vladimir Gusinsky and Boris Berezovsky were forced into exile after losing most of their media assets. It is striking that the Putin regime tried to move against these 'oligarchs' in a manner which sought to create the impression that an unbiased prosecutor and an independent judiciary in a *Rechtsstaat* review cases of ordinary civil economic disputes, tax evasion or fraud. But that the regime's efforts failed did not save those fallen from grace.

The downfall of these well-known businessmen opened the way to other actors. Among others, 'new oligarchs', mostly loyal to the regime, took their place, with many of them controlling and subsidizing mass media outlets. Furthermore, enterprises under the (direct or indirect) control of the state stepped in – creating the impression that they act on behalf of the authorities. The most notable actor seems to be *Gazprom*. The energy giant's media assets have increased considerably since 2000, including Gusinsky's former media holding company *Media-MOST* and the once respected daily paper *Izvestiia*. At the beginning of April 2006 reports surfaced that *Gazprom* was about to make two major new acquisitions: the *Kommersant* publishing house that for many years had been controlled by Berezovsky and which he had sold to his longstanding business partner Badri Patarkatsishvili less than two months earlier; and *Komsomol'skaia pravda*, the profitable daily paper with the biggest readership that was owned by the holding company *Prof-Media*, the media arm of the *Interros* conglomerate (Trapeznikov, Dolgosheeva and Voronina 2006; Parsons 2006).

In January 2007 Gazprom announced it was stepping back from the planned purchase of *Komsomol'skaia pravda*. *Prof-Media* also announced that it had sold a 60 per cent share of *Komsomol'skaia pravda* to the mysterious *ESN* group.[11] Possibly, the politically relevant daily paper may in the future, directly or indirectly, end up in *Gazprom*'s coffers, since *ESN* head Grigorii Berezkin reportedly often has acted as a *Gazprom* proxy (Elder 2007, p. 1). In September 2006 the *Kommersant* publishing house was sold to Alisher Usmanov, co-owner of the metals conglomerate *Metalloinvest* and president of *Gazprominvestkholding*, a subsidiary of *Gazprom*. Many suspect that due to his long-standing and close relations with the state-controlled gas monopoly, Usmanov's role was that of a *Gazprom* proxy, too. But this is far from certain – not at least since the publishing house is a profit-making enterprise (Gromov, Dediukhina and Silaev 2006).

Another example is *REN TV*. The development of *REN TV* ownership is interesting because the network started as an entertainment-oriented channel and slowly acquired a higher political profile during the first years of the new millennium. During the 1990s, this network had a low political profile and was not involved in the notorious 'media wars'. The majority of its shares were owned by *LUKoil*. In late 2000, *LUKoil* sold its *REN TV* stake to *EES* (Unified Energy Systems). In summer 2005, *EES* sold its 70 per cent stake to the steel giant *SeverStal'* and the channel's founders sold their remaining 30 per cent stake to the German *RTL Group* (RFE/RL Newsline, 8 July 2005). Two months later, *SeverStal'* sold half of its shares to *Surgutneftegaz* (ibid., 6 September 2005) – an oil company reportedly connected to the *siloviki*. Previously, neither *SeverStal'* nor *Surgutneftegaz* was known to operate in the media business.

A further reshuffle of ownership occurred in December 2006. Both *SeverStal'* and *Surgutneftegaz* sold the majority of their shares to a subsidiary of the bank *Rossiia*, now controlling the majority (52.5 per cent) of the shares of the channel (Dolgosheeva and Krampets 2007). Whether this change in ownership control took place with an eye to the approaching parliamentary and presidential elections and the potential use of *REN TV* as a political resource remains to be seen. In any case, it is striking that the newly appointed deputy director of *REN TV*'s information programmes, Aleksei Abakumov, previously worked for state-owned *VGTRK* and that the bank *Rossiia* appears to be very close to President Putin. Press reports indicate that many of the bank's former managers and co-owners received top government posts and jobs in state-controlled companies after President Putin assumed office (RIA Novosti, 13 April 2007; 'Udachnyi kooperativ' 2007).

A third example is the history of *TV-6*. A few months after *LUKoil*'s pension fund had initiated the closure of the channel by court decision, *TVS* took over *TV-6*'s frequency in June 2002. *TVS* was to be financed by the *Media-Sotsium* consortium. This group consisted of a whole range of representatives of big business, among them Anatolii Chubais, Oleg Deripaska, Roman Abramovich and others. *TVS*'s life span was in the end no more than a year. Soon, the financial problems of the channel became so acute and the disagreement between the shareholders so deep that Chubais sold his stake, leaving Deripaska as the dominant shareholder. In June 2003, the Media Ministry used *TVS*'s financial problems to justify cutting off transmissions, thereby ignoring the law which allows the closure only by the order of a court. Within days, *TVS* was replaced by a state-run sports channel (Belin 2003).

In sum, in Putin's Russia, there are no electronic media outlets with nationwide significance and politically relevant content that are not influenced – either directly or indirectly – by state agents. *Pervyi Kanal* and *Rossiia*, the TV channels with the largest audience share, are under firm state control. The other nationwide channels with relevant political content are controlled by people and companies loyal to and/or dependent on the government. The main reason for this development seems to be that in contrast to low-circulation print media, these outlets represent an overwhelming powerful political resource – not only during election campaigns. However, recent ownership changes at small high-brow newspapers like *Kommersant* or *Nezavisimaia gazeta* may indicate a growing desire on the part of the members of the political elite on the eve of the upcoming election season to dispose of a political resource pointing to a narrow circle, too.

In parallel to these changes in the ownership of some outlets during the Putin presidency, the state strengthened its administrative grip on the mass media. The first sign was the approval of an 'Information Security Doctrine of the Russian Federation' by the Security Council in September 2000 ('Doktrina' 2000), which was followed by normative acts restricting the operation of the mass media. The law 'On Counter-Extremism', for example, which came into force in July 2002, prohibits the 'dissemination of extremist materials via the mass media and the conduct of extremist activities by the mass media' ('On Counter-Extremism' 2002, Article 11). Articles 4 and 16 of the law 'On the mass media' were altered accordingly ('O vnesenii' 2002). From now on, 'the activity of a mass media outlet can be terminated' in accordance with the provisions of the law 'On Counter-Extremism'. The restrictions were justified by reference to the 'war on terror', meaning first of all the fight against 'Chechen terrorists'. An additional, potentially repressive legislative step can be seen in the revision of the law 'On Counter-Extremism' in July 2006 ('O vnesenii' 2006), which broadens the definition of 'extremism' even further. Consequences for the work of the mass media may result above all from the new clause that 'public slander directed toward individuals fulfilling the state duties of the Russian Federation or state duties of a subject of the Russian Federation' is considered 'extremist activity', too.[12]

The danger that is inherent in these (and other) legislative acts is their vagueness. In that way the authorities dispose of a pretext that can be used on political grounds. In any case official warnings were issued against media outlets citing violation of the law 'On Counter-Extremism', for example against *Nezavisimaia gazeta* for printing an interview with then Chechen rebel leader Aslan Maskhadov. In April 2007, the popular website *gazeta.ru* received an official warning for publishing an interview with Eduard Limonov, the leader of National Bolshevik Party – a party banned by court order a few months earlier (Yasmann 2007).

Such warnings – citing violations of the law 'On Counter-Extremism' or of any other law – can have serious consequences as repeated warnings lead to the closure of the media outlet in question. As for the broadcast media, for example, the authorized licencing body issued more than eighty warnings in 2004–5 alone (Kachkaeva, Kiriya, and Libergal 2006, p. 22). But there are alternative administrative measures in addition: media outlets that criticize the authorities frequently experience visits by the tax police, business inspectors and the like. The consequences of the increasing legislative and administrative pressure on the mass media need not necessarily to be the noisy closure or bankrupting of inconvenient outlets. Much more likely is a further growing tendency towards self-censorship.

With regard to the war in Chechnya, the Russian authorities learned the lesson of the first war (1994–96) very well. From the start of the second campaign, one of their main aims was to win the 'information war'. In sum, one has to acknowledge that state and military officials succeeded in this respect. Since the Chechen Republic was sealed off to a great degree by the state authorities, reporting from the war zone without 'guidance' by the Russian military became almost impossible. Simultaneously, Chechen fighters and civilians were effectively cut off from media access, thereby losing the opportunity to set forth their views (Belin 2004, pp. 133–6).

The last point concerns matters of personnel. In 2001, *Mediasoiuz*, a new union for journalists, was set up with the apparent backing of the authorities. The main aim of the new organization was attempting to split the established Union of Journalists of Russia (*Soiuz zhurnalistov Rossii*) and reduce its influence. This case is exceptional only in that an entirely new organization in the media sphere was founded. As Simons has pointed out, at least since mid-2002 the authorities have pursued the strategy 'of placing "reliable" people into key areas of media organizations' (2005, p. 2). As examples one might cite personnel changes in senior positions at *VGTRK*, *ORT* and *ITAR-TASS*.

Notwithstanding these trends during the Putin presidency, one has to admit that on issues where power is not entirely at stake, the Russian mass media can and sometimes do offer a wide range of viewpoints. This applies above all to print media outlets. However, the approaching election season would probably show whether the administrative (and economic) grip on the mass media was likely to intensify. Media monitoring on the eve of past parliamentary and presidential elections in Russia has demonstrated considerable bias (OSCE 1999, 2000, 2004a, and 2004b). In addition, 'virtual' political parties (and candidates) in post-Soviet Russia have repeatedly been created 'from above' shortly before the elections by (a section of) the political elite, and have subsequently been successful at the ballot box. For this Sarah Oates has coined the term 'broadcast party' (and 'broadcast candidate'). A 'broadcast party' differs from other newly created parties in that it is 'a political movement that relies heavily on television for its creation and electoral success – albeit not for its survival' (Oates 2003, p. 29). The Putin era serves as a prime example for this phenomenon. If one takes into account another finding – 'the curious duality between knowledge of bias, yet trust in state television' (Oates 2006b, p. 165) among ordinary Russians – the stunningly strong position of those 'in power' cannot be fundamentally contested.

Since the mass media and particularly television evidently played a major role in influencing electoral choice (Oates 2006a; White, Oates, and McAllister 2005) and considering that the political elite seems to believe in the usefulness of 'media engineering', there is little doubt that in the approaching election season the mass media will play a key role as a political resource. What role exactly is impossible to predict. A great deal depends – if Putin actually retires – on whether the overwhelming majority of the political and economic elites can unite behind a common presidential nominee or whether competitive struggles between elite factions are to be staged in public.

Conclusion

The peculiarities of the Russian polity and of the political and economic processes that took place during Russia's transition in the course of the 1990s had far-reaching effects on the operation of the mass media.

Since 1992, the overwhelming majority of the Russian mass media have become increasingly dependent on outside sponsors. The biggest banking and industrial groups 'supported' a significant number of them. Media investments by financial and industrial circles in Russia were aimed essentially at securing important economic and political dividends outside the media market. Entrepreneurs often made use of 'their' media as a political resource. This regularly led to biased coverage.

Crucial for the understanding of these processes are two factors:

(i) The political and economic system that had evolved in Russia by the 1990s could best be described as 'political capitalism'. This notion underlines not only that during the Soviet and Russian transformation political power was converted into economic power and wealth, and vice versa; it also points to the phenomenon of the interdependence and collaboration of leading economic and political actors in Russia. They had many opportunities to enrich themselves, and many of them were not really interested in further economic reforms and comprehensive democratization in Russia, yet profited from the privatization of the state.

(ii) Russian media law was seriously flawed. It was not difficult to find a range of contradictions and omissions as well as a number of problems to which the law provides no solution at all. This situation was no coincidence. It gave the political authorities as well as other actors extensive opportunities to exert pressure on the mass media. In this context, most Russian media outlets in the 1990s became more of an asset in political and economic warfare than a form of communication that conformed to the democratic precepts of the 'fourth estate'.

In a structural sense, the Putin presidency is mainly marked by continuities. Above all, many actors continue to view the mass media as a political resource. The conversion of political into economic power and vice versa still plays an important role. But since the interaction between politics and economics under Putin is characterized so far more by a 'bureaucratization of the economy': it is no longer big business but state actors for whom control of media outlets is of prior importance. With regard to media legislation, the basic deficiencies of Russian media law remain uncorrected and new legislative acts with vaguely defined terms were passed. This state of affairs makes media outlets vulnerable and gives the executive as well as other actors extensive room to manoeuvre. There are lively discussions about the creation of a public radio and television in Russia, but these ideas are limited to academic circles and certain NGOs. One should not expect the realization of such a project in the near future. In Russia, most mass media outlets with a political profile during the 1990s became and continue to be more an asset in political and economic warfare than an example of the normative democratic concepts of the 'fourth estate'.

Notes

1. For Wilson (2005, p. 43) the 'golden age' dates between around 1989 and 1996.
2. Fossato and Kachkaeva (1997–2000), for instance, provide a good synopsis of the big players on the Russian media market at the end of the 1990s in their series 'Russian Media Empires' I–VI.
3. This is not to say that these phenomena were unknown during the Soviet era. The crucial point here is that they acquired a specific significance after the breakdown of the Soviet Union.
4. The parliamentary and presidential elections in December 1999 and March 2000, respectively, can be seen as the turning point marking the beginning of a new paradigm (see below).
5. This holds true not only for national media outlets, but for regional media as well (Fossato 1997).
6. Basing themselves on a nationally representative survey, Stephen White and Sarah Oates came to the conclusion that television is 'the single most important source of political information and the most important source of information when voters make their choices' (White and Oates 2003, p. 36).
7. It was only at the end of June 1999, when by governmental regulation 'the licensing procedure was modified by establishing the compulsory

competition procedure for the award of broadcasting licences in cities with a population of more than 200,000 inhabitants' (Regulation of the Government 1999; Sklyarova 2003, p. 5).

8. Although in the last fifteen years the law experienced almost twenty modifications, it was not fundamentally revised. Article 32 remained unchanged.

9. For a detailed analysis of the regulations governing the issuance and revocation of licences, the governing bodies and – due to unclear and contradicting legislation – the impressive discretionary powers of executive authorities, see Grakhov and P'iankov 2006.

10. It should be noted that the media ministry issued two warnings to *ORT*, too, and that *ORT* easily won the resulting tender. Most analysts believe that the media ministry moved against *ORT* to create the impression of its own impartiality, i.e. not singling out a media company in opposition to the current regime.

11. It is striking that *Prof-Media* apparently tries to get rid of its shares in media outlets with a political profile whilst expanding its holdings in more entertainment-oriented television or internet media (Dolgosheeva 2006).

12. Admittedly, the clause is relativized by the provision that the fact of slander is to be confirmed by the decision of a court. Whether this hurdle provides sufficient protection for the mass media in political reality remains to be seen.

References

Åslund, Anders. 1996. 'Reform vs "Rent-Seeking" in Russia's Economic Transformation', *Transition* 2(2): 12–16.

Åslund, Anders, and Mikhail, Dmitriev. 1999. 'Economic Reform versus Rent Seeking', in Åslund and Martha Brill Olcott (eds), *Russia After Communism*, Washington, DC: Carnegie Endowment for International Peace, pp. 91–130.

Belin, Laura. 2001. 'Political Bias and Self-Censorship in the Russian Media', in Archie Brown (ed.), *Contemporary Russian Politics: A Reader*, Oxford: Oxford University Press, pp. 323–42.

Belin, Laura. 2002. 'The Russian Media in the 1990s', *Journal of Communist Studies and Transition Politics* 18(1): 139–60.

Belin, Laura. 2003. 'TVS: Another Failed Experiment in Private Television', *RFE/RL Report* 3(25), 26 June (www.rferl.org/reports/rpw/2003/06/25-260603.asp, accessed 26 June 2003).

Belin, Laura. 2004. 'Politics and the Mass Media under Putin', in Ross, Cameron (ed.), *Russian Politics under Putin*, Manchester: Manchester University Press, pp. 133–52.

Christophe, Barbara. 1998. 'Von der Politisierung der Ökonomie zur Ökonomisierung der Politik: Staat, Markt und Außenpolitik in Rußland', *Zeitschrift für Internationale Beziehungen* 5(2): 201–40.

Deppe, Jens. 2000. *Über Pressefreiheit und Zensurverbot in der Rußländischen Föderation: Eine Untersuchung über die gesetzliche und tatsächliche Ausgestaltung der verfassungsrechtlichen Freiheitsgarantie*, Dissertation, University of Hamburg,

Seminarabteilung für Ostrechtsforschung (www.russianmedia.de/dissertation/index.htm, accessed 18 April 2002).

Dinello, Natalia. 1998. 'Banker's Wars in Russia: Trophies and Wounds', *Post-Soviet Prospects* 6(1) (www.csis.org/html/pspvi1.html, accessed 27 August 1999).

'Doktrina informatsionnoi bezopasnosti Rossiiskoi Federatsii'. 2000. *Rossiiskaia gazeta* 187, 28 September.

Dolgosheeva, Yekaterina. 2006. 'Slovo dlia investora', *Vedomosti* 247(1774), 29 December.

Dolgosheeva, Yekaterina, and Gleb, Krampets. 2007. 'Koval'chuk-TV: "Surgut-neftegaz" priznalsia v prodazhe "Ren TV" ', *Vedomosti* 66(1840), 13 April.

Dunlap, Ben. 2001. 'Media and the Law', *Russia Watch* 6: 11 (http://bcsia.ksg.harvard.edu/BCSIA_content/documents/RW6-01.pdf, accessed 28 January 2004).

Elder, Miriam. 2007. 'Gazprom, Yukos and a Mystery Company', *Moscow Times* 3618, 20 March, p. 1.

Eyal, Gil, Iván Szelényi and Eleanor Townsley. 1998. *Making Capitalism Without Capitalists: Class Formation and Elite Struggles in Post-Communist Europe*, London/New York: Verso.

Fossato, Floriana. 1997. 'Russia: Media, Money and Power – An Analysis', *RFE/RL Report*, 26 September (www.rferl.org/features/1997/09/F.RU.970926152044.asp, accessed 17 June 1999).

Fossato, Floriana. 2001. 'The Russian Media: From Popularity to Distrust', *Current History* 100(648): 343–8.

Fossato, Floriana, and Anna, Kachkaeva. 1997–2000. 'Russian Media Empires I–VI', *RFE/RL Reports* (accessible via www.rferl.org/specials/archive/2005.asp).

Fossato, Floriana, and Anna, Kachkaeva. 1998. 'Russia: Media Empires Continue to Change Shape and Influence Politics', *RFE/RL Report*, 19 May (www.rferl.org/features/1998/05/F.RU.980519131854.asp, accessed 17 June 1999).

Goble, Paul. 1998. 'Russia: Analysis From Washington – The Economics Of Press Freedom', *RFE/RL Report*, 14 October (www.rferl.org.nca/features/1998/05.F.RU.981014124920.html, accessed 17 June 1999).

Grakhov, Nikolai, and Sergei, P'iankov. 2006. 'Deistvie litsenzii na teleradio-veshchanie: problemy i perspektivy pravovogo regulirovaniia', *Zakonodatel'stvo i praktika mass-media* 4 & 5 (www.medialaw.ru/publications/zip/140/1.htm and www.medialaw.ru/publications/zip/141/2, accessed 30 May 2006).

Gromov, Andrei, Anastasiia, Dediukhina, and Nikolai, Silaev. 2006. ' " – Tverdyi znak: Kakie by prichiny ni pobudili Alishera Usmanova kupit' "Kommersant" ", stavit' krest na unikal'nom rossiiskom mediaiavlenii rano', *Ekspert* 32(526), 4 September.

Hellman, Joel S. 1998. 'Winners Take All: The Politics of Partial Reform in Postcommunist Transitions', *World Politics* 50(2): 203–34.

Johnson, Juliet. 2000. *A Fistful of Rubles: The Rise and Fall of the Russian Banking System*, Ithaca, NY/London: Cornell University Press.

Kachkaeva, Anna, Ilya Kiriya, and Grigory Libergal. 2006. *Television in the Russian Federation: Organisational Structure, Programme Production and Audience. A Report prepared by Internews for the European Audiovisual Observatory, Strasbourg* (www.obs.coe.int/online_publication/reports/tv_russia_internews2006.pdf, accessed 1 June 2006).

Kagarlitsky, Boris. 2002. ' "Political Capitalism" and Corruption in Russia', *LINKS* 21 (www.dsp.org.au/links/back/issue21/Kagarlitsky.htm, accessed 30 May 2006).

McFaul, Michael. 1998a. 'Russia's Privatized State as an Impediment to Democratic Consolidation. Part I', *Security Dialogue* 29(2): 191–9.

McFaul, Michael. 1998b. 'Russia's Privatized State as an Impediment to Democratic Consolidation. Part II', *Security Dialogue* 29(3): 315–32.

Oates, Sarah. 2003. 'Television, Voters, and the Development of the "Broadcast Party" ', in Vicky L. Hesli and William M. Reisinger (eds), *The 1999–2000 Elections in Russia: Their Impact and Legacy*, Cambridge: Cambridge University Press, pp. 29–50.

Oates, Sarah. 2006a. *Television, Democracy and Elections in Russia*, Abingdon: Routledge.

Oates, Sarah. 2006b. 'Where's the Party? Television and Election Campaigns in Russia', in Katrin Voltmer (ed.), *Mass Media and Political Communication in New Democracies*, London: Routledge, pp. 152–67.

'On Counter-Extremism'. 2002. Federal'nyi Zakon Rossiiskoi Federatsii ot 25 iiulia 2002 g. No. 114-FZ 'O protivodeistvii ekstremistskoi deiatel'nosti', *Sobranie zakonodatel'stva Rossiiskoi Federatsii* 30, art. 3031.

'On the Mass Media'. 1992. Zakon Rossiiskoi Federatsii ot 27 dekabria 1991 g. No. 2124/1-1 'O sredstvakh massovoi informatsii', *Vedomosti S"ezda narodnykh deputatov Rossiiskoi Federatsii i Verkhovnogo Soveta Rossiiskoi Federatsii* 7, art. 300.

OSCE, Office for Democratic Institutions and Human Rights. 1999. *Russian Federation: Elections to the State Duma, 19 December 1999: Final Report.* Warsaw (www. osce.org/odihr/documents/reports/election_reports/ru/rus2-2.pdf, accessed 20 November 2002).

OSCE, Office for Democratic Institutions and Human Rights. 2000. *Russian Federation, Presidential Election 26 March 2000: Final Report.* Warsaw (www.osce. org/odihr/documents/reports/election_reports/ru/rus00-1-final.pdf, accessed 20 November 2002).

OSCE, ODIHR Election Observation Mission. 2004a. *Russian Federation Elections to the State Duma, 7 December 2003: OSCE/ODIHR Election Observation Mission Final Report.* Warsaw (www.osce.org/documents/odihr/2004/01/1947_en.pdf, accessed 1 February 2004).

OSCE, ODIHR Election Observation Mission. 2004b. *Russian Federation Presidential Election 14 March 2004: OSCE/ODIHR Election Observation Mission Final Report.* Warsaw (www.osce.org/documents/odihr/2004/06/3033_en.pdf, accessed 9 October 2004).

'O vnesenii'. 2002. Federal'nyi Zakon Rossiiskoi Federatsii ot 25 iiulia 2002 g. No. 112-FZ 'O vnesenii izmenenii i dopolnenii v zakonodatel'nye akty Rossiiskoi Federatsii v sviazi s priniatiem Federal'nogo Zakona "O protivodeistvii ekstremistskoi deiatel'nosti" ', *Sobranie zakonodatel'stva Rossiiskoi Federatsii* 30, art. 3029.

'O vnesenii'. 2006. Federal'nyi Zakon Rossiiskoi Federatsii ot 27 iiulia 2006 g. No. 148-FZ 'O vnesenii izmenenii v stati 1 i 15 Federal'nogo Zakona "O protivodeistvii ekstremistskoi deiatel'nosti" ', *Sobranie zakonodatel'stva Rossiiskoi Federatsii* 31, art. 3447.

Pappe, Iakov (ed.) 1998. *Finansovo-promyshlennye gruppy i konglomeraty v ekonomike i politike sovremennoi Rossii*, Moscow: Tsentr politicheskikh tekhnologii (www.nns.ru/analytdoc/fpg.html, accessed 27 August 1999).

Parsons, Robert. 2006. 'Russia: Gazprom's Expansion Plans Extend to Media', *RFE/RL Report*, 2 May (www.rferl.org/features/features_Article.aspx? m=05&y=2006&id=1714C4F9-3FD0-4E3E-A152-69A2651980E8, accessed 30 May 2006).

Pleines, Heiko. 1997. 'Entwicklungen im russischen Medienmarkt: Rundfunk und Presse zwischen staatlicher Kontrolle, wirtschaftlicher Krise und Konzentration', *Media Perspektiven* 7: 391–9.

Regulation of the Government of the Russian Federation No. 698. 1999. 'O provedenii konkursov na poluchenie prava na nazemnoe efirnoe teleradioveshchanie, a takzhe na razrabotku i osvoenie novogo radiochastotnogo kanala dlia tselei teleradioveshchaniia', *Sobranie zakonodatel'stva Rossiiskoi Federatsii* 27, art. 3382, 26 June.

Remington, Thomas F., Steven S. Smith, and Moshe Haspel. 1998. 'Decrees, Laws, and Inter-Branch Relations in the Russian Federation', *Post-Soviet Affairs* 14(4): 287–322.

RIA Novosti. 2007. 'Kremlin-Friendly Bank Takes Over Last Independent TV Channel', 13 April (http://en.rian.ru/business/20070413/63587625.html, accessed 14 April 2007).

Schröder, Hans-Henning. 1999. 'El'tsin and the Oligarchs: The Role of Financial Groups in Russian Politics between 1993 and July 1998', *Europe-Asia Studies* 51(6): 957–88.

Simons, Gregory. 2005. *Russian Crisis Management Communications and Media Management under Putin*. Uppsala: Institutionen för Östereuropastudier & författaren, Arbetsrapporter No. 85 (www.east.uu.se/publications/AR85GS.doc, accessed 25 March 2005).

Sklyarova, Yana. 2003. *The Russian System of Licensing of Television and Radio Broadcasting*, Strasbourg: European Audiovisual Observatory (www.obs.coe.int/online_publication/reports/ru_sklyarova.pdf.en, accessed 25 July 2005).

Staniszkis, Jadwiga. 1991. *The Dynamics of the Breakthrough in Eastern Europe: The Polish Experience*, Berkeley: University of California Press.

Tatur, Melanie. 1995. 'Interessen und Norm: Politischer Kapitalismus und die Transformation des Staates in Polen und Rußland', in Hellmut Wollmann, Helmut Wiesenthal and Frank Bönker (eds), *Transformation sozialistischer Gesellschaften: Am Ende des Anfangs*, Opladen: Westdeutscher Verlag, pp. 93–116.

Trapeznikov, Maksim, Ekaterina Dolgosheeva and Anfisa Voronina. 2006. ' "Kommersantu" nazvali tsenu: Badri Patarkatsishvili mozhet prodat' izdatel'skii dom', *Vedomosti* 58(1585), 4 April.

'Udachniy kooperativ'. 2007. *Novaya gazeta* 27, 16 April.

Utkin, E. A., and M. A. Eskindarov. 1998. *Finansovo-promyshlennye gruppy*, Moscow: EKMOS.

Vartanova, Elena. 2001. 'Media Structures: Changed and Unchanged', in Kaarle Nordenstreng, Elena Vartanova and Yassen, Zassoursky (eds), *Russian Media Challenge*, 2nd edn., Helsinki: Kikimora, pp. 21–72.

Weber, Max. 1980. *Wirtschaft und Gesellschaft: Grundriß der verstehenden Soziologie*, 5th rev. edn., Tübingen: J. C. B. Mohr (Paul Siebeck).

White, Stephen, and Sarah Oates. 2003. 'Politics and the Media in Postcommunist Russia', *Politics* 23(1): 31–7.

White, Stephen, Sarah Oates and Ian McAllister. 2005. 'Media Effects and Russian Elections, 1999–2000', *British Journal of Political Science* 35(2): 191–208.
Wilson, Andrew. 2005. *Virtual Politics: Faking Democracy in the Post-Soviet World*, New Haven/London: Yale University Press.
Yasmann, Victor. 2007. 'Pressure Mounting on Opposition, Media', *RFE/RL Russia Report*, 7(8), 24 April (www.rferl.org/featuresarticle/2007/04/8b75c144-21a1-4535-a4e5-0c1be66bf34c.html, accessed 25 April 2007).
Zasursky, Ivan. 1999. *Mass-media vtoroi respubliki*, Moscow: Izdatel'stvo Moskovskogo universiteta.

Part 3
Economy, Culture and Society

8
Russia's Asymmetric Capitalism in Comparative Perspective
David Lane

The disintegration of the state socialist system in Central and Eastern Europe after 1989 led the new leaders in these societies in alliance with those in the hegemonic capitalist world to create, on the ashes of state socialism, a social system having a capitalist market economy, a polyarchic polity and a pluralist civil society. These were the intentions of the political leaders thrust into power after 1989. What type of society has emerged is a matter of intellectual debate. In this chapter I shall consider only one aspect of the transformation: the type of capitalism that has developed in the postcommunist countries, and particularly Russia. Prior to the discussion of 'what type' of capitalism is the definition of capitalism itself. This is of significance because many commentators dispute whether capitalism has been introduced in some of the postcommunist countries.

Types of capitalism

Even before the 'varieties of capitalism' debate, which has evolved in the late 1990s, many have recognized different types of capitalism, and the ways modern capitalism evolved from other formations. Weber and Marx differentiated between booty capitalism, merchant capitalism, modern capitalism, monopoly capitalism, state capitalism, and 'pariah' capitalism, pursued by marginal trading groups such as Jews or Parsees in non-capitalist formations (Gerth and Mills 1948, pp. 66–7). The major distinction for Weber was between 'political capitalism' and modern capitalism. In the former, opportunities for profit are derived from 'the exploitation of warfare, conquest and the prerogative of political administration' (ibid., p. 66); profits are made from various forms of political domination. This is what many contemporary untheorized commentaries on 'mafia capitalism' and bureaucratic domination have in mind when they consider the post-socialist countries.

Weber defined modern capitalism as 'the pursuit of profit and forever renewed profit, by means of continuous, rational, capitalistic enterprise' (Weber 1970, p. 17). Capitalism is predicated on a market, formally free labour and a psychological predisposition to adopt rational economic conduct. By rational economic conduct he meant the making of profit and, for the labourer, the maximization of income. The 'ethos of the capitalist economic system, the spirit of capitalism' entails the avoidance of spontaneous spending for enjoyment and the continual reinvestment of profits for accumulation of capital. Similarly, Marx emphasized the role of accumulation. For Marx, the capitalist mode of production involved the continual growth of the forces of production: this was ensured by the extraction of surplus value (profit) through market competition of autonomous productive units (capitals).[1] Competition between companies (capitals) for profit leads to antagonistic relationships between owners of the means of production and sellers of labour (class conflict).

For both Weber and Marx, the economic system and economic institutions were the critical variables, but capitalism and the capitalist mode of production are not limited to economic institutions. Analysis has to understand the ways the economy is embedded in political and social institutions which provide leadership, scientific innovation, social cohesion and/or forms of division and conflict. Important components promoting cohesion in society are the state, class and ideology. A sociological interpretation would consider the integrative mechanisms in society, the institutions which maintain the cohesion of the system: a value system, a dominant bourgeois class, and associations not only promoting social, political and economic coherence but also sustaining a dynamic of development.

I would therefore propose to define modern really existing capitalism as: a system of production taking place for global market exchange, utilizing money as a medium which determines differentials of income, levels of investment and the distribution of goods and services; productive assets are privately (collectively or individually) owned, and profit leading to accumulation is a major motive of economic life. The state, which is embedded in a more or less pluralistic society, establishes an effective system of law which secures private property and rights of owners over the proceeds of production. A dominant legitimating ideology of polyarchy, which entails competition between parties and groups for influence over the legislature and executive arm of state government and a sphere of autonomy (including the economy) between the individual (or family) and the state. Individual states are located in a global market which itself exerts autonomous pressures on and limits the power of states.

Not all 'actually existing' capitalist countries share these features to the same extent or in the same ways, and this variation forms the basis of the varieties of capitalism approach. Marx is rarely recognized as a forerunner of theories of 'divergent capitalisms', but when comparing German capitalism to British capitalism, he pointed to the 'incompleteness' of capitalist development and the 'passive survival of antiquated modes of production' in the former country (Marx 1956, p. 9).[2] Also he noted the ways in which the needs of social solidarity modified the interests of capital and led to the growth of socialistic elements within British capitalism.[3] In contemporary societies there are many different categorizations of countries into types of capitalism depending on the criteria adopted by the writer (Coates 1999, pp. 643–60).[4]

Peter Hall and David Soskice are the major contributors to this field. They emphasize the role of institutions in influencing behaviour. Institutions, they claim, act as socializing mechanisms, confer power on actors, and provide a 'matrix of sanctions and incentives' (Hall and Soskice 2001, p. 5). The work of Hall and Soskice takes as a defining factor the ways in which the activities of firms are coordinated. They consider two ideal types of coordination of modern capitalism: liberal market (LME) and coordinated (CME) (sometimes referred to as 'organized') market economies. The liberal market model applies in the 'Anglo-Saxon' societies – the USA, UK, Canada, Australia and New Zealand. Firms here operate through competitive markets in all areas of economic life, with price signals, supply and demand being crucial economic indicators. There is a high level of complementarity between institutions and processes. Such economic systems have high levels of stock market capitalization, low levels of employment protection, high rates of paid employment and high income inequality. The economy is characterized by mergers and acquisitions which are facilitated through the stock exchange, trade unions are weak and labour is insecure. The market is the primary instrument of economic coordination.

In the second form of economy (CME) firms are coordinated through non-market relationships, including network monitoring based on exchange of private information and collaborative (rather than competitive) relationships between firms. For Hall and Soskice, Germany, Denmark, France and Japan are examples of such systems. They have high levels of employment protection, low stock market capitalization, relatively lower numbers of working hours and relatively low differentials of income inequality. Takeovers are relatively rare and trade unions secure the interests of labour. Companies are coordinated through vertical or horizontal associations of firms. While Hall and Soskice point to differences between sub-types of these economies (between, for example, Japan and Germany in the CMEs and between Britain and the USA in the LMEs), they contend that the similarities between the coordinating mechanisms and complementarity between them point to two generic types of economy.

Bruno Amable extends the analysis even further to include product-market competition, wage-labour and labour-market institutions, the financial intermediation sector and corporate governance, social protection and the welfare state (Amable 2003, p. 14). On this basis, Amable devises five types of capitalism (see Table 8.1). A *market based* one is equivalent to Hall and Soskice's liberal market economy. The distinguishing features of the *social democratic* model are moderate employment security, a high level of social welfare, widespread labour retraining and a coordinated wage-bargaining system. The *Continental European* system is similar to the social democratic model, but the welfare state is less developed, the financial system facilitates long-term corporate strategies, wage bargaining is coordinated, and labour retention is less possible than in the social-democratic type. The *Mediterranean model* has more employment protection and less social provision than the Continental European model; a workforce with limited skills and education does not allow for the implementation of high wages and high skills in industrial strategy. The *Asian model* (a variant of Coates's 'state'-led capitalism) is 'highly dependent on the business strategies of the large corporations in

Table 8.1:   Amable's five models of capitalism

Model	Country
Liberal market	Australia, Canada, UK, USA
Asian	Japan, Korea
Continental European	Switzerland, Netherlands, Ireland, Belgium, Norway, Germany, France, Austria
Social-Democratic	Denmark, Finland, Sweden
Mediterranean	Greece, Italy, Portugal, Spain

Criteria:
Product markets: (regulated, deregulated),
Labour markets: (flexible, regulated),
Finance: (stock markets, banks, property ownership),
Welfare: (extent and type of welfare state),
Education (extent and public/private type).

collaboration with the State and centralized financial system' (Amable 2003, p. 15). Labour is protected through possibilities of retraining and careers within corporations. There is an absence of social protection and also sophisticated financial markets; stability is provided by the large corporation.

Like the work of Hall and Soskice, these typologies have institutional complementarities. Different groups of societies have congruent economic, political and social institutions: they hold together as coordinated systems of capitalism. It is claimed that these models are useful to indicate the 'complementarity' between the institutional structure and type of economic activity. In Germany, bank capital enables long-term investment to be made, the educational system produces highly skilled workers, and special attention is given to quality engineering and machine tools. The American and British financial system and the competitive labour market enable mobility of labour and innovative research and investment. Companies which perform badly on the market can be bought out and this leads to economic and commercial innovation and change, especially when linked to financial markets with high propensities to make profits. The low educational qualifications of the Mediterranean workforce, limitations on temporary work and long-term contracts lead to a lack of mobility and relatively high levels of unemployment that in turn perpetuate low-pay industries.

While these models are useful tools for understanding capitalist societies, they are all based on stable and well-established economies, sharing (though in different ways) the component parts of modern capitalism described above: a market system, private property, banking systems in support of entrepreneurship and accumulation, developed welfare, regulatory states, competitive political polyarchy and civil society. They are predominantly concerned with advanced capitalist countries having relatively high levels of market development and a long history as capitalist countries. Even the Asian model includes countries such as Singapore (27th in world rank of GDP) and Korea (52nd), which are currently higher than any former state socialist society except Slovenia (46th). They do not consider societies in transformation moving from non-capitalist systems (as in Central and Eastern Europe), or industrial systems (as in China) that operate on a non-capitalist basis without free markets, individual entrepreneurship or money-based accumulation.

In the transformation of the post-socialist societies, non-capitalist features are taken from quite a different mould. They had forms of ownership and coordination quite unlike even undeveloped capitalist market societies. In the absence of a free market, the government was the major coordinator of the economy through extensive public ownership of resources, complete control over the issue of money and the direction of investment. Government direction largely determined levels of employment, wages, and division between personal and collective spending. The state socialist societies, before their disintegration, as a whole, had achieved relatively high levels of income and human development (United Nations Development Programme 1991, pp. 119–21).[5] A notable feature of these states was that the Human Development Index had a ranking well above the ranking of gross domestic product, indicating that resources had been channelled by the state to provide for education and health.[6]

This reflected the weakness of the market and the positive role of the state in directing resources to human development. Of course, the state socialist societies were below the top echelon of industrial states but they all had an advanced industrial base, high literacy and educational attainment and average life expectations of over 70 years – a consequence of adequate housing, food and health care. The 'legacy of socialism' provided a footprint quite different to that from which Western capitalist societies have evolved.

In postcommunist economies, as well as other developing ones, many components of capitalism are compromised by alien features – non-market economic relationships, the absence of a complementary ideology – disdain for private property and classes of entrepreneurs and capitalists. They are 'transiting' to capitalism. Analysis, then, must grasp not only the *type* of capitalism, but the extent to which capitalism has been constructed. To determine the scale of capitalism, we need to consider: the *extent* of private ownership of assets, the presence of a free market and price liberalization, the accumulation of capital, exposure to and participation in the global economy, mechanisms for the coordination of capitalist firms, and levels of income redistribution and inequality. (In this discussion, however, the psychological, political and ideological have to be excluded.)

In the early years of transformation in Russia, radical reformers like Anatolii Chubais and Grigorii Yavlinsky wanted to reconstruct the state socialist economy on the basis of capitalism and turned to the West for policy advice. The most favoured model was what has become known as the 'Washington consensus' (Williamson 1990). Advisers from the West advocated a transition to an Anglo-American type of capitalism. This involved the introduction of markets for commodities, assets and labour, a low level of government intervention in the economy, exposure to foreign competition, monetary stability and a free exchange rate.

Privatization of economic assets was to be introduced to create a self-motivated business class. The stock exchange would become a crucial institution channelling investment to companies to meet consumer demand. These policies would preclude the reproduction of the communist administrative class which, it was claimed, would replicate the institutional features of state socialism.

The adoption of Anglo-American neoliberalism was a rational strategy for the new radical reform leadership: it legitimated destroying the political and economic base of the old ruling classes as well as the formation of competing units on the domestic market; global competition would promote economic efficiency and industrial restructuring on the basis of comparative advantage. State activity was to be minimal, its role was to set the rules in which neoliberalism was to operate. This meant divesting state ownership and abstaining from intervention in the market. Local currencies had to be negotiable on world currency exchanges, and tariffs had to be minimal to allow foreign competition. Such an 'institutional design', moreover, ruled out other forms of capitalism such as that which had developed in Germany, Korea, Japan and Scandinavia. How far was this policy successfully operationalized?

The uneven transformation of state socialism to something else

By 2002 a market had been successfully introduced; price liberalization was either comprehensive or countries had only a small number of administered prices, at a level comparable to Western market economies. Only Belarus, Turkmenistan and Uzbekistan fell below these levels (EBRD 2003, p. 16).[7] Most of the transition countries had a private sector contributing to more than 60 per cent of their GDP (EBRD 2003).[8] Privatization[9] was less comprehensive: only 6 of the 27 countries had privatized 50 per cent or more of large-scale companies, and another 14 had achieved a 25 per level. For small-scale privatization, the figures were much higher: 21 had reached the levels of advanced industrial economies, and another 4 had comprehensive programmes ready for implementation. These figures, even for the most advanced countries still show a considerable level of state ownership and production: the most privatized (Hungary, Slovakia, Czech Republic and Estonia) had, in 2002, 20 per cent of GDP from the state sector.

Combining private sector share of GDP and extent of privatization, we may divide the post-state socialist countries into three major blocs. The top group, with levels of privatization scores of over 8 (i.e. by adding large- and small-scale privatization) and GDP private sector over 75 per cent, contains Slovakia, Hungary, Estonia, Czech Republic, Poland, and Lithuania. A second group of states has 60 or more per cent of GDP originating from the private sector and a privatization score of 6.5 or more: this group includes Bulgaria, Albania, Latvia, Russia, Armenia, Slovenia, Ukraine, Romania, Kyrgyzstan, Croatia, Macedonia, Georgia and Kazakhstan. A third group, with relatively little privatization or only schemes in preparation, and less than 60 per cent of private production in GDP includes Azerbaijan, Moldova, Tajikistan, Bosnia, Uzbekistan, former Yugoslavia, Turkmenistan and Belarus. The incidence of privatization and the private sector are highly correlated with a Pearson's r of .92. In the following discussion I exclude the third group of countries as they do not pass the threshold to qualify as modern capitalist societies.

In terms of these basic criteria – price liberalization and the extent of the private sector – Russia is a hybrid system. Prices of retail goods are determined by the market, with some exceptions – energy being the most important. In respect of the private sector, Russia is still very far from Western advanced societies described in the varieties of capitalism literature. The proportion of GDP contributed by the private sector in 2002 was 70 per cent (Hungary and Czech Republic 80 per cent); on a five-point scale, the privatization of large enterprises was 3.5 (Hungary was 4), for privatization of small enterprises the index was 4 (Hungary 4.5), price system, 4 (Hungary 4.5); foreign trade and currency exchange, 3.5 (Hungary 4.5); and anti-monopoly policy 2.5 (Hungary 3). For banking reforms Russia had particularly low indexes – only 2 for the liberalization of bank rates and 2.5 for the development of non-banking financial organizations (the comparative figures for Hungary are 4 and 3.5) (EBRD 2003, p. 4, Russian edition, accessed at the EBRD website). While Russia had discarded the system of state planning and is predominantly a market society, many areas of state control and production remain.

One of the major differences between the Anglo-American and Coordinated models of capitalism is extent of open trading of companies on the stock exchange. The extent to which companies have a transnational presence and are open to domestic and foreign ownership is dependent to a great extent on their stock market capitalization. This is a major feature of Anglo-American capitalism though less so for the German and Japanese. Stock marketization in the countries own stock exchanges (enabling takeovers as well as the raising of capital), with European comparisons, is shown on Table 8.2.

Here we note the early start to stock market capitalization in Hungary and Poland. All countries between 1990 and 1999, including Western

Table 8.2: Stock market capitalization

Country	Percentage of GDP		No. of listed domestic companies (2000)
	1990	*1999*	
Poland	0.2	19.1	225
Russia	0	18	249
Ukraine	0	2.9	139
Hungary	1.5	33.7	60
Czech	0	22.2	131
Other countries			
China	0.5	33.4	1086
Germany	22.2	67.8	933
Japan	98.2	104.6	2470
Turkey	12.6	60.7	315
UK	85.9	203.4	1945
USA	53.2	181.8	7651

Source: Adapted from World Bank, *World Development Indicators 2001*, pp. 278–80.

ones, have had a rapid increase in stock market capitalization. Russia and Ukraine were much behind the East European countries, where Hungary and Estonia (not shown in Table 8.2) were in the lead.

There are two major groups of post-socialist countries: a small group above the average of low income countries – Hungary, Moldova, Russia and Estonia (the highest with 26.7) – at a level comparable to the average of Latin American countries, although below Turkey. Russia is one of this group, coming second after Estonia. However, Russia is a special case because its figure is derived mainly from a small number of very large energy companies (such as Lukoil). Moreover, the emerging capitalism was much less firmly set in the stock market in comparison to the UK, USA and Japan. The extent of stock market capitalization is much lower even than in 'coordinated' countries such as Germany and precludes any form of economic coordination through the stock market.

The global perspective

One significant measure of the transformation of the former state socialist countries is the extent to which they have become part of the global market and participate in the global economy. Under state socialism, the presence of Soviet companies' affiliates abroad (such as Aeroflot or Moscow Narodny Bank) was very small. In 1991, the whole of the CIS had only 68 parent corporations and 2,296 foreign affiliates.[10]

These data are for the early period of the transition to capitalism for the former state socialist countries. By 2001, the numbers of transnational companies had grown considerably. On an imperfect information base, on a world scale, there were 64,592,000 transnational companies with 851,167 foreign affiliates. Of these, only 850 companies were reported in the six Central and East European countries; a total number of 255,442 affiliates of foreign companies were however operating in *all* the East and Central European countries. (In 2003, Russia had only 7,793 foreign affiliates in its economy and Ukraine 7,362, compared to Poland's 35,840 (UNCTAD 2002, p. 272), though data for the countries of the former USSR were incomplete, the scale of the difference with the central European countries would still hold.)

The companies formed after the collapse of state socialism have little presence in the world of transnational companies. After the collapse of the USSR, its new export orientated companies, such as Lukoil (now the largest Russian transnational company), have sought a global dimension, though their opportunities initially were limited. The Russian government under Yeltsin fixed a limit on foreign shares in Russian strategic companies (originally not more than 15 per cent of shares in Russia's oil companies, for example, could be foreign owned) and the state in different forms owned (and still owns) a very large proportion of assets. The largest companies in Russia are located in the energy sector, which includes the top five companies by market value and 19 out of the top 50 companies (*Kommersant reyting* 2003, pp. 93–6).

On a world scale, in the *Financial Times 500 Index* (capital market value) (FT Global 500 2003), the USA dominated with 240 companies, and Japan followed with 48. Russia had only five companies, all in the energy sector: Yukos ranked 144, Gazprom 169, Surgutneftegaz 280, Lukoil 294, Sibneft-Siberian 375. No other former communist country appeared in the list. If we turn to revenues earned as shown in the Fortune 500 (Fortune 2002), China had 11 companies, the UK 33, Japan 88, the USA again topped the list with 197 companies; of the former state socialist countries, there were only two – both from Russia: Gazprom (rank 236, no profits data), Lukoil (422, for profits it ranked 74). Even in the top 500 European companies (capital market value), there were only 10 companies from the former state socialist bloc: Telekomunikacja Polska (rank 170), Surgutneftegaz (214), Lukoil (231), Gazprom (232), Cesky telekom (310), Matav (Hungary) (326), Yukos (Russia) (336), Unified Energy (Russia) (383), Mobile Telesystem (Russia) (464), and PKN Orien (Poland) (482) (2002 data drawn from the FT website).

In terms of their foreign assets, the transnational corporations of the former state socialist countries are relatively minor companies compared to the Western TNCs. Of these, Russia has the top two in terms of foreign assets – Lukoil and Novoship. Their foreign assets are $4,189 million dollars and 964 million respectively (UNCTAD 2002, p. 112), this compares to the world's top company (Vodafone) with foreign assets of $221,238 million and General Electric (in second rank) with $159,168 million dollars (ibid., p. 86). Other countries in the top ten Central and East European states include the following in order: Latvia (Latvian shipping), Russia (Primorsk shipping), Croatia (Hvatska elektroprivreda), Slovenia (Gorenje Group), Russia (Far East shipping), Croatia (Podravka group) and Croatia (Atlantska Plovidva).

One further indication of the global reach of the companies founded after the fall of communism may be exposed by their listing on Western stock exchanges. This requires companies to satisfy certain internationally recognized legal and financial conditions which enhance the credibility of the company and makes it possible for companies to attract capital investment. Table 8.3 shows the number of companies registered on the London and New York Stock Exchanges in 2003. On the London Stock Exchange, in June 2003, 40 central and Eastern European companies were listed. On the New York Exchange a total of 472 foreign companies was listed, but of these only 6 originated from the former socialist countries of Central and Eastern Europe. The participation of the former state socialist countries again is small. The largest economy, Russia, has only three energy companies registered in London and five in New York, including energy, telecommunications and food. China and Brazil have a much more substantial presence.

When one turns to foreign investment as a proportion of gross capital formation in the private sector, one sees a quite different picture. For high income countries, the proportion of capital formation derived from FDI is relatively low: Japan has less than 1 per cent; the UK is exceptional with a much higher (25.8%) level. China (10.1%) is lower than the average (13.2%) for middle-income countries. The Central and Eastern post-socialist countries (the Czech Republic, Croatia, Hungary, Estonia, Poland, Slovakia, Latvia, Kazakhstan, Moldova, Bulgaria, Lithuania, Romania and Georgia) all have higher proportions of investment coming from abroad than middle-income countries; and all (except Belarus and Slovenia) have very much higher dependency than even low-income countries (averaging 3.9%). Those with a very low FDI as well as low rates of domestic investment are Ukraine, Georgia, Turkmenistan, Belarus, Russia and Slovenia. The low level of foreign investment as a share in

Table 8.3:   Listings on the London and New York Stock Exchanges (June 2003)

Country	London Stock Exchange	New York Stock Exchange
Poland	11	0
Russia	3	5
Hungary	4	1
Other countries		
China (excludes Hong Kong/China)	5	14
Japan	23	19
Turkey	9	1
UK	(2737)	52

On the London exchange:
Russia's three companies include: Tatneft, Gazprom, Lukoil.
Poland is more diversified: media agencies, banks (3), vehicle distribution, mineral extraction, construction, pharmaceuticals, oil and gas, software, telecommunication.
Czech Republic: telecommunications (2), banks.
Hungary: computer services, building, chemicals (2).
China: oil, minerals, construction, electricity (2).
On the New York exchange:
China included: oil petrochemicals gas coal mining (6), aluminium production, transport (3), communications (2), power plants, chemical products manufacturing,
Hungary: telecommunications,
Russian Federation: Oil and gas, telecommunications (3), food.
Source: NYSE website (www.nyse.com), listed on 2 April 2003, London Stock Exchange website (www.londonstockexchange.com), listed on 6 June 2003.

capital formation is lower than one might expect: this may reflect the bunching of investment for big projects and also the high level of capital export (WDI 2003, table 5.2, reporting a three-year average).

Levels of investment

A key variable in capitalist development is the level of investment both domestically and from the world market. The provision of credit to the private sector is a key indicator of the propensity of a capitalist system to invest. The amount of domestic originated credit to the private sector (expressed as a percentage of GDP) and the amount of foreign direct investment (FDI) (as a percentage of gross capital formation) is shown on Table 8.4.

In high-income countries the average level of domestic credit to the private sector, as a percentage of GDP, in 2001 was 137.4; for middle-income countries 57.9. The average for the post-socialist countries was

Table 8.4: FDI (capital formation) and domestic credit

	FDI/capital formation (%)	Domestic credit
Ukraine	10.3	13.2
Russia	3.6	15.4
Eur/Cas	13.8	21
Low income	3.9	24.1
Poland	15	26.5
Hungary	17.2	33.8
Czech Rep.	28.9	44.4
Middle income	13.2	57.9
Germany	8.5	122
China	10.1	127.2
High income	19.2	137.4
UK	25.8	138.8
USA	15.1	145.8
Japan	0.6	186.7

Source: World Bank 2003, tables 5.1 and 5.2

21; this is even below the average for low-income countries, which was 24.1. Domestic credit, of course, includes advances to the domestic sector as well as small businesses – most investment for companies originates from internal sources. These data then show both the underdevelopment of the banks as well as the low levels of consumer credit. The banks were not functioning to create credit for investment which is a major component for modern capitalism.[11]

Figure 8.1 and Table 8.4 bring out the striking international differences between the levels of domestic credit to the private sector. All the industrial countries are clustered at the right hand of the chart (Figure 8.1), and all have credit to GDP ratios of over a hundred; Japan has 190, China is also in this category (125). One feature these advanced countries all have is a very high level of domestic credit to the private sector. For the European transition countries, only the Czech Republic and Croatia (not shown on the chart) are near the level of middle-income countries and 13 are below the levels of even the low-income countries.

This discussion indicates that all the postcommunist societies have a severe lack of domestically sourced investment in the private sector. (As there are still considerable public sectors in these countries, this discussion does not apply to investment as a whole.) However, foreign direct investment is much greater than for other countries at a similar level of gross domestic product. This is consistent with the policy of the

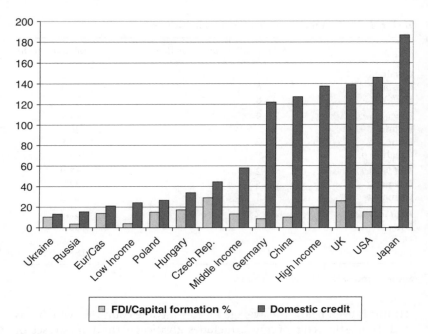

Figure 8.1:   FDI (capital formation) and domestic credit

last group of countries, which had the least foreign sales of assets. For the post-socialist countries as a whole, however, the very low levels of internal investment and accumulation indicate a serious impediment to their quest to become modern capitalist countries.

Foreign direct investment is only one aspect of the role of globalization, also of importance is the contribution of foreign investment to gross domestic product and employment and the structure of exports. One informative index here is the transnationality index. The transnationality index provides a very good measure of the involvement of countries in the global economy. It is calculated as the average of four ratios: FDI inflows as a percentage of gross fixed capital formation for the past three years, FDI inward stocks as a percentage of GDP, value added of foreign affiliates as a percentage of GDP, and the employment of foreign affiliates as a percentage of total employment. A high index indicates a significant economic dependence on foreign countries. As shown in Table 8.5, in 1999, the USA had a low index (8.2) and the UK 14.5; the lowest of the developed countries was Japan with 0.6. As one might expect from the earlier discussion, Russia was low down the list with an

Table 8.5: Transnationality index 1999

Japan	0.6 (lowest)
USA	8.2
Germany	10.6
UK	14.5
China	14.4
Czech Republic	17.6
Ukraine	4.8
Russia	4.6
Turkey	4.1
Hungary	27.6
Hong Kong (China)	98.4 (highest)

A high index indicates a significant dependence on foreign countries. The index is a composite average of four ratios expressed in percentage terms: average of FDI inflows as % of gross capital formation; FDI inward stocks as % of GDP; value added of foreign affiliates as % of GDP; and employment of foreign affiliates as % of total employment.

Source: Derived from UNCTAD 2002, *World Investment Report*, p. 275.

index of 4.6 and Ukraine 4.8 – both similar to Turkey with 4.1; Hungary was much higher with 27.6 and the Czech Republic with 17.6, which is even higher than China's 14.4, although Hong Kong (China) had an enormous dependency of 98.4 (disproportionately due to massive FDI inward stock) (UNCTAD 2002, p. 275).

This is an average of four different components of transnational activities: FDI inflows as a percentage of gross fixed capital formation for the previous three years (which helps to correct for large inward takeovers or projects in any one year); inward stocks as a percentage of FDI in the given year (2000), the value added of foreign affiliates as a percentage of GDP in a given year, and employment of foreign affiliates as a percentage of total employment (UNCTAD 2003, p. 6). The composition of exports measured in terms of primary and manufactured goods is a good indicator of the modernization of the economy as a whole. (Data for 1998–2000 indicate that Bulgaria, Moldova and the Czech Republic had over 30 per cent of gross fixed capital formation from FDI flows, and Latvia, Lithuania and Croatia were between 20 and 30 per cent: UNCTAD 2002, p. 70.)

Developed and developing countries do not differ on average in terms of their transnationality indexes: for the former it is 21 and for the latter 20.1. The indexes for former state socialist countries, however, are much lower, with an average of 13. Again there are important differences between the different blocs of countries. There is a small group of countries with a very low participation rate: Russia, Belarus and Ukraine have an index below 5. At the other end of the scale are the Czech Republic (24), Estonia (25) and Hungary (27) with rates above that of the average of high-income countries (21). These figures are probably explained by the low foreign ownership in the first three countries – even in the energy extraction industries (due to legal restrictions), and very high levels of foreign ownership in the second. Consequently, the three former Soviet republics have much less dependency on international trade. If one considers the proportion of employment by foreign affiliates (as a proportion of all employment), Hungary has a figure of 27.4 per cent and Latvia 10.4 per cent; the figures for Russia, Ukraine and Belarus are 1.6, 0.7 and 0.3 per cent respectively (UNCTAD 2002, p. 275)[12] – for Belarus, the lowest in the world.

The former state socialist societies have an export profile most similar to low-income countries. As a proportion of merchandise exports, primary commodities represent 45 per cent of low-income countries' exports, and in Central and Eastern Europe and the Commonwealth of Independent States, 42 per cent; high-income countries, on the other hand, have an average in this category of only 15 per cent and middle-income 35 per cent. There are, however, important differences between the postcommunist countries. Bulgaria, Lithuania, Latvia, Russia, Moldova, Kazakhstan and Turkmenistan constitute a group with a share of primary exports higher than the middle-income countries. At the other end, is a group with primary exports below the average level of high-income countries: these include Slovenia (the lowest with 10 per cent), Czech Republic, Hungary and Slovakia (15 per cent) – just below the United Kingdom (with 17 per cent).

Russia, Kazakhstan, Ukraine, Moldavia and Turkmenistan are countries with a high level of export of primary commodities but with a low level of gross domestic product and investment generated by FDI. These countries are even more dependent on primary sector exports than even low-income countries and are on a par with Columbia, El Salvador, Egypt, Morocco and Senegal.

The decline in the rankings in the Human Development Index for the former state socialist societies is partly a consequence of the great rise in inequality in these countries, and this in turn is highest for countries that derive a high proportion of their export earnings from the primary sector. The top five primary-sector exporting countries (Kazakhstan, Moldova, Azerbaijan, Turkmenistan and Russia) all have very high Gini coefficients. The correlation between share of primary exports and inequality is very high at +.689. This is probably explained by the low labour costs and low labour saturation in the oil and gas industries, and high incomes from oil exports being retained by few people, as a consequence of privatization. Possibly, the 'Dutch disease' syndrome, in which a high exchange rate may depress agriculture and manufacturing and consequently lead to unemployment, may be at work in these countries.

The evidence indicates that the postcommunist countries have moved into the world capitalist economic system. But they have not entered as members of the core states – rather they rest on the periphery. They have a negligible number of transnational companies. The Central European states (Hungary and the Czech Republic) are highly dependent on transnational companies for investment, income and employment. While Russia receives a considerable amount of FDI for its energy industry, it and Ukraine remain largely self-sufficient (or self-deficient) with respect to gross capital formation, value added and employment.

A key variable in capitalist development is the level of investment both domestically and from the world market. As noted above in the discussion of capitalism, the provision of credit to the private sector is a key indicator of the propensity of a capitalist system to invest and to grow. The average for the post-socialist countries was 21, below even the average for low-income countries, which was 24.1. The figures for Russia are among the lowest of all: 4 and 15. These data then show both the underdevelopment of the banks as well as the low levels of consumer credit. The banks were not functioning to create credit.

Two types of post-state socialist capitalism

Following the disintegration of state socialism, a market system based on private ownership and production for profit has been constructed in all but three of the former state socialist societies. There is no chance of a return to state socialism. The measures of reform have secured a high level of irreversibility: the planning mechanism has been destroyed, and the lynchpin of the political system, the Communist Party apparatus, dissolved. Whether these countries have moved to a modern capitalist system is open to question. The consequences of transformation have led to three blocs of post-state socialist countries, two of which are market orientated and have large private sectors and one small cluster of countries which preserve statist economies (Uzbekistan, Belarus and Turkmenistan, which are ignored in the following discussion). Despite the significant policies of destatization, the postcommunist societies all share in common a higher level of state control than market capitalist countries and most have stock market capitalization at the levels of very low-income countries. In terms of social development, the postcommunist states have fallen in the world rankings of human development.

Weber's claim that modern capitalism is distinguished by 'the pursuit of profit and forever renewed profit, by means of continuous, rational, capitalistic enterprise' (Weber 1970, p. 17; King 2003, pp. 3–30; Lane 2002, pp. 32–3) applies more to the first group than to the second. The first includes the Central European countries – Slovenia, the Czech Republic, Poland, Hungary, Slovakia and Estonia – all new members of, and having borders with, the European Union. These countries are approaching the levels of OECD countries with respect to marketization and privatization, they also have a very extensive participation in the global economy. This group is closest to the continental type of market capitalism, though it is more state led. They all have a low level of stock market capitalization and more developed welfare states, making them distinct from the Anglo-American countries. What is particularly import-ant, from the point of view of the transition to a self-sustaining capitalist system, is that a high level of accumulation of capital is sustained. The figures cited above (Figure 8.1 and Table 8.4) show the exceedingly low levels in all the former state socialist societies. Some, but not all, have very high exposure to the global market, which acts as an exogenous source of economic change. They resemble, and are likely to identify with, the continental European system as they all have embedded wel-fare states derived from the state socialist period. Economic coordination here is not through stock exchange capitalism, but is dependent on the state and also on companies with an international presence. Tutored by the conditionality requirements of the EU and the IMF, they have developed not only the economic preconditions of capitalism, but also the political and societal: an appropriate type of government, a civil society and an emerging bourgeois class structure.

A second model is that of a hybrid state/market uncoordinated cap-italism. This is a relatively economically poor group which has had an unsuccessful period of transition: Russia, Ukraine, Kazakhstan, Georgia, and Moldova. These countries have exceedingly high income differen-tials, and high levels of poverty and unemployment. They have the characteristics of low income, primary-sector exporting countries, with a very low integration into the global economy. They have particu-larly low levels of domestically sourced investment, though those with a large energy sector (such as Russia) have significant and disproportionate foreign direct investments. The form privatization has taken may lead to relatively few owners in extractive industries, such as oil, giving rise to great wealth on the one hand and, because of relatively low employment rates and ineffective redistribution policies, to poverty on the other. Economic policy should be concerned not only with efficiency, but also with equity. The move to the market and private ownership has significantly diminished equity in the postcommunist states – though less so for those bordering on the European Union than in those that lie beyond them.

A state-led scenario for Russia

In the Russian Federation, the initial period of privatization and destatization led to a weakening of the state and consequently to a period of 'chaotic capitalism'. A chaotic social formation may be defined as a social and economic system that lacks institutional coordination and promotes social fragmentation: goals, law, governing institutions and economic life lack cohesion. Its characteristics are uncertainty about the future, elite disunity, the absence of a dominant and mediating class system, criminalization and corruption, rent-seeking entrepreneurs, minimal political interest articulation and an economy in decline characterized by inflation, unemployment and poverty (Lane 2000, pp. 485–504).[13] As far as the economy is concerned in the Yeltsin and early Putin periods, 'state capture' by private interests was widespread. By state capture, we mean that private bodies are able to impose policies on the state that promote their own interests. Study of legislation has shown that regional legislatures were subverted by business interests having an adverse effect on development (World Bank 2005).

This state of affairs has been attenuated somewhat by the leadership of President Putin, who has sought to strengthen the role of the state in economic regulation. However, the economic system is far from being a modern wealth-creating one. It is a form of political capitalism.

In seeking greater stability for the future, the footprint of state socialism may 'fit' into a pattern of cooperative state-led capitalism. In the discussion of transformation to capitalism in the postcommunist countries, it is surprising that so little mention has been made of the non-Anglo-American forms of capitalism, discussed at the beginning of this chapter. Coordination in all modern economies is based on a combination of market, state, competitive and cooperative economic institutions. A possible scenario for the stability of Russia is an economy with a limited market economy, a regulatory state and cooperative economic institutions in which management has an important place and in which ownership is in the hands of interconnected state and private businesses and financial institutions. This kind of state-led capitalism might ensure accumulation. Not only will the state directly channel economic rents earned from export-oriented industries such as armaments, precious metals and energy, but also private and semi-private companies will indirectly be financed through state institutions and banks. A state-led development policy would involve support for the space and nuclear industries, computer software, arms production and aircraft. The private sector is unable to provide the long-term finance required to develop these industries. The key components of such a state-led system would be:

- *Driving forces*: State
- *Institutions*: Stakeholders: industrial management, leading capitalists, political elites, workers' collectives
- *Culture*: Nationalist
- *Solidarity*: Social compact, welfare state

Such a policy is not without critics. A free-market ideology and policy have been advocated by the Ministry of Finance, the Ministry of Economy and the Ministry for the Management of State Property and is supported by the IMF, leading Western governments, particularly the UK and USA, and international interests in financial corporations. Also, Russian successful companies in export industries, such as oil, who have been associated with radical market reformers in the government, have defined their interest in participating in a global economy – both as investors in foreign assets and in selling on world markets. In this context, outside political actors become a major determinant of the direction of economic change.[14] The 'conditionality' of support by international agencies such as the IMF and the European Union is usually in terms of a neoliberal form of economy.

At a more theoretical and general level, major criticisms of this approach come from those who hold that a one-way convergence is taking place between the different types of capitalism I have considered, with the direction of convergence towards the stock-exchange, shareholder profit maximizing Anglo-American system. The globalization of capitalism, it is argued, is inimical to a state-led negotiated form of capitalism, and it is claimed that cooperative-type economies of the German type do not lead to innovation. The growth of countries like Germany and Japan has declined in the 1990s and at the beginning of the 21st century they are restructuring in the direction of a competitive neoliberal type of capitalism. Many contend that such cooperative capitalism is a sure way to promote economic decline. Global convergence to a market-led capitalism, it is argued, is now under way and cannot be stopped without substantial costs to domestic economies. The political and economic space for state-led as well as 'cooperative' systems is limited. International financial organizations and international political gatekeepers, such as the IMF, OECD, World Bank and European Union, are able to impose their conditions on emerging countries. The argument here is two-fold: first, state-led corporatism is not efficient and second, its days are numbered anyway as it is severely constrained by the forces of globalization.

These arguments, I believe, are 'overdetermined'. While there certainly are trends towards convergence, there are also divergencies (Kitschelt, Lange, Marks and Stephens 1999, pp. 427–60). Production in an economy as large as Russia is local in character and regional companies and political actors have considerable scope for action independently of the global economy. With the exception of the extractive industries, the globalization of finance has had little effect on Russia. Governments may oppose free trade if it is not in their economic interests and maintain tariffs in support of home industries. As Joseph Stiglitz (2002) has pointed out, the developed countries demand trade liberalization and the elimination of subsidies while maintaining trade barriers and subsidies for their own products. The main advantages for adopting a model of organized market capitalism in Russia is that it may be able better to cope with competition on a world scale. Greater regulation (such as in the recent history of France) may lead to more effectively organized restructuring. A positive legacy of communism is high investment in human capital, which is a considerable asset in transformation. My own conclusion is that a state-led corporatist economy is by no means perfect but is the best system for Russia in its current circumstances.

Notes

1. This is 'a continuous connected process, of reproduction, [which] ... reproduces capitalist relationships: on the one side, the capitalist, on the other the wage-labourer' (Marx 1958, p. 578).
2. Preface to the first German Edition of *Capital*.
3. For instance he noted the role of the factory laws (the Ten Hours Bill) in England which limited the length of the working day as well as the role of the state in sanitation and housing.
4. For an overview see Coates 1999, pp. 643–60, and 2000; Hall and Soskice 2001; Amable 2003.
5. Data used are life expectancy at birth, adult literacy, mean years of schooling and gross domestic product. United Nations Development Programme. Based on data for the 1980s (before the fall of state socialist regimes), seven countries were ranked in the top UNDP 'high human development' category of 53

states: Czechoslovakia (ranked 27), Hungary (30), USSR (31), Bulgaria (33), Yugoslavia (34), Poland (41) and Albania (49), out of a total of 163 countries.

6. The USA, Denmark, Germany, Turkey and only Romania from the socialist states all had negative deviations (that is their human development rank was below their gross domestic product rank), whereas Hungary, Yugoslavia, Poland and Albania (and especially China) had very significant positive ones.

7. EBRD, *Transition Report 2003*, p. 16.

8. Here and following, data taken from EBRD 2003. The private sector's share of GDP includes estimates drawn from both official and unofficial sources of the extent of informal or not reported economic activity.

9. The EBRD estimated the extent of privatization, on a scale with 0 being no privatization and 4.5 (4+ in original) being comparable to advanced industrial countries. The data are shown separately for large-scale and small-scale privatization (two scales 0 to 4+). I have aggregated into one scale – being a total of nine (I have translated the original – and + signs to −.5 and +.5). The definition of a 'private' company includes companies which are not part of the state sector, but they certainly include companies in which various government agencies (local authorities, ministries) hold stakes.

10. The developed countries have transnational corporations in thousands (in 1991, the USA 3,800, Germany 6,984), with foreign affiliates in tens of thousands. Individual countries like Germany, Brazil and China, had more foreign affiliates than all the former state socialist societies put together.

11. On Russian banks, see Lane (2002, chapter 1, especially pp. 15–17).

12. These data are not given in the 2003 edition.

13. The present author developed this concept in an earlier article covering the initial period of transformation in the Russian Federation.

14. As Michel Camdessus has put it: 'I cannot emphasise strongly enough that Russia cannot afford to take this [corporatist] route' ('In Search of a Vision to Revitalize Reform', St Petersburg Economic Forum, June 16, IMF website: Russia, 16 June 1999).

References

Amable, Bruno, 2003. *The Diversity of Capitalism*. Oxford, Oxford University Press.

Coates, David, 1999. 'Models of Capitalism in the New World Order: the UK Case', *Political Studies* 47: 643–60.

Coates, David, 2000. *Models of Capitalism*, Cambridge: Polity Press.

EBRD, 2003. *Transition Report 2003*. London EBRD.

Fortune, 2002. European Edition, No. 15, 19 August.

FT Global 500, 2003. *Financial Times* 28 May, accessed at: http://specials.ft.com/ft500/may2001/FT37L797KMC.html.

Gerth, H. H. and C. W. Mills, 1948. *From Max Weber*, London: Routledge and Kegan Paul.

Hall, Peter and David Soskice (eds), 2001. *Varieties of Capitalism*. Oxford: Oxford University Press.

King, Larry, 2003. 'Shock Privatization; The Effects of Rapid Large-Scale Privatization on Enterprise Restructuring', *Politics and Society* 31(1): pp. 3–30.

Kitschelt, H., P. Lange, G. Marks and J. D. Stephens, 1999. 'Convergence and Divergence in Advanced Capitalist Democracies', in H. Kitschelt, P. Lange, G. Marks and J. D. Stephens (eds), *Continuity and Change in Contemporary Capitalism.* Cambridge: Cambridge University Press, pp. 427–60.

Kommersant reyting, 2003. *200 krupneishikh kompanii Rossii* 1, pp. 93–6.

Lane, David, 2000. 'What Kind of Capitalism for Russia? A Comparative Analysis', *Communist and Post-Communist Studies* 33: 485–504.

Lane, David (ed.), 2002. *Russian Banking*, Northampton MA: Edward Elgar.

Marx, K. 1956. *Capital*, Vol. 1. Moscow: FLPH.

Marx, K. 1958. *Capital*, Vol. 3. Moscow: FLPH.

Stiglitz, Joseph E. 2002. *Globalisation and its Discontents*. New York: Norton.

UNCTAD, 2002. *World Investment Report 2002: Transnational Corporations and Export Competitiveness*. New York: United Nations.

UNCTAD, 2003. *World Investment Report 2003*. New York: United Nations.

United Nations Development Programme, 1991. *Human Development Report*. New York and Oxford: Oxford University Press.

WDI, 2003. *World Development Indicators*. Washington DC: World Bank.

Weber, Max, 1970. *The Protestant Ethic and the Spirit of Capitalism*. London: Allen & Unwin.

Williamson, John, 1990. 'What Washington Means by Policy Reform', in Williamson (ed.), *Latin American Adjustment. How Much has Happened?* Washington DC: Institute for International Economics.

World Bank, 2005. *From Transition to Development. A Country Economic Memorandum for the Russian Federation, 2005*. Website: web.worldbank.org/WBSITE/ EXTERNAL/COUNTRIES/ECAEXT/RUSSIAN FEDERATION.

9
Killers and Gangsters: the Heroes of Russian Blockbusters of the Putin Era

Birgit Beumers

In recent years Russian cinema has advanced from one of the most underdeveloped to the fifth largest film market in the world. This chapter outlines first the rise of the Russian film industry that allowed the term 'blockbuster' to be applied once again to Russian cinema[1] before it explores the 'heroes' of the new Russian blockbusters in order to define their characteristic features.

I argue here that two paradigms characterize the new Russian blockbuster: first, the killer-cum-knight who operates within the criminal world and reinforces social justice in the absence of a competent and powerful police force; and second, the lawful killer whose biography contains an inherent flaw (criminal sentence, corrupted by evil), but who is part of the new legal system. The second paradigm chronologically follows the first, reflecting the development from police corruption of the late Yeltsin era to an attempt to instil trust in the police force in the Putin years, asserting that the forces need to be trusted and that individuals in the police force can defend the people from evil acts, whether these are terrorist attacks or the disasters brought upon by abstract, evil forces.

If the first generation of blockbusters presented the tasks of the killer as a game, then the second phase of blockbusters integrates reality and circumstance into the new rules established through the game, endowing the killer-guardsman with the powers of an ever-winning figure of a computer game. At the same time, the binaries of good and evil dissolve in the new hero, thus pointing at the integration (possible or real) of the criminal into the security apparatus, and by extension, into society.

This de-heroization (through attributing human flaws to the hero) ties in with the popularization of former (Soviet) heroes through exhibitions, serials and other forms of mass culture, which serves, as the French historian Sophie Wahnich (2005) has argued regarding war heroes, to remove the hero from his pedestal and integrate him into the 'ordinary' community in order to allow for people's emotional involvement with his suffering rather than encouraging a respectful distance vis-à-vis his feats.

The elevation of the killer to a figure in a game, however, creates a new, virtual hero who bears little resemblance to real life in his action, but is humanized through his flaws of the past. As Yevgenii Gusiatinsky (2004) has argued, contemporary films do not show reality as it is: rather, they create an artificial and empty space which creates the abstract conditions necessary for a game.

The sociologist Lev Gudkov has written extensively about the Russian's self-perception, arguing that the victim complex is one defining feature of the Russian character: attributes of submissiveness and passivity are approved in this value system, whilst the criminal with his activity and decisiveness rejects the role of the victim and marginalizes himself from society (Gudkov 2004, p. 106). The marginalized criminal is eventually reintegrated into society as a lawful killer. However, the former criminal who turns into a guardian of good remains a 'guardsman': watching over borders between reality and game, between the group he now belongs to ('us') and the criminal world ('them'). His position between past (crime) and future (safety) underscores this transitional role. In this ability to cross borders lies the specificity of the hero.[2] I therefore explore the attributes of blockbuster heroes as representative of the assimilation of the hero figure of American blockbusters into Russian cinema, and, on the other hand, of the integration of active traits of character (hitherto associated with crime and violence) into society.

The making of blockbusters

In 1996 Russian film production statistics showed an all-time low in the number of films produced (usually around 150 per year) of 28 feature films. At the same time, piracy dominated the sales sector to almost 100 per cent, leading the Motion Pictures Association of America (MPAA) to pronounce a boycott on Russian distribution, depriving it of Hollywood's A-movies, which in turn triggered an even higher level of piracy for those much-wanted films. In October 1996 the first refurbished cinema, fitted with the Dolby Stereo System, opened in Moscow: the Kodak Kinomir.

Unable to deal with a defunct exhibition sector, with a non-existent distribution network, with piracy and crime that put at risk Russia's negotiations with the World Trade Organization (WTO) and led to the MPAA's boycott, most critics avoided writing about that bleak reality which doomed the film sector – and criticized instead their own film-makers. Many debates on Russian film in the latter part of the 1990s were dominated by the function of the filmmaker in the new Russia. There was a fascination with the role of Russian cinema between art and commerce, between education and industry, between propaganda and business. In the eyes of the state, which still financed most films (as had been custom in the nationalized industry for over seventy years of Soviet rule), cinema remained in those days a most powerful means of expressing moral values and providing guidance. At the same time, people began to recognize cinema as a business that could potentially, one day, make a profit. The dilemma of cinema appeared to rest in its situation between the fetters of ideology and capital. The first initiatives in speaking directly to an audience were undertaken in advertising, and the transition from clip-maker to successful filmmaker represents a natural development that applies to many of Russia's contemporary directors of 'blockbusters' (Timur Bekmambetov, Yegor Konchalovsky, Fedor Bondarchuk, to name but a few).

Looking back over the history of Soviet cinema in the 20th century there is little doubt that cinema possessed the potential for guiding viewers towards ideals, be they political, moral or other. But there are larger issue at stake: should filmmakers be *expected* to create models for the people to believe in? It may not have been pleasant and entertaining to watch modern Russian films of the mid-1990s that refused to comply with the call for a 'positive hero' and instead showed a gruesome and blackened reality (*chernukha*). However, the use of cinema for the projection of a national identity in the spirit of Socialist Realism was then, and remains today, extremely problematic. Nikita Mikhalkov's words at the Fourth Congress of the Filmmakers' Union in May 1998 echoed this call for a positive hero and the perception of cinema as a means of instilling moral values:

> But to serve the Fatherland does not necessarily mean to serve the regime. That is why today we can state so openly: cinema has betrayed its audience, has left it to the mercy of fate, has rejected its love! (Mikhalkov 1999, p. 50)

Using the example of the US film industry, whose success, Mikhalkov suggested, lay in the creation of positive heroes that the American nation identified with, Mikhalkov neglected the fact that America is proud of its cinema also because it is a $3.5 *billion* profit-making industry – not just a myth factory. Mikhalkov was leading the Russian film industry into another *grande illusion* – the make-believe that the American government supports the film industry because of its nice stories and muscular heroes rather than the economic advantages it provides.

In Mikhalkov's opinion, cinema should portray the bright future of a country that was, in 1998, in the midst of an economic crisis following the collapse of the currency. Cinema should punish the evil-doers, the killers, the traitors, while Russia's legal system was attempting to formulate new laws that had yet to be implemented, and while the police was the loser in the fight against video piracy – causing a loss of $275 million in 2003 which was minimally reduced to $224 million in 2005, accounting for 70 per cent of the DVD market (Galetski 2006), not to mention crime. Cinema should create a virtual reality, a perfected reflection of the crisis surrounding Russian society in those days. And Mikhalkov proposed to do just that.

First, he took the chair of the Filmmakers' Union and led it, in seven years, to a deplorable state: the sale of the sanatorium at Krasnaia Pakhra did not cover the refurbishment cost of the house of veterans in Bolshevo; the attempt to gain control over the Cinema Centre (Kinotsentr) led first to a conflict with the Confederation of Filmmakers' Unions of the CIS and then to the eviction of the Museum of Cinema. The House of Cinema, the gathering place for film professionals, will be demolished. Thus, the Filmmakers' Union has failed to provide support for those who most needed it: the veteran Soviet filmmakers, living on a meagre pension and unable to afford medical care; at the same time, property issues impoverished the Union instead of bringing benefit.

Under Mikhalkov's presidency the Moscow International Film Festival became an annual event in the attempt to maintain its status as an A-category festival, while the festival venues have deteriorated as festival organizers refused categorically to deal with commercial outlets until 2006 when the festival was held in the October multiplex. In October 2004 Mikhalkov forced his re-election as chairman of the Filmmakers' Union in a non-quorate late-night session. Less than a year later, Mikhalkov took temporary 'creative' leave. Second, Mikhalkov made his own contribution to the 'blockbuster' industry with *The Barber of Siberia*, costing $45 million to produce and grossing $2.6 million in Russian box office over four years, less than one million admissions in co-producing France, and without securing US distribution. Designed to restore faith in Russia as a nation, *The Barber* was one of the biggest flops in Russian film history, as Mikhalkov's ambitious plans for the film industry turned into one of the greatest shams. As the abstract debates over the role of cinema continued, the industry began to recover in quite concrete terms.

With Putin in office, the Russian economy stabilized and the cinema sector began to grow. First and foremost, the exhibition sector expanded rapidly. In 2002 a nine-screen multiplex in central Moscow, Formula Kino, opened after a long construction period in the square in front of Kursk station. The first Kino Star cinema opened in September 2003, owned by Rising Star, a joint venture between the US-based National Amusements and Paul Heth's Soquel Ventures; it seats 3,100 spectators in eleven cinemas. A twelve-screen multiplex, Kino Star, opened in December 2004; and a third multiplex with 14 screens is planned in St Petersburg, followed by the lease of space from Ikea Mega in both Moscow and St Petersburg (Franklin 2003, 2005; Mitchell 2006). The first nine-screen multiplex of Cinema Park opened in January 2004 and is owned by ProfMedia (part of Potanin's InterRos Group, 80 per cent) and Mikhalkov's TriTe (20 per cent) with 1,186 seats; another six-screen cinema opened in December 2004 (Kay 2004; Franklin 2005).

The steady growth of the number of cinemas and multiplexes affects above all the major cities: in 2005 Moscow counted 216 screens (over a population in excess of 10 million), followed by St Petersburg with 59 screens and Yekaterinburg with 21 screens. Moreover, the growth of cinema multiplexes is limited to a few exhibitors, such as Formula Kino (going up from nine screens in 2003 to 64 in 2004); KinoMax (with 24 screens), Kino Star (increasing its screens from eleven in 2003 to 23 in 2004) and Cinema Park with 15 screens.[3] Ticket prices reach on average $11 – compared to a US average ticket price of $2.60 (*Screen Daily* 23 September 2003). In addition, UPI ventured onto the Russian market in February 2005 (Frater 2005). These developments make the Russian film market a considerable player in world cinema distribution. Moreover, the national distribution network expanded vastly to cater for a growing number of exhibitors; it is dominated by five companies, namely Gemini (with its German director Michael Schlicht), Karo Film, Cascade, UIP, and Central Partnership (with director Ruben Dishdishian).

In recent years the Russian film industry has risen literally like the phoenix from the ashes: in 1997 it had a box office turnover of $6 million ('Blokbaster', p. 5); by 2002 the box office grossing had reached $112 million, seeing an increase of 70 per cent to $190 million for 2003. In 2004 box office grossing amounted to $268 million (Franklin 2004, 2005; Galetski 2005). In 2005 it reached $340 million, and projections predict $840 million by 2009 (Brown 2007). In 2007 Russia was the fifth highest grossing cinema market with an estimated $580 million box office.

In the light of the alleged inability of Russian filmmakers to speak to their audiences and Mikhalkov's attack on the *chernukha* films, it should be expected that the box office in those cinemas would be achieved largely by American films. However, in 1996 there was an all-time low of some 25 films produced in Russia (compared to an average of 150 films in the post-war Soviet era), but the number of new films has been steadily picking up since 1998. By 2000 films were largely financed by independent producers and backed by television, although many still receive subsidies from Goskino or its successor FACC (the Federal Agency for Culture and Cinematography). Films are produced by small, independent companies, as well as by large corporations. Many production studios (e.g. 'Debiut' [Debut], 'Zhanr' [Genre], 'Krug' [Circle], 'Luch' [Ray], and 'Ritm' [Rhythm]) are former production units of Mosfilm (still state-owned); others are independent studios using the production facilities at larger studios (e.g. Slovo in Moscow, CTB and Troitsky Most in Petersburg). Major television channels, such as ORT/Channel One, RTR, NTV with its (now independent) film production arm NTV Profit (Production Firm of Igor Tolstunov), and CTC have developed powerful film production arms. These companies often make a profit through the production of television serials and finance films with commercial potential that they then air on their channels. Central Partnership has ventured into serial production and launched their own series 'Nash novyi serial' (Our New Serial). The large independent studios produce blockbusters in order to finance art-house operations: Sergei Selianov's CTB has produced Alexei Balabanov's and Alexander Rogozhkin's blockbusters as well as debut films; Yelena Yatsura and Sergei Melkumov's Slovo has produced Il'ia Khrzhanovsky's art house debut *4* as well as Dmitrii Meskhiev's festival winner *Our Own* (*Svoi*, 2004) and Fedor Bondarchuk's blockbuster *Company 9* (*9-aia rota*, 2005); Nikola Film of Igor Kalenov has produced Alexander Sokurov's films as well as the popular comedies of Dmitrii Astrakhan; and Sergei Chliants's Pygmalion has produced Petr Buslov's mega-hit *Bimmer* and its sequel *Bimmer 2* as well as art house-films by Kira Muratova or Alexander Veledinsky.

As production is on the rise, so is the share in Russian films at the box office which stands at 30 per cent (Brown 2007): for a share of 20 per cent of titles released (58 Russian and 292 other), the Russian films gross 28.5 per cent ($86.8 million for Russian films over $217.6 million for non-Russian films) (*Action*, May 2006).

Alexei Balabanov's *Brother* (May 1997) was the first Russian film that was successful to the extent that it managed to recoup most of the production cost through video release, television rights and international sales at a time when the distribution network in Russia was still ailing. Although *Brother* was a 'blockbuster' in its own time, it cannot be compared in theatrical release figures to films of 1999 and 2000. The *Brother* sequel was released on 11 May 2000 and, with a budget of $1.5 million, grossed $1.1 million in the CIS territory alone; it achieved top rankings in the video sales figures for 2000 (Segida and Zemlianukhin 2004).

In the first years of the new millennium the distribution of Russian films picked up further. Yegor Konchalovsky's *Anti-Killer* (6 April 2002) cost $3 million in production plus an additional $220,000 for the publicity campaign; it was released in 42 prints, grossing $1.3 million. The sequel *Anti Killer 2: Anti-Terror* (release 25 November 2003) made $2.6 million at the box office with 162 copies; it was the most lucrative film for the first quarter of 2004 (Segida and Zemlianukhin 2004). Petr Buslov's *Bimmer* (*Bumer*, 28 June 2003) grossed $1.6 million and reached the fifth place in video releases for 2003 (Segida and Zemlianukhin 2004; Franklin 2004). The sequel, *Bimmer 2*, was released in 2006 (*Bumer-2*, 7 March 2006), proving the popularity of *Bimmer*, further underlined by the official release of a Goblin translation[4] entitled *Anti-Bimmer*.

The year 2004 brought the breakthrough for Russian cinema in the revived market. Art-house movies regained the attention of international festivals, with Andrei Zviagintsev's *Return* (*Vozvrashchenie*, 2003) winning the Venice Golden Lion in September 2003, Alexei Popogrebsky's and Boris Khlebnikov's *Koktebel* being awarded the title FIPRESCI Best Film of the Year in 2004, and Dmitrii Meskhiev's *Our Own* winning three awards at the Moscow International Film Festival 2004 as the 'best film I have seen in a long time', according to jury chairman Alan Parker (see Slatina 2004; Rozhdestvenskaia, 2004). This was followed in 2005 by the victory of another Russian film at the Moscow International Film Festival: Alexei Uchitel''s *Dreaming of Space* (*Kosmos kak predchuvstvie*). Russian mainstream cinema conquered its audiences at home too. The teen crime-comedy by Ruslan Bal'tser's *Don't Even Think* (*Dazhe ne dumai*, 31 March 2003) grossed just under a million, but its sequel already made a greater impact in spring 2004 with $2.3 million box office grossing. Vladimir Khotinenko's *72 Meters* (*72 metra*, 2004) about the Kursk tragedy grossed $2.6 million, while *Night Watch* (*Nochnoi Dozor*, released 11 July 2004), which cost $3.5 million and was released in over 300 copies, grossed $14 million in four weeks and a total of $16 million through theatrical release alone. *Night Watch* crossed the $10 million threshold of box office grossing, which was achieved partly through a massive PR campaign and rigid anti-piracy surveillance that made pirated copies of the film invisible in the streets. The film showed clearly that Russia was ready for home-grown blockbusters. As the sequel to *Night Watch* was delayed in production and the rights for a remake and a prequel to the trilogy sold to Fox for $6 million, other blockbusters followed suit in rapid succession.

In December 2004 *Countdown* (*Lichnyi nomer*, dir. Yevgenii Lavrent'ev) announced itself as the new 'blockbuster'. Released on 12 December 2004, it grossed $4.5 million. On 27 February 2005 *Turkish Gambit* (*Turetskii gambit*, dir. Djanik Faiziev) opened and grossed a total of $19 million at the box office, outstripping *Night Watch*. On 20 March 2005 *Shadowboxing* (*Boi s ten'iu*, dir. Alexei Sidorov) was released, grossing $8.2 million. In April the releases of Yegor Konchalovsky's *The Escape* (*Pobeg*) and Filipp Yankovsky's *Counsellor of State* (*Statskii sovetnik*) brought in $3.5 and $7.5 million respectively; Balabanov's spoof *Blind Man's Bluff* (*Zhmurki*), released in June 2005, grossed $4 million. The mega hit *Company 9* (*9-aia rota*), directed by Fedor Bondarchuk, a former clip-maker and son of Sergei Bondarchuk (*War and Peace*), was released on 29 September and grossed $19 million in the first fortnight of its run. Released on 1 January 2006 as the 'first film of the year' *Day Watch* (*Dnevnoi dozor*) opened on 518 screens and grossed $27.9 million. *Bimmer 2* opened in March 2006 on 444 screens and grossed $12.5 million, underlining again the viability of sequels (see Table 9.1).

These figures show the massive increase in grossing and the potential for film to become a branch of the Russian industry, while they also reflect the ability of Russian filmmakers to reach their audiences. These blockbusters appeal to audiences, largely 14–25 year olds with an urban background. But what heroes and what actions do these films show that attract such large audiences, notably at home, and not abroad? Why do they all deal with crime and criminals? Are they blockbusters because of the plot, because of star actors, or because of the genre? And what are the main features of the three mega-hits listed above?

The action hero, as we have seen, is a concept alien to the Russian character. Russians define themselves in the first instance vis-à-vis an enemy, real or imagined, to assert their national identity (Gudkov 2004, p. 555). Gudkov shows that the attributes 'criminal' and 'strange, alien' rank highest (63 and 41 per cent) amongst those applied to the new Russia, as opposed to a very low rating (12 and 8 per cent respectively) in connection with the Soviet regime. The Soviet system is perceived as 'ours' by 32 per cent of the survey group, whilst only 3 per cent would use this attribute for the new Russian administration. Thus people associate crime with 'other', not 'ours' and perceive the current power structures as alien to the people (ibid., p. 151).

Table 9.1:   Blockbusters: budgets and box office

Title	Release	Budget (est.)	Screens	Gross (mill.)
The Barber of Siberia	20 Feb 1999	$45 mill.		$2.6
Brother 2	11 May 2000	$1.5–2 mill.		$1.1
Anti-Killer	6 Apr 2002	$2 mill.	42	$1.3
Don't Even Think	31 Mar 2003			$1
Bimmer	28 June 2003	$1 mill.	59	$1.6
Anti-Killer 2: Anti-Terror	25 Nov 2003	$3 mill.	162	$2.6
72 Meters	Mar 2004	$1.6 mill.		$2.6
Don't Even Think 2	Apr 2004			$2.5
Night Watch	11 July 2004	$3.5 mill.	318	$16 [$31world]
Countdown	12 Dec 2004	$7 mill.		$4.5
Turkish Gambit	27 Feb 2005	$4 mill.	319	$19
Shadowboxing	20 Mar 2005	$3.5 mill.	274	$8.2
The Escape	3 Apr 2005	$1.8 mill.	270	$3.5
The Counsellor of State	24 Apr 2005	$4 mill.		$8
Blind Man's Bluff	5 June 2005		244	$4
Velvet Revolution	14 Sept 2005	$7 mill.		$7.2
Company 9	29 Sept 2005	$9 mill.	361	$25.6
Day Watch	1 Jan 2006	$4 mill.	518	$27.9 [$32 world]
Bimmer 2	7 Mar 2006		444	$12.5

Two important points result from this observation: Russia values its film industry with reference to the United States, establishing itself as economically ambitious and energetic. On screen, however, Russian filmmakers create heroes with few positive features or potential to set moral standards, and/but transpose these heroes into abstract spaces that are both similar and different from contemporary Russia. There is thus an ironic distance with regard to the 'model' of the American action movie. In these ambitious blockbusters the audience chooses its models of behaviour and thus signals its critique of, or attitude towards, modern Russian society.

Night Watch and *Day Watch* are based on the trilogy by Sergei Luk'ianenko, a little-known sci-fi writer from Kazakhstan, whose works subsequently became bestsellers. *Night Watch* deals with the conflict of good and evil, using the genre of an action movie with elements of horror (vampires, spells and so forth), peppered with a good deal of suspense. The film stars Konstantin Khabensky, who is widely known from his roles in the television serial *Criminal Petersburg* and his work on the theatrical stage. His hero Anton Gorodetsky has an essential flaw, but despite this he is a major guardian figure. *Turkish Gambit* is based on the best-selling novel by the crime writer Boris Akunin and stars a completely unknown actor, Yegor Beroev, in the lead (compare to *Counsellor of State* where the popular Oleg Men'shikov plays Fandorin). Fandorin is an intelligent investigator, but he is prone to human weakness and error. *Turkish Gambit* is a spy thriller in the style of the Soviet 'Red Western' and thus tapping into an established popular genre. *Company 9* is an anti-war and action movie, starring Fedor Bondarchuk (see above) and based on a film script by Iurii Korotkov, which was subsequently published. It is a movie about soldiers with human flaws, but who nevertheless fight for their fatherland. The common denominator of these films is the characteristic of the hero, who is an essentially good person with an inherent human flaw. He does not try to overcome this flaw, but accepts it as part of his personality. It is also noteworthy that all three films are driven by a male cast; indeed, if there are a number of male stars with huge popularity in Russian cinema (Oleg Men'shikov, Gosha Kutsenko, Konstantin Khabensky, Fedor Bondarchuk, Andrei Panin, Alexei Serebriakov as the vanguard, followed by Alexei Chadov, Alexei Panin, Dmitrii Diuzhin, Andrei Merzlikin, Viktor Sukhorukov and Kirill Pirogov), then there are only a few actresses who have starred in a number of blockbusters (Viktoria Tolstoganova, Renata Litvinova, Liubov' Tolkalina and Chulpan Khamatova). The absence of leading actresses is also obvious in national festival and academy awards in the category 'Best Actress'.

The just killer

Balabanov's *Brother* and the sequel *Brother 2* playfully engage with the genre of the action movie. The plot of *Brother* concerns a killer with a good heart who reinstates justice and fights evil. The cast includes no stars, but unknown and unprofessional actors; with the exception of Viktor Sukhorukov the cast became known as a result of the film.

The film tells the story of Danila Bagrov, who returns to his provincial hometown from army service. When he gets into trouble with the police his mother sends him to visit his elder brother, Viktor, in St Petersburg. Viktor is a killer, who enlists Danila to shoot the 'Chechen' mafia boss. While carrying out the task Danila realizes that his own brother has betrayed him; at the same time an unknown woman tram driver, Sveta, helps him. Danila subsequently has an affair with Sveta, but she stays with her violent husband. Danila shoots the 'Chechen' and bails out his brother. Danila is a professional killer, but he is also a knight who helps the poor, suppressed and underprivileged. Having conquered the criminal world of St Petersburg, he leaves for Moscow.

Brother defines a new type of hero, who upholds no moral standards at all.[5] On the one hand, Danila possesses skill, strength and courage. He knows how to use guns, he is physically fit enough to fight, and his actions display a sense of military logistics. He helps the poor: he defends an old man, Hoffman, against a racketeer; he helps the conductor collect a fine from two Caucasians travelling on a tram without a ticket; and he shoots at Sveta's violent husband. A man of action, he is ruthless to his enemies. In the tradition of the romantic hero, he is a knight who keeps his word. In the criminal world he is a killer. He combines within himself the contradictions that lie at the heart of the 'Russian idea': the right to judge and the compassion to redeem.

Balabanov creates not only a lovable killer, but he also debunks the socialist myth, which sees the hero as part of a historical process: Danila has no role in society at large. A true killer, he is a loner, an individual acting without a reason, an outsider ('Proshchai, oruzhie', Rutkovsky, p. 16). Moreover, Balabanov rejects the *chernukha* model, which perceives man as a victim of circumstance and therefore essentially non-heroic. The new hero is no victim, but makes no choices either; he lives on the spur of the moment and acts according to circumstances, but 'we do not see a man who really overcomes himself and circumstance' ('Proshchai, oruzhie', Dmitrii Bykov, p. 7).

Danila offers neither a lead to the future, nor does he have a past. If he does have a history, it is the fictional biography of Bodrov Jr's previous hero, the soldier of the Chechen war, Vania Zhilin of Sergei Bodrov Sr's *The Prisoner of the Mountains* (*Kavkazskii plennik*, 1996). At the beginning of *Brother* Danila claims that he spent his army service as a scribe in some office, but his knowledge of firearms and his carefully planned manoeuvres reveal this to be false. Indeed, *Brother 2* confirms that Danila has served in Chechnya. Danila is a young man hardened to the realities of life by his experience of war. He rewrites his past and his personality at leisure: he is like a blank page onto which any story could be written, which is reflected in the technique of blackouts that fragments the film into episodes and allows it to be reassembled in almost any order. Danila is deprived of psychological depth and the choice of a non-professional actor reflects Balabanov's need for a façade rather than a character. Danila is a construct, a figure whose path can be reassembled, whose origin lies in fiction, who hears the sounds of a virtual world. Danila is a figure out of a virtual game, appearing at the right time and in the right place to be a 'saviour' or a 'killer', protecting the good in human nature and punishing the evil characters.

At the film's opening Danila accidentally walks into the location of a clip for the rock group Nautilus Pompilius's latest album 'Wings' (Kryl'ia). Later he literally marches into lead singer Slava Butusov's[6] flat: he seeks to identify with the group, but fails to realize that he lives in a different world. In both cases, he crashes back into reality: at the police station, bruised and beaten; and into a murder scene in the neighbouring flat. Nautilus's music functions as a leitmotif for Danila's journey to St Petersburg. Like Danila, Nautilus came from the provinces to the northern capital in the 1990s; in St Petersburg Danila finally acquires a compact disc of 'Wings' that he plays on his walkman. He lives in the world of Nautilus's music and only partly apprehends the reality that surrounds him. The songs endow the film with a dream-like quality. Bagrov's movements are paced by the rhythm of the music and appear to be executed unconsciously. Nautilus's songs are about daydreams that allow an escape from the crippling effect of reality; the wings that enable man to fly have been severed, leaving only scars ('Wings'). The songs used in the film are all from those albums that Danila fails to acquire in the music shop. In other words, the spectator hears the music Danila wishes to hear on his player but has actually not yet managed to acquire. The hero lives in the sound system of another world, in which he is immortal: the CD player literally saves his life when it deflects a bullet.

Brother 2 takes Danila to Moscow, where his 'brother'-in-arms, Kostia, with whom he served in the Chechen war, is murdered as he tries to help his twin brother, a hockey player in the NHL who is being exploited by the American mafia boss Mennis. The theme of fraternity resounds in the slogans 'save our brothers' and 'we don't desert our own'. Danila and Viktor (who now works for the police in his home town) travel to Chicago to free Kostia's brother Mitia from the grip of capitalist exploitation. Like the Russian fairy-tale hero Ivan who gets to his object of desire (usually a princess to marry) by doing good deeds on his way to engage magic assistance, Danila also rescues the Russian prostitute Dasha, befriends an American truck-driver, sleeps with the black television presenter Lisa Jeffrey, and recovers the money from Mennis. Danila has an innate understanding of social justice: he never acts to enrich himself, but to help others. All of Danila's actions serve to punish the exploiters and rehabilitate the exploited, asserting right over wrong – and Russia over America.

While Viktor beats up a Polish-speaking cop and holds forth about Ukrainians and niggers, using the same abusive language that Danila had used for the Caucasians in *Brother*, Danila encounters nice Americans, such as Ben Johnson, Lisa Jeffrey, the New York taxi driver and the Chicago policeman. The Russians he meets rip him off, such as the car salesman in Brooklyn. If for Viktor power lies in money (representing the American ideal), then for Danila it lies in the truth (representing the Russian ideal). Therefore Viktor stays in the US while Danila returns to Russia.

Danila's comments disclose the television image as essentially flawed: the pop icon Irina Saltykova[7] falls for Danila precisely because he is not a fan. Lisa Jeffrey is worried about the media repercussions of the accident, yet she also genuinely cares for Danila. The TV interview with Kostia, Il'ia and Danila alleges that they have enjoyed themselves in the Chechen war. Media are thus shown in a negative light, distorting both reality and personality.

In *Brother 2* Danila never behaves according to real time and place: he fires around in the Chicago nightclub as though playing a game; he intimidates the American gun dealer in a staged manner; and he overwhelms Mennis, ironically, with his eloquence. For Danila, shooting is like a computer game where the enemy lurks around every corner and behind each door. Danila is playing, as it were, a virtual game with his gun. Indeed, Danila lives largely in an artificial world of music and media, while he has no grip on the real world: in the same way as he stargazed at the lead singer Slava Butusov in *Brother*, in the sequel he does not know who Irina Saltykova is, how to find Kotelnichesky Embankment, or what roaming means. His lack of education and culture transpire from his comments (he does not know Saltykova's music), just as much as from the Viktor's comments (he says that Filipp Kirkorov[8] is Romanian – he is Bulgarian). After all, the Bagrovs are sons of a common criminal, who venture into the great criminal world. Danila overcomes the new Russians who have gained their wealth by cheating on the common people. He shows loyalty to his brother(s), to his family, to his people. Naïve and good hearted, Bagrov avenges and rescues Russians from capitalism.

Many critics have accused Balabanov of nationalism, especially citing the comments on black arses and niggers (Dondurei 1998; Matizen 1997). Yet while Balabanov clearly promotes a Russian way of life, the American and Russian people are not schematized: there are good and bad men and women on both sides. Rather, the public and private images are split: there are stars and those who are not. Playing Bagrov, Bodrov left his own stardom and cult status aside and played the simpleton, who has no aspirations to stardom: 'I am both sky and moon to myself' ('ia sam sebe i nebo i luna'), as Auktsyon's film score 'The Road' ('Doroga') begins.

Danila demythologizes the world of stars: all people are the same, and even stars seek human attention and love (like Jeffrey and Saltykova). On the other hand, by associating himself with the media stars Danila ascertains that he shows just his façade.

Bagrov re-establishes social order and redistributes wealth: he is a modern Raskol'nikov, with the difference that he does not act out of a need to prove himself a superman. He knows that he is a superman in his virtual computer world of killers and gangsters. The comparison with Ivan the Fool helps shed light on Danila's almost mechanical execution of his actions: if the morphology of fairy tale suggests a (fictional) journey, it appears that Danila's journey too is only imaginary: whether he acts in his mind or in reality remains unresolved. All the shootings are choreographed and paced to the soundtrack that intoxicates Danila and that speaks of ideals to which he aspires. If, in the first part, he walks onto the location and into the virtual reality of the film clip, in the second part he moves comfortably in the media jungle and, with his leisurely and unassuming manner, demythologizes the pop icons.

The issue remains of whether Danila is a killer or whether he is just playing a game. Is he in Russia, as he claims on his mobile phone, saying he is in Tula when he arrives in New York, in Biriulevo when he roams the streets of Chicago, 'running' just before he gets to O'Hare airport; and eventually, as he boards the return flight to Moscow, he books a table at the Metropol for dinner. Igor Mantsov has pointed out that Balabanov reasserts Moscow as the centre of the universe, an approach that dominated the geopolitical ideas of the 1920s and of Soviet cultural discourse in general (Mantsov 2000). Balabanov here resurrects the concept of Moscow not as the centre of socialist ideology, but of a practical and humanist socialism, which redistributes wealth and fights against crime. Balabanov is, I would argue, not a nationalist, but a political left-winger.

The *Brother* films became blockbusters because they created a new, virtual hero who lived not in reality, but in a world where he plays a game according to his own rules. Bagrov's world resembles the virtual world of Viktor Pelevin's *Generation P* (*Pokolenie P*) with a media-manipulated Yeltsin figure; likewise, he could be part of Vladimir Sorokin's world of clones in *Rosenthal's Children* (*Deti Rozentalia*) or the film script *Four* (*Chetyre*). Thus, the first paradigm of the new Russian blockbuster encompasses the parody of an action movie by transposing the plot into a virtual reality (like a computer game) with a plot about a killer who creates new rules. The killer's actions and his conduct increase the popularity of the actor, who consequently acquires the status of a cult figure.

A variation of this paradigm can be seen in Sergei Bodrov Jr's debut film *Sisters* (*Sestry*, 2001). Bodrov tells the story of two girls, Sveta (Oksana Akinshina) and her younger half-sister Dina. Sveta loves shooting as a sport and dreams of becoming a sniper while Dina is a spoilt little girl who plays the violin and is the pride of her gangster-daddy. Suddenly Sveta has to protect herself and Dina from some gangsters who come after Dina's father. Sisterhood, like brotherhood, involves protecting the weak from the hostile reality and maintaining the child's fairy world. However, in the crucial situation Sveta does not have to fire at a human target: she does not (yet) have to kill. However, she is able to transfer her skills acquired in the world of sport and games to a real situation.

In Balabanov's *Blind Man's Bluff* (*Zhmurki*, 2005) today's businessmen are shown to be yesterday's criminals. The film is a parody on the rise of corrupt individuals to key business roles in the late 1990s, while former mafia bosses are degraded to caretakers. Balabanov plays a game with social roles, but in contrast to other blockbusters *Blind Man's Bluff* is set in the immediate past and not the present. For Balabanov, society remains corrupt, and he mocks his colleagues' unwillingness to see this: Balabanov's characters are flatly drawn and deprived of any depth; they are players in a game that never ends; only its players change. Balabanov's *Brother* is a landmark in the development of the Russian hero for the future blockbuster, as is clear from the remarks in the 2002 roundtable at *Iskusstvo kino* 'Proshchai, oruzhie': it is a complex character straddling borders between 'us' and 'them', good and evil, submissive and aggressive, whose action drive is brought out only because of the contact with an 'enemy' (Caucasians, Americans), which functions as catalyst for the creation and definition of a national myth (Gudkov 2004, p. 566).

The legitimate killer

In the first paradigm the killer was a criminal, who had human flaws and who acted out of a sense of social justice and therefore became a knight. The second paradigm inverses the first: the hero operates within society, within its judicial system, and has a licence to kill. He does not confuse real and virtual worlds, as the killer of the first paradigm who acted in detachment from reality.

The second paradigm presents the killer-policeman, the killer who belongs to the forces of good. These films use the genre of an action movie without elements of irony or parody. Into this category fall *Anti-Killer* and the sequel *Anti-Killer 2: Anti-Terror*, which were a considerable success at the Russian box office, although they have not been distributed abroad. Both films were based on the crime novels by Danil Koretsky. The former police lieutenant Korenev (nickname 'Lis', or Fox), played by the popular actor Gosha Kutsenko, has been set up and arrested for abuse of power. Having served his sentence, he is released from prison and tries to assess the new constellation of power in the criminal world in order to disperse the mafia gangs. The criminal boss, Shaman, has ordered the murder of Fox's friend and former colleague. Shaman is a new player in the criminal world, who does not follow the codes of the old mafia bosses, Father, King, and Cross. Into this mafia war of old and new clans erupts the violence of Ambal (played by the actor Viktor Sukhorokov, who specializes in evil and dark characters), a brutal gangster whose level of pain has been reduced significantly by a lobotomy. Ambal has no values, no understanding of the order of the criminal authorities and knows only the force of his gun. In many ways, Konchalovsky's tale of Fox's revenge on the mafia is a continuation of the amoral killer of *Brother*, but this time the killer operates in the real criminal world and he is an ex-cop. Alone, Fox is capable of taking on hundreds of criminals at once.

In the sequel *Anti-Killer 2* Fox has returned to the police force and married a medical doctor, Liuba. The Chechen commander Aduev has been arrested, and this arrest puts in danger the entire city: Aduev's son Uzhak seeks revenge and tries to free his father, and to this end he prepares a chemical attack on the town's water supplies. Indeed, Uzhak is a terrorist leader: he orders the widow of a Chechen fighter to blow herself up in front of the mayor's office; he shoots his father in a crucial moment when they disagree; he liquidates his own people when they become useless. Uzhak takes Fox's wife Liuba as a hostage and Fox has to save her before the military destroy both the dangerous terrorists and the hostage. In a fistfight, Fox single-handedly overcomes the dangerous terrorist Uzhak. Konchalovsky creates a story that transforms the allegedly corrupt cop into a guardian angel with qualities of a superman. However, even Fox has doubts in the system: he had been disappointed by the police force, which had alleged his involvement in mafia crime for which he served a term in prison. Throughout the first film Fox reinforced good in a world of evil, and acted outside the police force and among criminals, establishing order and doing alone the work that the police should do. In the second part Fox is again part of the police force, but he fights his superiors and the bureaucrats that surround him. His human flaws are clear: he is an ex-prisoner, a friend of the mafia bosses, and a man in love. Fox is an individual who asserts his understanding of good and evil, of right and wrong; he is a hybrid between criminal and policeman. Fox maintains that the function played by man in society is irrelevant as long as the individual is prepared to fight for and defend his ideals.

The reality of *Anti-Killer* is relative and abstract, remote from the here-and-now. As Dmitrii Komm observed, not all social classes are part of this world, but only marginal groups: *Anti-Killer* 'comprises only four groups of citizens: bandits, cops, tarts and victims' (Komm 2002, p. 23). Moreover, the space is sterile and lacks a clear indication of time. Here Konchalovsky elevates the marginal criminal world as typical for the whole of Russia, avoiding the issue of Russia as a country with a lost identity, defining instead its enemy.

The paradigm of the policeman who once was in prison and becomes a legitimate killer acting in the name of social order also applies to another mega-hit, *Night Watch*. Here the killer is a soldier of the good forces, but once upon a time he too was tempted by the evil world. Timur Bekmambetov's[9] *Night Watch* (*Nochnoi dozor*, 2004) and *Day Watch* (*Dnevnoi dozor*, 2006) are based on Sergei Luk'ianenko's gripping fantasy sci-fi thriller and address the fight between good and evil, between the worlds of light and darkness, which is explained in a historical prologue (Languedoc in 1342). Since ancient times the world is ruled by a constant fight between good and evil. In modern days fortune-tellers, magicians, and vampires act as representatives of the evil forces, while the light people work as engineers for Gorsvet (City Light).

Anton Gorodetsky (Khabensky) works for Gorsvet and helps protect Moscow and its inhabitants from disaster, catastrophe and evil. But once upon a time, in August 1992 he wanted to revenge his wife and kill their unborn child. To this end he turned to the dark forces and employed the sorceress Schulz, who was prevented from casting the spell by the forces of light. Twelve years later Gorodetsky fights on the side of 'light' for Gesser (played by Oscar-winning director Vladimir Men'shov). On a mission to protect the boy Yegor he kills the vampire Andrei, who had enchanted a girl and made her long for Yegor's blood. The woman vampire seeks to destroy Anton for having killed her beloved. Anton's attention turns to Svetlana, who (despite a name that is derived from 'svet', for light) also belongs to the 'others': she has cursed herself for hating her sick mother and wanting her death. Svetlana's curse leads to an explosion, which cuts the power supply for the whole of Moscow, and it almost causes an aircraft to crash; but Anton turns Svetlana's curse away in time. When he finally tries to rescue Yegor, the boy has to make a choice between the good and evil forces – and in a twist of events he turns to the evil forces.

Night Watch contains all the ingredients of an American action movie (such as *Terminator*), while expanding the fantasy component. The visual rendering of the funnel (*voronka*) in the form of crows (*vorona*) is only too reminiscent of Hitchcock's horror movie *Birds*. The difference between the worlds of good and evil, light and dark, is never drawn in black and white and avoids absolutes and stereotypes. Thus, doubt, weakness, and human flaws rule the world of the light forces: Anton not only has a flaw, having sinned when he tried to kill his unborn son, but he also befriends his 'dark' neighbour, who supplies him with pig's blood from the family butchery. The Gorsvet engineers Tiger and Bear are easily tempted by Yegor to transform into the animals that their names represent – just for fun, neglecting their responsibility. It is amusing to see the division between light and dark reflected also in the divide between high and low culture: the light forces have their agent work in the Bolshoi Theatre, while the pop star Alice assists the head of the dark forces, Zawulon. Ultimately, nobody is without a flaw. Yet it is crucial to confess to that flaw and stand by it: when Svetlana does this, the world is saved from darkness and the aircraft lands safely.

Day Watch sees the struggle between light and dark continued in the search for the chalk of fate that allows Anton to turn time back and undo the spell cast in 1992, thus annihilating the years between the collapse of the USSR and the present, making possible Anton's reunion with his estranged wife and a fresh start, undoing the economic and social turmoil of the 1990s.

The paradigm of the killer who lawfully fights evil and defends good involves a human flaw in the character. The lawful killers are played by already well-known actors, like Gosha Kutsenko and Konstantin Khabensky. Anton tried to kill his wife and unborn child; he lies to his son, asking whether he wanted to kill him; he kills the vampire Andrei. His colleagues too have such flaws: Semen arrives too late to prevent the explosion in the power plant; and Ignat fails to enchant Svetlana. There is both good and evil in all of us, and it is a question of dominance of one of the two forces. Zawulon exercises no force over the boy when the latter chooses the side of darkness. Bekmambetov creates a hero with a human flaw that is ultimately neither disguised nor belittled, but it allows him to fight for the light forces, to be a 'hero'. Mikhail Ryklin aligns the light forces with their slightly Soviet mannerisms to the Soviet past, while he compares the dark parasites who feed on the blood of the (Soviet) past to the new Russian bourgeoisie: 'The hidden code of the *Watches*...lies in establishing a link between the death of the USSR, which the light ones perceive as something alive and real, and the wild capitalism which is symbolised by the dark ones' (Ryklin in Kupriianov and Surkov 2006, p. 47).

Night Watch has become part of popular culture, as once upon a time the television serial *Seventeen Moments of Spring* (*17 mgnovenii vesny*, 1973, dir. Tat'iana Lioznova) and its hero, Stirlitz, or the revolutionary hero Chapaev: the story of Anton Gorodetsky is wittily summarized in the song 'Nochnoi dozor' by Sergei and Vladimir Kristovskie of the group Umaturman v gorode N (Uma Thurman in the City of N).

It is important here to note the possibility of choice, allowing former sinners (like Anton and Fox) to return to a normal life and devote their lives to the defence of the system, granting both of them the licence to kill. The lawful killer is a hero because he takes on forces that are superior or equally strong, and yet they master the situations. The lawful killer is allowed to integrate into society as long as he is ready to defend its values with his own life. The readiness to pay that price endows both Fox and Anton with heroic qualities, even if they are just soldiers doing their job.

The blockbusters that followed *Night Watch* continue the above pattern both for the plot and for the hero. *Countdown* fictionalizes the terrorist attack on the Dubrovka Theatre Centre, but with a different ending: through the efforts of one individual, a former special agent, the siege ends without victims. *Shadowboxing* shows the triumph of a boxer over the mafia, even though he has to pay a price and serve a prison sentence before returning to his new-found love – and, in the sequel, to boxing. In *Counsellor of State* Fandorin triumphs over the terrorists that make 1880s Russia an unsafe place, while *Turkish Gambit* is a spy thriller where Fandorin overcomes Russia's enemy in the East. *Velvet Revolution* shows two officers of the special forces who uncover the corruption of their own boss and save the world from illegal arms deals and terrorism. *Company 9* is set during the Afghan war, underlining the braveness of the soldiers in their fight for the fatherland even after it has abandoned its territorial pursuits. All these blockbusters revolve around plots that are removed in time: *Night Watch* through the historical prologue and the flashback to Anton in 1992; *Gambit* and *Counsellor* through their setting in the 1880s, both in Russia and Central Asia; *Company 9* through a geographically remote setting and the temporal distance to a regime (the USSR of the 1980s) that no longer exists. In all these films the heroes are victorious, but they pay for their victories and they are ready to die. The hero of cinema under Putin becomes a flagship of the regime: he inspires trust in the population and reassures the viewer that Russia is a safe place. His human flaws make him 'one of us', thus inspiring further heroic feats.

Conclusion

I have identified here two paradigms for the new Russian blockbuster: first, the hero of the Yeltsin years, the killer-knight who operates within the criminal world and reinforces social justice in the absence of a competent and powerful police force. Second, the hero of the Putin era, the killer-policeman, who has an inherent flaw in his past. More than often films show an improvement from killer to knight, thus cradling the viewer in the illusion that there is a chance for reintegration of killers in society, and that society needs forceful, active, decisive individuals.

Gudkov argues that such active and assertive features are extraneous to the Russian national character, which is defined instead by a victim complex. I suggest that these films are blockbusters because they project, in a real or virtual world, in a historical or contemporary setting, the assimilation of those features into the Russian character. This development suggests a rapprochement between 'ours' and 'them', or American characters, and, by extension, a rapprochement of the cultural and economic features that facilitate film distribution. It brings the American superman closer to Russian audiences and prepares the path for action hero qualities (crucial to the genre of the action blockbuster) to become part of the characteristic features of the Russian counterpart.

The second paradigm chronologically follows the first that had acknowledged the social chaos of the Yeltsin era when the police was corrupt. The second paradigm tries to instil trust in the police force, asserting that individuals can defend the people from evil acts, terrorist attacks or the disasters brought upon the world by the 'other', evil world.

If the Yeltsin blockbusters presented the plot as a game, in which the individual has no role, but a mechanical function, then the blockbusters under Putin apply to the real world the new rules of the killer who elevates himself to a defendant of justice. The killer-heroes deal with specific, localized tasks, and this explains to some extent the limited (national) appeal of some of these films (such as *Anti-Killer*): they are needed to confirm a social order to the Russian people, but not the outside world. *Night Watch* and *Day Watch*, which ventured onto the international market, draw on universal concepts of good and evil, thus making these films internationally viable.

It is worth noting that full-length animated films based on Russian folk epics have recently been quite successful, grossing between $4–5 million, They explore the adventures of the energetic, active, and fearless Russian heroes of Alesha Popovich, Dobrynia Nikitich or Il'ia Muromets, and signal that heroic and active qualities as inherent in Russian folk characters are also gaining ground in children's cinema.

Notes

1. See the roundtable discussion 'Blokbaster: perevod na russkii'.
2. In Russian folklore Baba Yaga is such a guardian: she inhabits a transitional space (the hut on chicken legs that can turn and offer or deny access to the land of the dead). Baba Yaga is ambiguous: she can be good or evil.
3. Source: Dodona Research, *Screen International*, 24 June 2005, p. 23.
4. Goblin translations are parodic dubs of blockbusters by Dmitrii Puchkov. These first appeared in MPEG 4 format only and were illegally produced and sold in subway passages. By contrast, *Anti-Bimmer* was produced by CTB and released on VHS and DVD.
5. For a full discussion, see Beumers 1999 and 2007.
6. Viacheslav (Slava) Butusov, born 1961, formed the band Nautilus Pompilius in Sverdlovsk and moved to St Petersburg in 1988. Danila has purchased the album 'Wings' (Kryl'ia), 1995; the soundtrack is from the albums 'Yablokitai', London 1996 and 'Atlantida', 1997.
7. Irina Saltykova's songs include 'Grey Eyes' (Serye glaza) with an erotic video clip; Saltykova is the advertising 'face' for 'Life Style' condoms.
8. Filipp Kirkorov, born 1967 in Varna; graduated from the Gnesin Institute in 1988; since 1994 married to pop star Alla Pugacheva.
9. Bekmambetov made advertising clips for the 'Bank Imperial' in the 1990s; he directed *The Arena* (USA, 2001, produced by Roger Corman), which starred the 'Playboy Playmates' Karen McDogal and Lisa Dergan.

References

Anon. 2003. 'Russia "an untapped opportunity for cinema industry"', *Screen Daily*, 23 September.
Beumers, Birgit. 1999. 'To Moscow! To Moscow? The Russian Hero and the Loss of the Centre', in *Russia on Reels*, ed. Beumers, London: Tauris, pp. 76–87.
_____ 2007. 'Brat', in *24 Frames: The Cinema of Russia and the former Soviet Union*, ed. Beumers, London: Wallflower, pp. 233–41.
'Blokbaster: perevod na russkii'. 2005. Roundtable, *Iskusstvo kino* 12: 5–23.
Brown, Colin. 2007. 'Russian film – Eastern promise', *Screen Daily*, 16 February.
Dondurei, Daniil. 1998. 'Ne brat ia tebe, gnida . . .', *Iskusstvo kino* 2: 64–7.
Franklin, Anna. 2003. 'US Exhibitor looks to cash in on Russian multiplex boom', *Screen Daily*, 19 September.
_____ 2004. 'Russian renaissance prompts increase in state support', *Screen Daily*, 21 January.
_____ 2005. 'Russian box office surges over 40% in 2004', *Screen Daily*, 17 January.
Frater, Patrick. 2005. 'UPI set up operations in Russia', *Screen Daily*, 23 February.
Galetski, Kirill. 2005. 'Behind the curtain: the Russian box office boom', *Screen International*, 13 May.

_____ 2006. 'Sinking the pirates', *Screen International*, 5 May, p. 12.

Gudkov, Lev. 2004. *Negativnaia identichnost'*, Moscow: NLO.

Gusiatinskiy, Yevgenii. 2004. 'Krizis kak zhanr', *Iskusstvo kino* 2: 33–5.

Kay, Jeremy. 2004. 'Russia's Cinema Park opens first multiplex in Moscow', *Screen Daily*, 23 January.

Komm Dmitrii. 2002. 'Uzhe ne protokol', *Iskusstvo kino* 12: 19–23.

Kupriianov, V. and M. Surkov (eds) 2006. *Dozor kak simptom*, Moscow: Falanster.

Larsen, Susan. 2003. 'National Identity, Cultural Authority and the Post-Soviet Blockbuster: Nikita Mikhalkov and Aleksei Balabanov', *Slavic Review*, 62(3): 491–511.

Mantsov, Igor'. 2000. 'Zvezdy i soldaty', *Iskusstvo kino* 11: 60–7.

Matizen, Viktor. 1997. 'Skromnoe ochorovanie ubiitsy,' *Seans* 16: 41.

Mikhalkov, Nikita. 1999. 'The Function of a National Cinema' [1998], in *Russia on Reels*, ed. B. Beumers, London: Tauris, pp. 50–3.

Mitchell, Wendy. 2006. 'Rising Star starts building Russia's largest multiplex', *Screen Daily*, 21 June.

'Proshchai, oruzhie'. 2002. Roundtable discussion, *Iskusstvo kino* 11: 5–21.

Rozhdestvenskaia, Kseniia. 2004. 'Russkoe stalo glavnym', *Gazeta.ru*, 28 June. http://www.gazeta.ru/2004/06/28/oa_125267.shtml. Accessed 8 May 2007.

'Russian Box-Office 2006: All is yet to come'. 2006. *Action*, May, p. 1.

Segida, Miroslava and Sergei Zemlianukhin. 2004. *Fil'my Rossii 1992–2003. Igrovoe kino/TV/Video*. Moscow: Dubl'-D.

Slatina, Elena. 2004. '"Svoi" i chuzhie', *Novye Izvestiia*, 29 June. http://www. newizv.ru/news/?id_news=7668&date=2004-06-29&grade=3. Accessed 8 May 2007.

Wahnich, Sophie. 2005. 'Les musées d'histoire du XXième siècle en Europe', *Etudes: Revue de Culture Contemporaine*, July–August: 29–42.

Web site

Screen Daily is the daily Internet bulletin of *Screen International*. See also: www.imdb.com; www.kinoros.ru; www.videoguide.ru; www. kinobusiness.ru.

10
Drug Abuse and HIV/AIDS in Russia

John M. Kramer

> Narcotics have become weapons of mass destruction in a war. They can be compared to the atomic bomb, poison gases, and deadly viruses. The number of victims in this war is shocking.
>
> (Oleg Kharichkin, Deputy Director of the Federal Service to Control the Trade in Narcotics and Psychotropic Substances (Interfax, 16 June 2005))

While charged rhetoric of this kind may seem hyperbolic, Russian officials commonly employ it, using terms like 'crisis' and 'threat to national security' to describe the impact of drug abuse on their society. Many ordinary Russians harbor similar concerns about drug abuse. Thus, when asked in a July 2005 nationwide poll of 2,107 residents of Russia with a statistical margin of error not exceeding three per cent to identify the 'most alarming' problems facing Russia today, 29 per cent of respondents cited 'the growth of drug abuse,' ranking it fifth in a list of 26 problems they identified, just behind the 'crisis in the economy,' named by 33 per cent of respondents, and ahead of such a well known problem as 'corruption and bribery,' named by 24 per cent of respondents (Levada Center data consulted at www.levada.ru).

The close link between drug abuse and the spread of HIV/AIDS in Russia fuels these concerns. As of February 2007, Russia officially had registered 376,825 individuals, of whom 80 per cent were aged from 15 to 30, as HIV positive (Russian Federal AIDS Center 2007). Yet Russian officials readily concede that the actual number of Russians with HIV is far higher than the officially registered figure. Thus, Vadim Pokrovsky, director of the Russian Federal AIDS Center (the 'RF AIDS Center') and Russia's leading expert on the subject, estimated in September 2005 that there could then be upwards of a million individuals living in Russia with the AIDS virus (ITAR-TASS September 26, 2005). The World Bank has estimated that Russia could have upwards of 2.3 million HIV positive people by 2010 and 5.4 million such people by 2020 if it does not soon begin to implement an effective program to prevent the spread of the virus (*AIDS Journal* 2005).

Of the 269,821 individuals officially registered as HIV positive between 1996 and 2003, 136,564 of them – just over 50 per cent of the total registered – were injection drug users ('IDUs') who contracted the disease through the use of shared injection equipment. IDUs constituted a substantially larger share – upwards of 85 per cent – among the 158,950 officially registered HIV cases between 1996–2003 where the main risk factor in contracting the disease could be determined. In contrast, in the United States only 17 per cent of individuals identified as HIV positive between 2001–2004 contracted the disease through intravenous use of drugs (*Washington Post*, August 13, 2006, p. A7).

This chapter amplifies on these themes by examining in turn the following aspects of drug abuse in Russia: (i) its scope; (ii) its links to HIV/AIDS; (iii) official responses; and (iv) its prospective status and implications for the spread of HIV/AIDS.

Scope

Only when Mikhail Gorbachev became General Secretary of the Communist Party in March 1985 did Soviet officials begin abandoning their hitherto oft-repeated ideological mantra that social pathologies such as drug abuse flourished only amidst the moral vacuity and alienation of capitalism. As part of Gorbachev's well-known policy of *glasnost'*, official commentaries now began acknowledging publicly that drug abuse both existed in the USSR and had its roots at least partly in the imperfections of socialist society itself (Kramer 1991, p. 96).

Yet, as with data on HIV/AIDS, officials readily admit that the actual extent of drug abuse in Russia is substantially higher than official data portray. Specialists writing in an official publication of the Russian Federation's Ministry of Health suggested applying a multiplier of between 20 and 50 to the official data on drug abuse to gain a clearer picture of its actual extent (Entin et al. 1999, p. 73). More commonly, commentaries suggest a multiplier of between eight and ten.

The problematic state of these data arises primarily because they are based upon individuals officially registered at state-run narcological clinics with a diagnosis of either 'drug abuse' or 'drug addiction.' Such a system has manifest inadequacies because drug abusers in Russia – even

Table 10.1: Individuals newly registered at narcological clinics with a diagnosis of drug addiction and drug abuse, 1999, 2003

	Per 100,000 population		2003 to 1999 (per cent)
	1999	2003	
Drug Addiction	41.9	16.1	−61.6
Including from:			
Opiates	37.9	13.0	−65.6
Cannabis	1.7	1.8	8.2
Cocaine	0.2	0.0	−97.0
Psychostimulants	0.7	0.3	−57.1
Other Narcotics	1.4	0.9	−36.4
Drug Abuse	36.1	22.8	−36.8

Source: Adapted from Evgenia Koshkina, 'Rastprostrannennost' osnovnykh narkologicheskikh zabolevanii v Rossii v 1992–2003 gg.,' *Voprosy narkologii*, 2 (2004): 55.

more so than their counterparts in other countries – have compelling disincentives to register with the authorities. These disincentives include the possibility of being subject to mandatory treatment for their affliction in prison-like facilities run by the police, the revocation of their drivers' license, and denial of admission to institutions of higher learning. The system also entails a 'catch 22' which leads to substantial undercounting of drug abusers because individuals can only be registered at narcological clinics in cities or towns where they legally reside. This excludes, by definition, those millions of individuals who either reside illegally in Russia or have no narcological clinics to offer them treatment in their legally registered places of residence.

What the official data do reveal is a steady increase, at least during the 1990s, in individuals registered at narcological clinics. Thus, in 1999 there were 41.8 individuals per 100,000 population who registered at narcological clinics for the first time, up from just 3.9 per 100,000 population in 1991 (United Nations Office for Drug Control and Crime Prevention 2001, p. 8). However, these data suggest that drug abuse may have peaked in the late 1990s with a substantial decrease being recorded thereafter in the number of individuals per 100,000 population newly registered at narcological clinics with a diagnosis of either 'drug addiction' or 'drug abuse.' A similar decrease occurred regarding newly registered individuals with addictions to specific drugs, including opiates (see Table 10.1).

Some officials have hailed these data as evidence of the efficacy of the government's anti-drug policies (*Izvestiia*, October 21, 2003). Yet other officials have expressed considerable skepticism about these data. For example, referring specifically to the approximately fourfold decline since 2000 in youths aged 15–17 officially registered with a diagnosis of 'drug addiction,' Evgenia Koshkina, deputy director of the RF Ministry of Health's National Scientific Narcological Center, flatly contended that such a decline 'cannot be' reflective of the actual state of affairs (quoted in *Kommersant-daily*, October 23, 2003, p. 7).

The available evidence strongly supports this latter assessment. First, there are no validated precedents worldwide for such reported declines in the magnitude of drug abuse over such a short period of time. More fundamentally as it applies specifically to Russia, Russia has not implemented the effective anti-drug measures which proponents credit for the unprecedented reported decline in the incidence of drug abuse (see below). Consequently, it is far more plausible, as Koshkina of the Health Ministry has contended, that the reported decline in drug abuse and drug addiction actually reflects a 'loss of faith in the effectiveness of treatment' at narcological clinics among drug abusers, who increasingly turn to private clinics for anonymous treatment or forego any treatment whatsoever (ibid.).

The problematic state of official statistics on the subject has prompted other, invariably higher, estimates of the actual extent of drug abuse. Since 2005, sources have typically employed a figure of about six million individuals who, depending on the denotation of the source, are 'drug addicts,' 'drug abusers,' 'drug users,' or 'drug dependent' people. For example, Viktor Cherkesov, Chairman of the Federal Service to Control the Trade in Narcotics and Psychotropic Substances (FSN), has used the six million figure to denote the number of people who 'use drugs more or less regularly,' with between 1.5 million and 1.8 million of this number being 'drug addicts' (RIA–Novosti, November 3, 2005).

One suspects that the six million figure is actually a convenient statistical artifact which officials employ to acknowledge both that they disbelieve the official data on drug abuse and do not know the real extent of this pathology but assume it is substantially higher than the official portrayal of it. Seemingly more credible are data from a national survey on drug use which the RF Ministry of Education conducted and reported on in 2003 (RF Ministry of Education 2004). The core of the study comprised a statistically representative national sample of 5,000 individuals aged 11–24 who were surveyed anonymously on their drug-related behavior and attitudes. The Ministry also surveyed 565 'experts' on the same subject working in various drug-related capacities as well as analyzing drug-related statistics culled from sundry official sources.

Overall, it estimated that approximately 6.5 million individuals in Russia consumed some type of illegal drug at least two to three times per month, while upwards of 1,800,000 of them consumed such a drug at least two to three times a week and were thereby deemed 'dependent' on it. If these data roughly reflect the actual situation, then the prevalence rate in the overall population for past month illicit drug use is approximately 4.5 per cent while the rate among those deemed 'dependent' on drugs is approximately 1.3 per cent. Within the age cohort 15–64 – the cohort typically considered most likely to use illicit drugs – these prevalence rates are approximately 6.4 per cent and 1.8 per cent. By way of an – admittedly rough – comparison, in the United States an estimated 8.1 per cent of Americans aged 15 and over engaged in past month use of an illicit drug in 2005 (United States Substance Abuse and Mental Health Services Administration 2006, Highlights).

The data on drug-related behavior among those aged 11–24 are especially interesting given that they derive from the largest reported statistically representative national survey on this subject ever conducted in Russia.

Overall, upwards of 30 per cent of the sample reported use of an illicit drug at least once in their lives. The average age at which such use began was 14, down from 17.8 in 1993. Regarding the key indicator of past month drug use in assessing the present level of usage, 13.1 per cent of the sample, equivalent to approximately 4,200,000 individuals in the age cohort 11–24, reported using illicit drugs at least two to three times in that time period. In comparison, in the United States, the *2005 National Survey on Drug Use and Health* reported that 9.9 per cent of the sample aged 12–17 acknowledged past month use of an illicit drug (ibid.). To be sure, the Russian and American data are not comparable given the substantive methodological differences in their compilation. Nevertheless, they are suggestive that drug use among the young in Russia may be approaching and perhaps even exceeding comparable levels found in the United States.

Table 10.2 provides data on the different types of illicit drugs that individuals reported consuming. While drugs from the cannabis family (such as marijuana) were the most commonly consumed illicit drug, increased consumption of opium-based derivatives and cocaine correlated strongly with an increase in the reported frequency of illicit drug consumption. Based on data gathered from the survey, researchers estimated that in 2002 the age cohort 11–24 spent almost US$2.5 billion to satisfy its illicit

Table 10.2:   Consumption of illicit drugs and of psychotropic substances (by type in per cent)

Substance	Frequency of Consumption		
	1–3 times in life	*2–5 times per month*	*No less than 2–3 times per week*
Cannabis	80.6	82.2	60.0
Opiates	12.4	25.4	44.6
Cocaine	4.2	8.7	15.2
Hallucinogens	5.4	8.1	5.6
Psychostimulants	2.2	8.1	11.8
Inhalants	4.4	2.2	15.9
Medicines	2.9	10.3	9.7
Others	4.6	3.5	3.1

Source: RF Ministry of Education, Center for Sociological Research, *Otsenka narkosituatsii v srede detei, podrostkov i molodezhi* (Moscow, 2004), Part 2, p. 6. Based on a reportedly statistically representative national sample of 5,000 individuals aged 11–24. For a discussion of the methodology employed in conducting the survey, including data on the composition of the sample, see ibid., Part 1, pp. 4–5.

drug habit while the figure for the entire population was approximately US$4.1 billion.

Links to HIV/AIDS

Two key links exist between drug abuse and the spread of HIV/AIDS in Russia. First, as noted, many abusers engage in dangerous drug-related behavior that places them at an elevated risk of contracting the virus. This behavior primarily entails the frequent sharing of injection equipment to ingest heroin and sundry locally-produced drugs. For example, in selected surveys among IDUs in Ekaterinburg, 86 per cent of respondents reported sharing injection equipment, while in Tol'iatti and Moscow this figure was 84 per cent in the former and between 35 per cent and 41 per cent in the latter (United Nations Development Program 2004, p. 31). In other studies, approximately one third of IDUs reported sharing such equipment in the four weeks prior to being interviewed (Lowndes et al. 2003, p. 51). Typically, such equipment is either unsterilized or poorly sterilized so that the HIV virus passes easily among those sharing the equipment if any of their number already has contracted it. Other common high risk practices that often produce the same end include injection with preloaded syringes, distribution of drug solutions from one syringe to another (so-called front or back loading), and the drawing up from a common pot of a drug solution into which the IDUs may even have placed drops of their blood to clarify it.

Estimated HIV positive prevalence rates among IDUs in some Russian cities already have reached staggering levels, including Irkutsk (65 per cent), Tol'iatti (56 per cent), Tver' (55 per cent), St Petersburg (36 per cent), and Moscow (28 per cent) (United Nations Development Program 2004, p. 16). Overall, in 2005, 9.3 per cent of the 369,600 IDUs registered with state narcological clinics throughout Russia were HIV positive. The respective figure exceeded five per cent in 37 of the 86 federal subjects of Russia, including in ten of them where it exceeded 20 per cent (Koshkina and Kirzhanova 2006, p. 56). UNAIDS considers that a concentrated epidemic of HIV has broken out in an at-risk group for the disease when the HIV prevalence rate within it exceeds five per cent. Considering that the World Health Organization, in a 2003 study, estimates that there could be between 1.5 and 3.5 million IDUs in Russia, mostly using heroin, this suggests that between 1.0 per cent and 2.4 per cent of the entire population of Russia is at an elevated risk of contracting the AIDS virus solely through high risk drug-related behavior (United Nations Development Program 2004, p. 26).

Crossnational data provide perspective on the magnitude of this high risk behavior in Russia. Thus, no other country except Russia in the aforementioned World Health Organization study, which included all of the states of the former Soviet Union and communist Europe, had a highest estimated IDU prevalence rate that exceeded 2.0 per cent nor a lowest estimated prevalence rate that exceeded 0.8 per cent. Separately, the United Nations *World Drug Report 2006* ranked Russia, together with Mauritius, third worldwide, behind only Iran and Kyrgyzstan, in the percentage of its population aged 15 to 64 who abused opiates with an estimated prevalence rate of 2.0 per cent (United Nations Office on Drugs and Crime 2007, pp. 383, 384).

Similar comparisons with the member states of the EU are even more striking. There, in 2004 the European Monitoring Center for Drugs and Drug Addiction (EMCDDA) estimated that there were between 850,000 and 1,300,000 IDUs out of a total population of approximately 456,000,000 in these states (EMCDDA 2004). In other words, even using absolute figures, the *lowest* estimated number of IDUs in Russia exceeds the *highest* estimated number in the EU, which has a population more than three times larger than that of Russia. Using prevalence rates to account for the substantial disparity in population between Russia and the EU is even more instructive. Thus, the prevalence rate for even the lowest estimated number of IDUs in Russia is upwards of 3.5 times greater than the same rate for the highest estimated number of IDUs in the EU. Comparing the highest estimated number of IDUs in Russia to the same estimated number in the EU yields a prevalence rate in the former approximately 8.5 times greater than in the latter.

In contrast to these exceedingly troubling data, official statistics indicating a sharp decline between 2001 and 2003 of approximately 55 per cent in the incidence of newly registered HIV cases and of 75 per cent in those cases specifically attributable to injection drug use paint a much more optimistic picture of the present state, and prospective evolution, of this pathology. Overall the incidence of newly registered HIV cases declined by upwards of 60 per cent in 2006 compared to 2001 (Russian Federal AIDS Center 2007).

Officials typically offer two hypotheses to explain these declines. First, and less plausibly, some contend that they merely are a consequence of the sharp decline since 2001 in the officially registered number of 'drug addicts' and 'drug abusers.' Thus, responding to a question about why the incidence of newly registered HIV cases has been declining, a high-ranking official in the RF Ministry of Health contended, 'I wouldn't say it's our work but there clearly are fewer new drug addicts' (quoted in the *Moscow Times*, November 28, 2002, p. 1). As the evidence presented in this study indicates, the only thing that has 'clearly' declined is the number of officially registered such individuals, with no demonstrable evidence available that this datum accurately reflects the actual situation.

Second, some officials argue that HIV has become so pervasive among IDUs in selected Russian cities as to reach a point of 'saturation' (*nasyshchenie*), thereby resulting in the declining number of newly recorded HIV cases overall and specifically among IDUs (*Meditsinskaia gazeta*, October 31, 2003, p. 10). This argument offers at best only a partial explanation for the observed phenomenon given that reported HIV prevalence rates among IDUs in many cities and regions are far below any level that could reasonably be considered one of 'saturation' and that data on such prevalence rates in many areas of the country are simply nonexistent. Reflecting on these latter circumstances, a recent United Nations report explicitly argued that there remains 'ample space' for the AIDS virus to grow among Russian IDUs (United Nations Development Program 2004, p. 17).

In reality, both Pokrovsky of the RF AIDS Center and Murray Feshbach, America's leading expert on the AIDS problem in Russia, offer a much simpler and convincing explanation for the reported decline in HIV incidence. Stated succinctly, starting in 2000, Russia has substantially reduced the number of individuals, specifically including IDUs, that it annually tests for the AIDS virus. In Pokrovsky's words, declines in the incidence of newly registered HIV cases 'may be associated merely with changes in the constitution of the tested group' (*Meditsinskaia gazeta*, October 31, 2003, p. 10; Feshbach and Galvin 2005, p. 12).

The second link between the spread of AIDS and high risk drug behavior is even more threatening. Thus, IDUs rank among the so-called 'high risk core transmitters' of the virus – that is, groups at elevated risk of contracting the disease who then transmit it to so-called 'bridging groups' composed of non-IDUs through (commercial or noncommercial) sexual intercourse. In turn, members of these non-IDU 'bridging groups' interact sexually with other non-IDUs who may then contract the virus and spread it even further into the general population.

The city of Tver', which has experienced an outbreak of HIV among the general population, illustrates how this process unfolds. In explaining the outbreak, the head of the regional AIDS Center contended that 'this is the echo of past drug problems' (quoted in the *Christian Science Monitor*, August 17, 2004). He noted that in a survey conducted in 2000 among regular drug users, including IDUs, 63 per cent of the sample reported having regular sexual contacts with individuals not themselves drug users. Reported condom use rates in this study were 40 per cent. HIV already pervades IDUs in Tver': among IDUs tested in 2002 at both a local needle exchange program and an official narcological clinic, HIV prevalence reached approximately 55 per cent (UNDP 2004, p. 16).

Several factors extant in Russia increase the likelihood of HIV transmission through sexual contact between IDUs and non-IDUs. Thus, most IDUs are relatively young – several studies report the average age of first injection at between 16 and 19 years – with the concomitant potential to engage in frequent sexual activity (Rhodes et al. 2000). Then, too, the Russian IDU population appears fluid and dynamic rather than stable and persistent given that not all IDUs are frequent injectors, but rather may engage in injection on a short-term and experimental basis. In a situation in which HIV prevalence and incidence are already high among IDUs, such inexperienced IDUs may be especially prone to HIV infection by engaging in risky drug-related behavior that more seasoned IDUs shun. When these HIV positive IDU 'short timers' migrate back into, and again become part of, the non-IDU population, they then can pass the virus into the latter population through sexual intercourse. That many IDUs are unaware of their HIV positive status facilitates this mode of transmission. For example, a 2000 survey in Tol'iatti among IDUs found that 56 per cent of them were HIV positive and approximately 75 per cent of these infected individuals were ignorant of their condition (Reuters, September 13, 2002).

Finally, many IDUs are also found among other key 'high risk core transmitters' of the virus, including prostitutes, prisoners, and so-called mobile populations such as homeless children. For example, studies among female IDUs in selected Russian cities estimated that between 15 per cent and 50 per cent, depending on locale, engaged in commercial sex work (Lowndes, et al. 2003, p. 52). In Moscow, an estimated 40 per cent of the capital's 70,000–80,000 female prostitutes are IDUs and 15 per cent of them tested positive for HIV (*Boston Globe*, February 10, 2002). Among females aged 15–17 being held at a juvenile detention center in Moscow, 46 per cent of them reported engaging in commercial sex work and 11 per cent of them reported past 12 month injection drug use (Shakarishvili et al. 2005, p. 59). Reportedly, the situation is even worse in St Petersburg where of an estimated 65 per cent of all female prostitutes, most of them IDUs, are HIV positive (Webster 2003, p. 2133).

Russia's prisons, where high risk drug-related and sexual behavior are common, have become notorious incubators for HIV. In 2006, 38,841 inmates in Russian prisons, most of whom were IDUs, were HIV positive (RF Ministry of Justice 2007). The HIV prevalence rate in that year of 4.5 per cent was well above what UNAIDS considers the 'breakout' rate for a generalized epidemic. Survey research data reflect the behavior that leads to such rates of infection: one survey, which the prominent Western NGO 'Doctors Without Borders' conducted among seven Russian prisons in 2000, found that 43 per cent of inmates had injected drugs, 50 per cent of the IDUs shared injection equipment, and 10 per cent of them had penetrative sexual intercourse with other prisoners (UNDP 2004, p. 34). These practices directly threaten the general population, given that upwards of 300,000 individuals – some of them undoubtedly HIV positive, even if unaware of it – are released annually from Russian prisons and become potential transmitters of the virus to unsuspecting sexual partners.

The very limited data available on the drug-related behavior of the estimated one million *bezprizorniki*, or homeless children, suggest that more research is urgently needed to illuminate this group's role as a transmitter of the AIDS virus. A St Petersburg NGO working with such children conducted several surveys which found that HIV prevalence among them in 2000 was 8 per cent while by 2002 it had increased to 10.4 per cent (Human Rights Watch 2004, p. 26).

A final bridging group crucial for spreading the AIDS virus widely in the general population comprises non-IDUs who have sexual intercourse with both IDUs and non-IDUs. Almost no reliable data exist on the extent and nature of such activity in Russia. However, circumstantial evidence suggests this is widespread given that in 2006 heterosexual intercourse constituted the main risk factor, where one could be determined, in contracting the virus in 31 per cent of the officially registered HIV cases, up from barely 3.3 per cent in 2000 (Russian Federal AIDS Center 2007).

Government responses

The RF government has responded to drug abuse in ways that are strikingly reminiscent of the response that was characteristic of the USSR. In both cases, the response has been exceedingly limited, consisting mostly of repeated vows to rid society of this evil pathology without any meaningful measures to realize this end. Emblematic of these circumstances were four widely heralded but essentially unimplemented federal programs promulgated between 1992 and 1998 to combat drug abuse.

In 2002, the government promulgated another program – this time through 2009 – to combat drug abuse. Its stated goal is to reduce the consumption of narcotics and psychotropic substances in 2010 by 16 per cent to 20 per cent compared to 2003. For the overall period 2005–2009, the program envisions spending only 3.62 billion rubles (approximately US $127 million or 89¢ per capita of the Russian population) to implement all of its measures (RF Governmental Resolution No. 561, September 13, 2005).

The anti-drug measures that have been enacted primarily seek to limit the supply of drugs through highly punitive legal measures rather than by reducing demand for drugs regardless of how widely available their supply might be. This stress on so-called 'supply side' measures should continue given that the aforementioned anti-drug program for 2005–2009 targets almost 50 per cent of its planned expenditures to sundry law enforcement agencies, including the FSN, the Ministry of the Interior and the Federal Security Service.

Many of these 'supply side' measure are embodied in the 1998 law 'On Narcotics and Psychotropic Substances,' the only law in the RF devoted exclusively to drug abuse. Its punitive provisions include criminalizing the possession of even miniscule amounts of 'narcotics and other psychotropic substances without a doctor's prescription,' which, if interpreted literally, precludes the use of such common analgesics as alcohol-based cold medicines. It also mandates the compulsory treatment of

individuals deemed drug addicts in government run facilities and prohibits the public dissemination of information on the production, use,
and sale of illegal drugs.

The FSN takes an equally punitive approach to drug abuse. Chairman Cherkesov is a former high-ranking official in the KGB who had
been responsible in Soviet times for hunting down political dissidents.
Officials with similar 'Chekist' backgrounds pervade the ranks of the
FSN from senior level management to staff positions in the field. Not
surprisingly, under these circumstances, the FSN publicly has opposed
many policies widely used and proven effective worldwide to reduce the
harm from drugs. Such policies include employing current and former
drug users as peer educators in drug treatment programs, maintaining
the anonymity of persons using needle exchange programs, weaning
addicts from heroin by providing them with less threatening drugs such
as methadone, and disseminating information on safe drug use practices
and behavior.

A May 2004 official decree mandating administrative liability, rather
than the hitherto harsh criminal penalties, for individuals possessing very small quantities of illegal drugs for personal use represented
a salutary break from this highly punitive approach to drug abuse
(*Kommersant-daily*, May 13, 2004, p. 17). One motivation for the revised
legislation may have been to relieve the severe overcrowding of Russia's
prisons by no longer incarcerating individuals for what often amounted
to little more than casual drug use – a laudatory objective given the
notorious role of Russian prisons as breeding grounds for high risk core
transmitters of the AIDS virus.

Yet the revised legislation engendered vociferous opposition, especially
from the FSN whose deputy head called proponents of the legislation
lobbyists for the drug cartels (*Moscow News*, May 13, 2004, p. 8). Such
opposition doomed the May 2004 legislation and in February 2006 newly
promulgated legislation reintroduced criminal liability for possession of
even small quantities of illegal drugs for personal use (*Kommersant-daily*,
February 2, 2006, p. 1).

Cherkesov of the FSN reports that the principal task of law enforcement
agencies is to interdict the flow of illegal drugs from both domestic and
international sources and destroy the organized criminal groups which
he claims are increasingly dominating the illegal trade in drugs. To these
ends, in 2006 FSN personnel confiscated upwards of 90 tons of illegal narcotics and psychotropic substances, exposed almost 90,000 drug-related
crimes, and suppressed more than 600 organized criminal groups in the
drug trade (Cherkesov 2007, p. 1).

Yet many critics contend that these seemingly impressive figures are actually a façade masking serious shortcomings in the fight against drugs. They especially assail the authorities for arresting and incarcerating almost exclusively individuals possessing small quantities (often amounting to little more than 'micro-particles,' according to a spokesman for the RF Ministry of Justice) of illegal drugs for personal use or petty drug dealers, but never the 'Big Fish' who control the illegal drug trade (quoted in *Kommersant-daily*, November 26, 2004, p. 7). Such actions are both ineffective in attacking the root sources of the drug trade and pernicious by incarcerating tens of thousands of individual drug users where the rampant high risk drug-related and sexual practices in Russia's prisons place them at elevated risk of contracting the AIDS virus.

Internationally, the most relevant anti-drug initiatives to combat the AIDS virus target the flow of what the Secretary of the RF Security Council calls the 'narkotsunami' of heroin and opium reaching Russia from Afghanistan for sale locally and for re-export to world markets (quoted in *Krasnaia zvezda*, February 19, 2005, p. 17). In 2005, Russian law enforcement personnel seized approximately four tons of heroin which mostly originated in Afghanistan (*Moskovskaia pravda*, April 13, 2006, p. 1). That Russia seizes no more than an estimated five per cent of the illegal narcotics from Afghanistan entering its territory places the magnitude of this trade in perspective.

To combat it, Russia has pursued bilateral and multilateral initiatives among states both in the region and in the West to create an 'anti-drug' belt surrounding Afghanistan. Bilaterally, Russia has concluded anti-drug pacts with key Central Asian transit states, including Kazakhstan, Kyrgyzstan, and Tajikistan. The FSN has announced plans to open an office in Afghanistan to enhance cooperation with colleagues there to combat the international drug trade. Russia is also cooperating with the United States on the 'Southern Border Project' which entails the establishment of three mobile drug interdiction task forces based at strategic points along the Afghan border with Kazakhstan.

Tajikistan represents a key transit point in this drug trade given its long, geographically challenging, and porous border with Afghanistan. Russia has used this circumstance in part to justify the deployment there since 1992 of its 201st Motorized Division and upwards of 10,000 military personnel (many of them ethnic Tajiks under contract) to guard the border and interdict the drug trade. Both the United States and the EU are similarly involved in these pursuits: in 2005 and 2006, the United States has pledged US $9.5 million and the EU the equivalent of US $11 million to strengthen border security and combat the drug trade (Interfax-AVN, February 26, 2005).

Overall, between 1998 and 2003, Russian and Tajik border personnel seized upwards of 30 tons of 'drugs and narcotics,' including 16 tons of heroin. Tajikistan now ranks third in the world in the volume of heroin that it seizes annually. Yet these impressive statistics must be placed in perspective: whereas Tajikistan seized 5.6 tons of heroin in 2003, a respected Western source estimates that as much as 80 tons to 96 tons of heroin from Afghanistan transited Tajikistan that year (United States Department of State 2004).

Further, in July 2005 Tajikistan assumed full responsibility for guarding its borders with Russian personnel serving only in an advisory capacity. The head of the UNODC admitted that he was a 'little worried' about Tajikistan's capacity to perform this task effectively, although he acknowledged that Tajikistan's status as a sovereign state 'demands such a step' (quoted in *The Russian Journal*, May 28, 2004). Unfortunately, these fears have proven justified with Tajikistan seizing upwards of 60 per cent less heroin transiting its border from Afghanistan in 2005 compared to 2003 (United Nations Office on Drugs and Crime 2005, p. 8).

Russia also has pursued sundry multilateral initiatives to combat the drug trade in Afghanistan and the surrounding region. To this end, representatives from Russia, UNODC and the North Atlantic Treaty Organization (NATO) met in October 2004 under the auspices of the NATO–Russia Council to examine 'the challenges posed by the exponential growth of opium production in Afghanistan ... and stability in the region and in the broader Euro-Atlantic area' (www.nato.int, October 28, 2004). In a concrete expression of such cooperation, in January 2005, the EU and UNODC jointly pledged US $9 million to 'fight the drug trade' in Central Asia by providing technical aid to anti-drug bodies in the region (Interfax-Kazakhstan, January 27, 2005). In March 2005, representatives from UNODC, Russia, the United States, the United Kingdom and all states in the region, including Afghanistan and Iran, met in the Turkmen capital Ashgabat to discuss the need for a 'common front' against, and other 'urgent questions' related to, the drug trade and drug abuse in the region (www.eurasianet.org, 2005). The Shanghai Cooperation Organization (SCO) – whose membership comprises Russia, China, Kazakhstan, Kyrgyzstan, Tajikistan, and Uzbekistan – pursues similar ends through its Regional Antiterrorism Center (RATS) based in Tashkent, Uzbekistan. RATS is exploring the possibility of cooperating with both the United Nations and the Organization for Security and Cooperation in Europe on anti-drug initiatives.

Yet despite all these punitive efforts both domestically and internationally to suppress the supply of illegal drugs, their use in Russia, as President Putin has admitted, 'continues to grow' (*www.President.Kremlin.ru*, January 21, 2005).

Indeed, many critics contend that the entire official response to drug abuse is deeply flawed because of its overwhelming stress on a 'supply side' strategy at the expense of a 'demand side' or preventative strategy designed both to reduce the incentives individuals have to abuse drugs and mitigate the harm to themselves when they do so. As the director of the RF Ministry of Health's National Scientific Narcological Center contends:

> We seem to crack down on the supply of drugs all the time, instead of trying to do something to decrease the demand for drugs. This is a difficult task that involves working with schools, parents and young people themselves. You cannot just hire 40,000 new police officers to deal with it and then say that the job is done. (*www.Russiaprofile.ru*, June 23, 2005)

There has been some official support – at least rhetorically – for a 'demand side' strategy. Thus, Cherkesov of the FSN contends that there soon will be 'far more ... addicts' if Russia 'does not engage in work to reduce demand' (*Izvestiia*, March 25, 2004). Some concrete steps have been announced to implement this rhetoric. Each of the republics and regions of the Russian Federation has now elaborated a complex program stressing demand reduction and prevention work to combat drug abuse, including establishing a special department to coordinate this work among young people. That said, a recent survey of these programs concluded that only 25 of them were then operating effectively (RF Ministry of Education 2004, Part 6, p. 6). The RF Ministry of Health has announced plans to open 250 modern drug rehabilitation centers and the RF Ministry of Education plans to open the first five such centers in Russia devoted exclusively to the treatment of adolescents. If these plans are realized, they represent a salutary first step in improving the typically dismal state of government run narcological clinics, which one former drug abuser accurately described as 'inhumane – no medicines, no care, the places are dirty and cold, they just keep you there' offering 'treatment' that consists of little more than going 'cold turkey' to rid their patients of their affliction (Human Rights Watch 2004, p. 47).

There also have been stepped-up efforts to educate the population, especially young people, to the dangers of abusing drugs and more positively, to promote a healthy style of life incorporating physical exercise, a nutritious diet, and eschewing habits, specifically smoking and the abuse of alcohol and illicit drugs, harmful to that end. In pursuit of these goals, the government plans to allocate between 2005–2009 239 million rubles (approximately US $6.6 million) to pay for public service advertisements with anti-drug messages in sundry mass media outlets. The RF Chief Sanitary Physician explicitly promised that the campaign would include outreach programs to teach drug abusers about the dangers of sharing needles and related drug-injection equipment (RIA-Novosti, July 6, 2004).

To promote the campaign in the mass media, a group called 'Sport Against Narcotics' enlists prominent personalities from the world of sport to make public interest advertisements under the rubric 'I Chose Sport,' rather than a sedentary style of life (RF Ministry of Education 2004, Part 7, p. 4). Specific efforts, even including the UNODC, have targeted the Russian Orthodox Church for a far more active role than hitherto in anti-drug initiatives. In response, Russian Orthodox Patriarch Aleksii II publicly has decried both 'drinking and drug addiction' as part of the pervasive moral decay afflicting society which he considers the root cause of the looming demographic crisis threatening the very existence of Russians as a people (RIA-Novosti, December 14, 2004). An especially promising initiative involves a United States Agency for International Development-funded project called 'Healthy Russia 2020' which pursues wide-ranging efforts via mass media, educational pamphlets, school based programs, and an internet portal to enhance public awareness of the virtues of both making healthy life style choices and avoiding risky behaviors, specifically including those that can lead to the contraction of AIDS (for details see *www.fzr.ru*). Even the FSN has joined these efforts, sponsoring a nationwide television and internet telethon featuring prominent public personalities promoting the message 'Say No to Drugs!' (RIA-Novosti, December 18, 2004).

What is to be done?

While these initiatives are welcome, much work still must be done before Russia has in place a comprehensive demand-side strategy to combat drug abuse and stanch a potential AIDS pandemic. To devise such a strategy, four imperatives are especially pressing.

First, Russia must expand substantially facilities where IDUs anonymously can obtain sterile syringes and receive a wide range of other services, including counseling on safe sex and drug use practices and referrals to medical professionals for health-related issues and questions. Considerable empirical evidence worldwide demonstrates the utility of such programs in decreasing the sharing of needles, reducing the prevalence of HIV, Hepatitis C and other blood-borne infections, and providing IDUs with requisite therapeutic and medical services. For example, studies on this subject in the United States estimate that upwards of 65 per cent of all HIV infections arising from contaminated needles could be prevented if every addict had access to a clean needle (*Washington Post*, August 13, 2006, p. A7).

Overall, no more than an estimated 75 such facilities existed in Russia at year end 2003, with only 56 of the federal units reporting at least one of them operating there (Human Rights Watch 2004, p. 17). By one estimate, such facilities reach no more than one per cent of IDUs in cities where they are located (Lowndes et al. 2003, p. 51). Yet the future of even these few facilities has become problematic, because the FSN has targeted them for closure for allegedly violating the 1998 drug law's stricture against engaging in 'open propaganda to use drugs' (*Washington Post*, June 13, 2004, p. A24).

Second, Russia must include so-called 'substitution therapy,' wherein IDUs are given methadone, a synthetic analog of heroin, as part of a comprehensive drug treatment and prevention program. Current Russian law prohibits the use of methadone, classifying it, along with other opiates such as heroin and morphine, as a Schedule One narcotic drug. Three United Nations conventions similarly classify methadone as an 'illicit' drug. In contrast, three United Nations agencies – the World Health Organization, UNAIDS and UNODC – have endorsed substitution maintenance therapy based on methadone (or another opiate substitute) as a 'critical component of community-based approaches in the management of Opioid dependence and in the prevention of HIV infection . . .' (World Health Organization 2004).

Indeed, methadone substitution has proven an effective tool in fighting heroin addiction and AIDS in many countries, including in those that are signatories to the aforementioned United Nations conventions criminalizing its use. The principal virtues of methadone are that it both suppresses craving for the far more physiologically damaging heroin and can be ingested orally, thereby eliminating injection, which has proved a principal transmission mode for blood-borne infections such as the AIDS virus. The FSN's Cherkesov, similar to his position on needle exchange programs, adamantly opposes the introduction of methadone maintenance therapy even on an experimental basis as has been done in Sverdlovsk region (interview, *Ekho Moskvy Radio*, July 3, 2004).

Third, Russia must develop an effective, affordable, and widely available program of anti-retroviral ('ARV') treatment for individuals living with AIDS, including those who are active IDUs. When administered appropriately, this therapy has dramatically reduced morbidity and mortality rates among AIDS sufferers. It may also help stem an AIDS pandemic because individuals receiving this treatment have lower viral loads which may make them less infectious and likely to transmit the virus to others.

At present, ARV therapy is rare in Russia and almost never includes IDUs even when it is available. Justifying these circumstances, Russians officials argue both that the overall cost of ARV treatment is prohibitive and that IDUs in particular are poor candidates for it because they allegedly lack the discipline to comply with the requisite regimen to administer it. In contrast, American investigators using the Russian cities of St Petersburg and Barnual as their test cities employed a mathematical model to assess the public health benefits and economic costs of sundry ARV therapy strategies among HIV positive individuals. Their model conclusively demonstrated that the most effective strategy was to provide ARV therapy to both IDU and non-IDU HIV positive individuals. In the judgment of the investigators, such a strategy if implemented nationwide 'could dramatically reduce HIV incidence among the general population in Russia, would yield enormous population-wide health benefits, and would be economically efficient' (Long et al. 2006).

Finally, a critical need exists for Russia to generate accurate data on the scope and etiology of drug abuse and AIDS both individually and in their relationship to one another. Ironically, Russia has pursued a highly punitive strategy towards these pathologies that seems almost perversely designed to prevent the realization of this end because it only drives such core transmitters of the AIDS virus as IDUs underground, terrified to reveal their condition to the authorities. Absent requisite accurate data, policy makers literally are 'flying blind' in their efforts to combat drug abuse and AIDS.

Yet in this otherwise mostly depressing picture, a ray of hope appeared in April 2006 when RF Russian President Vladimir Putin for the first time acknowledged publicly the critical significance of a possible AIDS pandemic for the future welfare of Russia. Putin singled out 'above all' the key need to 'work with high-risk groups' – in which he presumably included IDUs – to explain to them 'the danger and risk' they run of becoming HIV positive (Reuters, April 22, 2006). Subsequently, Putin promised that by 2010 'all HIV carriers' in Russia will have access to ARV therapy 'if programs now in the making are implemented' (RIA-Novosti, July 16, 2006).

Putin's actions represent a salutary and absolutely essential first step if Russia is to develop an effective response to its emerging AIDS crisis, including attacking it at its roots through meaningful initiatives to combat drug abuse overall and high risk drug-related behavior in particular. This study has demonstrated the critical need to center such a response on a 'demand side' strategy emphasizing initiatives both to reduce the incentives individuals have to abuse drugs and to mitigate the harmful consequences that may arise when they do.

References

AIDS Journal. 2005. No. 54: www.aidsjournal.ru.

Cherkesov, Viktor. 2007. '*Ob itogakh operativno – sluzhebnoi deyatel'nosti FSKN Rossii v 2006 godu zadachakh na 2007 god,*' posted on an official website of the RF government 'Net Narkotikam': www.narkotiki.ru.

EMCDDA (European Monitoring Center for Drugs and Drug Addiction). 2004. *Annual Report 2004: The State of the Drug Problem in the European Union and Norway*: www.emcdda.eu.int.

Entin, G. M. et al. 1999. 'Situatsiia s potrebleniem alkologia i narkotikov v Rossii v 1994–1997 gg.: dinamika i prognoz,' *Voprosy narkologii* 1.

Feshbach, Murray and Cristina Galvin. 2005. *HIV/AIDS, TB and Coinfections in Russia: An Analysis of the Statistics*, United States Agency for International Development, January.

Human Rights Watch. 2004. *Lessons Not Learned: Human Rights Abuses and HIV/AIDS in the Russian Federation*, April 28: www.hrw.org.

Koshkina, E. A. and V. V. Kirzhanova. 2006. *Osobennosti rasprostranennosti narkologicheskikh rasstroistv v Rossiiskoi Federatsii v 2005 g* 2.

Kramer, John M. 1991. 'Drug Abuse in the USSR,' in Anthony Jones et al., *Soviet Social Problems*, Boulder CO: Westview.

Long, Elisa et al. 2006. 'Effectiveness and Cost-effectiveness of Strategies to Expand Antiretroviral Therapy in St Petersburg, Russia,' *AIDS*, November 14.

Lowndes, Catherine M. et al. 2003. 'Conditions for Widespread Heterosexual Spread of HIV in the Russian Federation: Implications for Research, Monitoring and Prevention,' *International Journal of Drug Policy*, February.

RF Ministry of Education, Center for Sociological Research. 2004. *Otsenka narkosituatsii v srede detei podrostkov i molodezhi*, posted on an official website of the RF government 'Net Narkotikam': www.narkotiki.ru.

RF Ministry of Justice, Main Directorate of Corrections. 2007. 'HIV Positive Inmates in the Penal System of the Ministry of Justice in the Russian Federation 1994 through 2006,' posted on the website of AIDS Foundation East West: www.afew.org.

Rhodes, Tim, et al. 2000. *Behavioral Risk Factors in HIV Transmission in Eastern Europe and Central Asia*, UNAIDS: www.unaids.org.

Russian Federal AIDS Center. 2007. Official data posted on the website of AIDS Foundation East West: www.afew.org.

Shakarishivili, A. et al. 2005. 'Sex Work, Drug Use, HIV Infection, and the Spread of Sexually Transmitted Infections in Moscow, Russian Federation,' *The Lancet*, July 2.

United Nations Development Program. 2004. *HIV/AIDS in Eastern Europe and the Commonwealth of Independent States*: www.undp.org/hiv.

United Nations Office for Drug Control and Crime Prevention. 2001. *Annual Field Report 2000–Russia*: www.unodc.org.

United Nations Office on Drugs and Crime. 2005. *Illicit Drug Trends in the Russian Federation in 2005*: www.unodc.org.

——— 2007. *World Drug Report 2006*, Volume 2, Statistics: www.unodc.org.

United States Department of State, Bureau for International Narcotics and Law Enforcement Affairs. 2004. 'Tajikistan,' in *International Narcotics Control Strategy Report, 2004*: www.state.gov.

United States Substance Abuse and Mental Health Administration. 2006. *2005 National Survey on Drug Use and Health*: www.oas.samhsa.gov/nsduh.

Webster, Paul. 2003. 'HIV/AIDS Explosion in Russia Triggers Research Boom,' *The Lancet*, June 21.

World Health Organization. 2004. 'Substitution Maintenance Therapy in the Management of Opoid Dependence with HIV/AIDS: Position Paper': www.who.int.

Index